10-96

(We're on the way)

10-96

(We're on the way)

40 True Stories That Can
Help Save Your Life

Conrad M. Gonzales, Jr.

Retired San Antonio Firefighter/Paramedic

Copyright

Preregistration Number: PRE000010446
Effective Date of Preregistration: 08/27/2018
Class(es) of Work: Literary Work in Book Form

Title: 10-96 (We're On The Way)

Conrad M. Gonzales, Jr.
ISBN-13: 978-0692191453
ISBN-10: 0692191453

Book Editor: Stephanie Rodriguez
Printed by Createspace, An Amazon.com Company
Available from Amazon.com and other bookstores
Available on Kindle

This book is a compilation of stories and events during my career as a firefighter, paramedic, and safety educator with the San Antonio Fire Department and San Antonio AirLife. I also included pre- and post-fire department events and other "hats" I wore then and now.

My stories and events will show how you can help save your own life, the lives of your family, and the lives of others.

The title *10-96* was a ten-code used for many years in fire departments throughout the country.
In San Antonio, 10-96 signified that we were "on the way" or responding to a call after being summoned by the dispatcher.

This book is dedicated worldwide to:

All future, active, retired, volunteer, and deceased first responders, EMTs, paramedics, firefighters, police officers, sheriff deputies, DPS troopers, nurses, doctors, flight paramedics-civilian and military, air medical pilots, physical therapists, and all medical professionals who deal with ill and injured patients; and those who have lost their lives in the line of duty working to save the lives of others.

This is a special and heartfelt dedication to all my brother and sister firefighters in New York City who perished on 9/11 and to the law enforcement officers who, along with the firefighters, made that last call. I dedicate this book to their families, the husbands, wives and children; to the occupants of both towers who lost their lives and to those who survived. I know there are many survivors who exited the buildings and looked into the eyes and faces of those first responders going up the stairs and into the chaos not knowing they would meet their fate. The looks on their faces, I am certain, are etched into your minds and hearts. We pray for you, and we pray for them.

Finally, I dedicate this book to all the families I have served on and off duty, both living and deceased. To those whose hands I held while they were in pain; to those whose hands I held as they were dying; to those I provided comforting words when they lost a loved one; to the babies I saved and those I couldn't; and to the baby I baptized in the back of the ambulance.

This is for you.

Table of Contents

Chapter 1
"Please, save my babies!"

On a warm summer night at Fire Station No. 9, I decided to go to bed early, as usual. I always made it a point to try to get some sleep in the event we were up all night responding to calls. However, some of the guys at the fire station usually stayed up late shooting pool or playing ping pong upstairs, or just BS-ing in the dorm.

There were no barriers to drown the voices and laughter from these more active guys and no respect for those who wanted to get some shuteye. Sleep was of essence for me for I had no idea what kind of night we would have. This one night, I finally had to cover my head and ears with a pillow, and I dozed off.

It was around 2 a.m. when the three tones alerted us for a house fire in our "regular alarm" district. A regular alarm consisted of 3 motors (fire engines) and one ladder truck. I was on No. 9's motor as a firefighter. The motor had all the fire hoses and equipment to extinguish the fire and the ladder truck had all the lights, ventilation equipment, extrication tools, and, of course, the ladders and the 100-foot extension ladder.

We donned our boots and pants, and we slid down the fire pole into the day room and then ran to the motor. I put on my coat and fire helmet and strapped on my safety belt at the back of the truck - yes, the *back* of the fire truck - and stood up holding onto the bar for dear life as we sped out of the fire station. The fire truck was a 1959 International that had only two front seats, one for the captain and the engineer who drove the fire truck. That

1

night, I was the only one riding the back of the fire truck as the other firefighter was on vacation. (It was lonely at the back!)

As we drove down the main street, I could see smoke billowing and an orange glow in the distance. It was a rather clear night with a half moon, and I could see the moon being obscured by the smoke.

When we pulled up to the house, I saw a lady in a robe yelling, "My babies are inside! My babies are inside!"

As we were the first fire truck on scene, without hesitation and without putting on any breathing apparatus (we only had one) and without a fire hose, the captain and I rushed into the front door as the fire was toward the rear. The smoke was thick. We both crawled on our hands and knees to work our way to the back of the house.

Even with our firefighting bunker gear and helmet, I could feel the heat as we maneuvered toward the back of the house. The smoke was thick, and we could hear the fire roaring close by. I was starting to cough as the smoke was filling and searing my lungs.

Then I heard a faint cry.

I yelled to my captain, "Cap, I hear something in this room! I'm going to the left!"

He responded, "OK! I'll go to the right!"

The cries were getting closer. I finally reached the faint cries and reached for a bundle on a bed but couldn't see what I was grabbing. All I knew was that I had the bundle of "faint cries" in my arms.

I shouted to my captain, "Cap, I've got it!"

"OK, I'm going out through the window!" he yelled back.

I could hear him gasping and coughing. The smoke was thickening and stabbing at our lungs. Fortunately, I took a quick right which led me into the hallway that led me back to the front room and out the front door. My eyes were burning. I was coughing up sputum, and it was running out of my nose. I could barely open my eyes as I stumbled off the front porch making sure I didn't fall on the "bundle" I was holding.

The lady came running up to me yelling, "My babies! My babies! Thank you for my babies!"

I could barely see and hear her. I was taking my helmet off, throwing up, and tearing my coat off to get some air and cool down.

She kept yelling, "Thank you for saving my babies, sir! Thank you - my babies are safe!"

After wiping my face, and mouth, and spitting up black sputum, my eyes focused and I could see her babies were... three small kittens!

Yes, three small kittens.

I dropped to my knees and thought, "Kittens! I almost killed myself for some damn kittens!" With an unsteady gait, I walked to the back of the fire truck and sat there on the running board, still trying to catch my breath.

All this unfolded in a matter of five minutes.

The second fire truck pulled up and proceeded to drop the hoses, connect to a fire hydrant and started to fight the fire. One of the firefighters from the second motor stopped to ask me, "Are you OK?" I said, "Yeah, three damn kittens, dude!"

As he ran off to join the other firefighters, the woman came up to me again. This time, she had the bundle of kittens and stretched her right arm to hug me.

She exclaimed, "You saved my kittens! How can I ever thank you?"

I responded, "You're welcome, ma'am."

She showed me the kittens that were wet and purring. They were looking at me as if they were thanking me.

I said as I patted one of the kittens, "Nice kitty... nice kitty."

Lesson Learned - Don't Get Burned

1. Please tell firefighters who or what may be inside the house that needs to be rescued or retrieved. While we all love pets, firefighters have been injured and killed saving someone's "fur babies." We want you, your family AND all of us to live a long happy life.
2. Let firefighters know where your family or pets may be. Which room? Did they go next door? Try to give us the most accurate information possible.
3. If you've exited a fire and you've left behind someone or something, PLEASE - do NOT go back inside! Once you are out, STAY OUT and call 9-1-1. Do not, I repeat, DO NOT go back inside a burning building.
4. Have an escape plan. Sit down and write one out with your family, and practice it together. Try it from various locations. Would you use a door or a window? Can you exit onto a roof or deck? Practice! Fire prevention is a major key to survival.
5. Install smoke alarms!

Small Disclaimer: I love pets, and many of us are willing to help them when we are safely able. I was not implying kittens *shouldn't* be saved - we just need to hear you say kittens/puppies/pets - NOT "babies!"

Chapter 2
No Time for Bad Jokes

On a bright and sunny Sunday afternoon, we were planning supper and getting our grocery list together at the station. It was around 2 p.m. when we received a call for a "still alarm." A "still alarm" is when they just send one fire truck. The "still alarm" was for a grass fire around four miles from the fire station. Again, I rode solo on the back of the old fire truck as we sped down the access road to get on the highway.

Getting onto the highway and having a "bird's eye" view of the terrain to my right, I could see a little smoke in a field to my right. I thought, "Wait, we got a different address. Are we passing this one up?"

Without the capability to communicate with my captain and the engineer (driver) I was unable to point out the smoke that I noticed. Minutes later, I saw the smoke in the direction of the address we were going to. Upon our arrival, we saw not only one grass fire, but three.

"What is going on here?" I thought to myself.

My captain, who looked ninety but was actually sixty-three years old yelled, "Get the red line!" The red line is the smallest hose on the fire truck which handles small fires such as dumpsters, piles of brush or lumber, and grass. I unreeled the red line and proceeded to extinguish the grass fires one by one.

"We have an arsonist here, Gonzales!" yelled the captain.

My captain was an old German fellow who, on my first day said to the rest of the firefighters at the station,

"We finally got us a Mexican on my crew!" The guys laughed at him and responded, "Yeah, Cap, and there's more comin' too!" More laughter followed, except for my captain.

We extinguished the three grass fires, reeled the red line hose back onto the fire truck and headed back to the station. Remember the smoke I saw in a field to my right on our way to the grass fires? Well, upon returning and going back to the station taking the same highway, I noticed the smoke again. This time, it seemed like there was more smoke and getting thicker and blacker. Again, not being able to communicate with the captain and the driver standing on the back of the fire truck, I couldn't relay that message to them.

After we backed into the station, I stepped off the back of the fire truck, and approached my captain as he was getting out of the front cab. I asked him, "Say, Cap, did you see that smoke off to the right by Roland street in that big field?"

He responded, "What about it?"

I asked him, "Don't you think we should go check it out before it gets any bigger?"

His response? "Don't worry about it. They'll call us."

I said, "Yeah, but it may get worse."

He asked, "Who's the Captain here, Gonzales?"

"You are, sir."

"That's right!" he said.

I said no more. An hour had passed when the tones rang and the fire department dispatcher voice rang out, "Number 9, number 9, respond to the same area you were at earlier. You have multiple grass fires again."

My captain walked over to the counter where the radio was and responded, "10-4. Number 9 is 10-96." This is a 10-code meaning "We're on the way."

I ran back and put on my coat and helmet, hopped on the back, strapped on the safety belt, and we hit the road. Destination: same place, same route.

As we were getting on the access road again, I could see that the smoke I saw earlier was billowing even more. I also noticed the captain and the driver looking to the right at the increasing smoke. We arrived and saw five different grass fires. Again, we proceeded to each one and extinguished the fires.

My captain said, "Damn arsonists! They never quit, do they Gonzales?"

I said, "I guess not, Cap. Did you see the smoke again on our way in?"

He quipped, "I said they'll call us, Gonzales!"

I said, "Yep, Cap. Sorry, I forgot. You're the captain."

We proceeded to reel the hose back in and headed back the same way. And, there it was again! This time I could see flames and the smoke was thicker, blacker, and now spreading even more. And there was no hesitation from my captain to stop and check it out.

We backed into the station and once more, I asked, "Cap?"

He yelled this time, "I don't want to hear it, Gonzales! I told you - they'll call us!"

I rolled my eyes and thought, "Conrad, you gotta be ready to work your ass off this afternoon so you better eat something real quick." Since the firefighter had not returned with the groceries, I went to the vending machine and bought a Coke and reached for my bag of snacks in the fridge.

Well, my hunch finally came to fruition. Another hour passed when the call came in. "Number 9, number 9, respond to Roland and IH-10 for a brush fire."

As I walked past my captain to get to the fire truck, he said, "I told you they would call us!" I didn't respond.

Now, when we arrived we pulled up onto the access road. I saw the fire had spread. To get to the fire, I had to jump a four-foot fence and pull the red line 100 feet over the fence. My captain was "pushing" the hose because he was just a tad too old to jump the fence.

We only had one breathing apparatus on the fire truck. Yes, back in those day, that was the minimum to carry on the fire truck. One breathing apparatus, and no, I didn't put it on. You were called a wuss if you did. No *real* firefighter used one according to these old guys!

I could see that the closest flames were about four to five feet high, and I had to extinguish what was in front of me before I could maybe... *maybe* ...reach the flames across. However, extinguishing the flames in front of me was my priority. I was able to put out what was in front of me but not beyond. So, in other words, this grass fire was NOT under control.

I yelled, "Say, Cap! We're gonna need some more help. The fire is spreading beyond us!"

He asked loudly, "You can't handle it, Gonzales?"

I said, "Cap, the fire is spreading beyond our reach! We'll need someone to get it from the other side!"

Well, I don't know how he did it, but next thing I know, he had climbed over the fence to see for himself. (To this day, I don't know how he jumped that barrier!)

As the Captain was walking toward me and stepping over burnt grass and rubble that I had extinguished, he picked up a burnt toilet seat that was broken in half. He picked up the toilet seat and brushed some of the soot off and said: "Hey, Gonzales! You see this half toilet seat?"

I yelled, "Yeah, Cap!"

He yelled, "It belongs to a half-ass fireman!" He proceeded to laugh at his own joke.

I said out loud, "That's a good one, Cap!" I felt the need to affirm and give a small laugh since he was the captain.

Now the fire had spread on the other side of the field, and the captain was still adamant not to call for backup. I continued dousing the embers in front of me and when I turned to my right, I noticed the wind started to change direction - drastically. The wind speed was picking up!

I yelled to the captain, "Hey, Cap! We're really gonna need some help here, and fast! The wind's changing direction!"

Now, he was standing on the other side of the fence close to the fire truck.

"How the hell did you get over the fence so quick, Cap?"

"Don't worry about it!"

I turned and saw the flames getting higher and noticed the tall grass and brush burning toward the path I had used to get to the fire.

I thought, "Shit! I better get outta here!"

I started running back and dragging the red line behind me so the hose wouldn't burn. But the flames were too fast for me and I dropped the hose and ran back to the fence as fast as I could.

As I was running, I could feel the heat to my left as the flames were getting closer. Then, I just about crapped my pants when I saw the fire truck pulling away! They had already unhooked the red line from the fire truck!

I yelled, "Hey, wait for me! Wait for me!"

I couldn't believe I was being chased by a brush fire and they were leaving me behind!

I yelled, "Hey, Cap! Hold on!"

They kept going down the access road!

I finally reached the fence and the flames were only thirty feet to my left! I had my bunker coat on but not my bunker pants (just uniform pants) as we usually fought grass and brush fires back then with only our coats, helmet, and boots.

I reached the fence and scrambled over. I couldn't get a grip on the fence with my firefighting rubber boots, I took them off and threw them clear over the fence and was just in my socks. I jumped over.

"Thank God!"

But - now my bunker coat was caught on the fence! I couldn't get loose, so I started to unclip my coat from top to bottom. I thought, "Shit. My ass is gonna burn on this fence!"

Finally, as the flames neared, I was able to break free from my coat and run toward the access road and the fire truck. I looked back and my coat was on fire!

I caught up to the fire truck and cursed my captain and the driver.

"Why the f---k did you all leave me?!"

The Cap said, "We can't have a fire truck burn!"

"Wow!" I yelled. "You motherf--kers left me to burn? You assholes!"

Talk about livid! I could not believe what had just happened!

What did the captain decide to do? He now called for some help! Finally! He literally almost cost me my life!

This fire turned out to be a third alarm fire with nine fire trucks, three brush trucks, three ladder trucks, three chiefs and the Assistant Chief who came from the downtown headquarters.

Total manpower: fifty-eight firefighters, three EMS units with six paramedics and three EMS supervisors. Total time at the scene: 36 hours.

All this resulted from the lack of common sense and stubbornness of one officer. Needless, irresponsible and totally incomprehensible. This is when I said to myself, "I'm gonna study and get promoted to get the hell outta this station. This guy is gonna kill me someday!"

Lesson Learned - Don't Get Burned

Just because you're at the bottom of the totem pole, like a rookie firefighter, if you see something that is not safe, LET SOMEONE KNOW!

If you have to bypass the chain of command, that's what you have to do.

All this could have been avoided; fortunately, no firefighter was injured or killed.

If you are a supervisor and one of your subordinates' notices something that is unsafe...LISTEN TO THEM! They may be saving LIVES or PROPERTY.

Chapter 3
Diving Deep

It was a sunny Saturday afternoon as we relaxed at the fire station. It was common to think of a weekend to chill out, lift weights, study for promotion, or play basketball or paddleball.

I was detailed to the ladder truck as a replacement for a guy on vacation. The ladder truck always had to be manned by four men. I was the fourth. My station, Station #9, had twelve firefighters manning a motor (pumper truck), and ladder truck, a district chief and his driver.

The ladder truck (with the 100-foot extension ladder) was responsible for overhauling a home, which is cleaning a house after the fire. They also were responsible for ventilating a home from smoke, extricating victims from car crashes and tearing down sheetrock during and after a fire to check if fire had spread into an attic. They had grappling hooks to retrieve bodies from the bottom of lakes or rivers when there was a drowning.

The pumper, or motor, carried all the hose for extinguishment of the fire. From small fires using the red line to major fires using the larger hoses, all necessary equipment was carried on the motor.

The call came in around 4:00 p.m.

Dispatcher: "Truck 9, Truck 9, respond to Southside Lions Park, respond to Southside Lions Park for a possible drowning. EMS and PD are on the way. 29's motor is also responding".

I donned my coat and we jumped on board the ladder truck and we were 10-96… on the way.

The park is located on the southeast part of town. It is a nice quaint park situated on six hundred acres with a lake and a winding road that circles the lake. Many people from the area would go to the park for picnics, walking, running, or just leisurely cruising through the park.

As we pulled into the park, we were directed by a park ranger (now Park Police) to the area where the "possible drowning" was suspected. We drove up, and we saw a very distraught family yelling and screaming at us, "Where the hell have you all been?!"

It took us around ten minutes to arrive from about five miles away. Unfortunately, getting cursed was very common as people think we "take our time" getting to the scene, which is not true, but in times of stress during an emergency event, it seems like it takes an eternity for emergency services to arrive. I'm sure if you've ever had to call 9-1-1 you know what I mean.

Ignoring the cursing, we stepped off the fire truck. Yes, we hadn't even gotten off the fire truck when we were approached by the family and friends that were cursing at us.

My officer, a captain, the engineer (driver of the fire truck), the other firefighter and I proceeded to ask, "Where is the victim?"

The mother yelled, "He's in the middle of the lake! He was trying to swim across with my other son but then he got tired and went under!"

I responded, "How long has he been under water?"

She yelled, "Too f---ing long! How do I know? Just go get him!"

Back in those days (1978), we had no rescue craft, runners, helmets, or fancy water rescue equipment like they have now. All we had, if we were lucky, were two life jackets and rope.

Captain Jack, as I called him, told me, "Conrad, go get the rope!" He called for the dispatcher to get a dive team out there. Well, back then, it would have taken an hour or more to respond. The fire department had no dive team and that was the responsibility of the police department or the "body recovery" team.

I replied, "Got it, Cap!"

I went to the back of the ladder truck and reached into a compartment where we had ropes. I grabbed it along with a life jacket. I went to the edge where my crew and the family were standing.

I told Cap, "Here you go, Cap!"

He looked at me and asked, "Do you swim?"

I answered, "Yes."

Captain Jack said, "Good, because we don't."

I looked at the other two firefighters and they just smiled and said, "You got it, Tarzan!" and grinned.

I thought, "Damn... Well, somebody's gotta do it and we can't waste any more time."

I was a certified lifeguard at one time. However, it's a little different when you can just step into a clear sparkling pool rather than walking barefoot into a murky, muddy lake with tangled weeds, and no way of knowing the depth.

I proceeded to tie the rope around my waist and I ditched the life jacket knowing that I was going to dive to the bottom of the lake. I took my boots and socks off as well as my fire department shirt and T-shirt. All I had on was my pants and underwear. Undressing to the last few items of clothing was going to ensure that I wasn't going to be weighed down.

Knowing I was taking a chance of stepping on glass or bottles, I walked gingerly into the water. I waded around ten to fifteen feet when it started getting deeper and up to my waist. I still had thirty yards to get to the point where they thought he went under. With the rope tied around my waist, I told the firefighters to pull me up if I didn't come up for some reason or another. I told them I was going to go under, feel the bottom (if I could reach it) and then come up for air.

I started treading water and swam my way to the area.

I heard the family and bystanders yell, "Right there! He should be right there!"

"OK!"

I thought, "Okay, Conrad, gotta go under now." I thought, "Please help me find this kid, Lord."

I took a deep breath and dove underwater. When I took swimming lessons as a young kid and in my lifeguard class, I learned how to "deep dive" by making sure my legs were up in the air and the weight of my legs would take me under.

As I was going down, I tried opening my eyes to try and see where to go.

I thought, "Damn! I can't see a thing!"

I closed my eyes and swam around seven to eight feet and felt… the bottom of the lake. I was feeling and looking for this kid not knowing what I would be grabbing at all. Scouring the bottom and feeling nothing but weeds and mud, I had to go up for air.

With the rope tied around my waist, I thought at least I have a lifeline and the guys could pull me out in the event I should get into trouble. But, "trouble" was the least of my concerns at the time. I just needed AIR. I hurried to the surface where I gasped and took a few breaths. I could hear the family yelling. "Did you find him?"

I yelled, "No!"

I made sure I swam straight up to get my bearings and swim over a few more feet so I wouldn't search the same area twice. I took a deep breath and went under again.

I scoured the bottom feeling some small weeds, a bottle, and mud. My eyes were still closed. I was still praying, "Please, Lord, let me find this kid!"

My lungs were running out of air and I had to come up again. Fortunately, it was daylight and I could see the surface as I was coming up for air. I thought to myself, "I'm glad it's not dark! I would not have done this if it was dark and without any lights at all!"

I surfaced and took a brief rest.

I heard, "Did you find him?" again.

I responded, "No, not yet!" I was treading water.

I took another deep breath and went under again. As I reached the bottom, I was thinking, "I can't be doing this all afternoon. He's probably dead…" The victim had been underwater for over thirty minutes now.

I was reaching desperately when I spread my arms out to feel the bottom. Then, suddenly I felt something very strange. I put my hand flat on his face! I just about screamed underwater!

I put my feet on the muddy bottom and pushed myself up toward the surface; I went up so fast the firefighters told me I looked like a bass that had just been hooked by a fishing line! They said my body was half way out of the water. I was thrashing with my hands and swallowing water as if I was drowning!

I yelled, "I found him!"

I could faintly hear the bystanders cheering and clapping. I was thrashing in the water still trying to get control of myself.

After a moment or two, I finally regained my composure and thought, "Okay, Conrad, no need to rush. The guy is gone. Control yourself!"

I knew I had to go under and get him. I had to focus on using what strength I had left to go back down and retrieve his body.

I took a deep breath and went under again. The Lord was with me as I got to the bottom; I immediately felt his upper torso. I grabbed hold of his hair and swam up. That was a technique I learned as a lifeguard: Grab the victim by the hair so they don't grab a hold of you. At this point, there was no struggle. He was presumably dead.

I finally reached the surface and continued to swim pulling him by the hair. I reached the edge with the firefighters pulling the rope that was tied around my waist. When I was about five feet from the edge, the firefighters along with some family members, waded into the water to assist me. They grabbed me and grabbed the kid.

I stumbled to the ground when the family started yelling to the paramedics, "Please, do something for him! He's gonna die!"

The paramedics told the family, "Ma'am, it's too late. He's already gone."

They started yelling and cursing at us, including the paramedics.

"You assholes! You don't want to save his life! What the f--- are you here for?"

One of the police officers had to restrain a family member when they started to aggressively approach us. Another officer yelled, "Ma'am, he's already gone! There's nothing more they can do! Please, stay back!"

One of the paramedics checked for a pulse and placed him on a cardiac monitor, and he was pronounced dead at the scene. Back then, the only person to be able to pronounce someone dead was the medical examiner, however, if we felt that there was no way to successfully revive someone, we would place the patient on a cardiac monitor and send the ECG reading to the cardiologist on call at University Hospital. From the hospital, they would be able to "see" the straight line and instruct us not to proceed with resuscitative efforts.

As all this was going on, I was sitting on the back of the fire truck. Someone, and still today I have no idea who, put a towel around my neck as I was bending over and trying to catch my breath. Whoever you are out there: thank you for your kind and angelic gesture.

I dried myself off and one of the paramedics brought my clothes to me and told me, "Great job, rookie."

I said, "Thanks."

We packed up and waited for the medical examiner's office to come and take the body. We tried to comfort the family but to no avail. They were distraught and overcome with grief. I wish we could have done more.

Lesson Learned - Don't Get Burned

How did all this happen?

The victim and his brother had been drinking and were going to walk around the lake. They decided they wanted to swim and race across the lake to the area where they had their picnic. They jumped into the water and started to swim across. To get to their picnic they had to swim a good forty yards. Being intoxicated, one of the brothers started to struggle. The other brother tried to help him stay afloat but was being pulled down. He had to let go and his brother went under and did not surface. The other managed to get to shore and ran to call for help.

Alcohol, poor judgment, and being naïve can be a fatal mix. That was the case in this tragic event. My sympathy goes out to the family.

However, could this drowning have been prevented? Of course. Picnics, family gatherings, and alcohol do not mix. How many times have you heard of people drowning or diving into unknown depths at a river or lake? Too many times, I have read about incidents exactly like this. Alcohol is a major contributing factor to many near-drowning incidents and drowning deaths. Many have died or suffered paralysis when drinking and diving into shallow water not knowing the depth.

Please, don't drink and swim, because you could drown. It's not worth it.

Chapter 4
The Full Moon

There is a myth or belief that when there is a full moon, people tend to get crazy. Yes, the dreaded full moon. The werewolves - er, people - come out in full swing. Car crashes, domestic violence, burglaries, fires, crime in any fashion seems to spike when that full moon rises. When I drove to the station knowing it would be a full moon that night, I had to emotionally prepare myself for a busy shift. The firefighters and paramedics saw the hype firsthand.

It was common to hear remarks from the boys at the station such as, "Hey, guys, it's gonna be a full moon tonight! Better get your ass ready 'cause we'll be working our asses off! And some of you guys need to work your ass off or get on a diet!"

When I arrived at my assigned fire station around 11:30 in the morning, I was told by my captain that I was going to be detailed to *another* station. I thought, "Great! I get to ride on a bench seat and not freeze my behind standing up in the back of the fire truck! Yes!"

On my way to my detail station, I was excited about my upcoming "comfort." Even though the seat was not totally enclosed, I could still ride next to the roaring engine but stay warm with the engine right next to me!

Well, wishful thinking! I pulled into the parking lot and noticed they had a spare fire truck sitting in the stall of the station. I thought, "Damn, I spoke too soon!" The spare fire truck had only a cab for the officer and the driver. I had to stand on the back… again! I proceeded to unload my gear and walked into the station. The captain, a seasoned veteran of over thirty-five years, greeted me and said, "Conrad, Welcome! Are you in on supper? It's just you, myself, and the other rookie!"

I responded, "Yes, only if you're cooking!"

He replied, "Of course, I'm cooking! The detail guy don't cook! He said he could make egg sandwiches!"

The captain, as mentioned, was a seasoned firefighter and one of the best cooks in the department! Anything you wanted... he cooked. And what a baker! Cakes, pies, and cookies were not out of the ordinary after supper! (That's my excuse for gaining weight in the department!)

The houses in that area were built in the early 1900s and made of nothing but solid wood. They were very intricate in style with high ceilings, no insulation, wrap-around porches, and more. Very nice but older homes. And there were those few older homes that were vacant or abandoned.

That afternoon, we handled a few small fires: two dumpster fires, a car fire, and a couple of grass fires. It got more complicated when the day included a house fire.

That night around 9 p.m., I walked to check on my car in the parking lot and looked up at the sky.

"Yeah, that moon sure is full and bright; it's going to be a busy night!"

(OK, I like to write poetry so excuse my short poems and phrases now and then.)

Then I walked back upstairs to the dorm. I looked around and thought, "I should sleep soundly. The Captain has his own room and the other rookie is on the other side of the dorm!" We had the whole station to ourselves. I made my bed, set my boots next to me, and got under the covers. I said my prayers as I put my head on my pillow.

"Dear Lord, please keep me safe tonight. Take care of my children and family and let me sleep until daylight!" That was my prayer before I went to bed at the station. I fell fast asleep.

The alarm sounded at 2:00 a.m.

The dispatcher came over the PA system throughout the station.

"We have a regular alarm...regular alarm in 6-0's district for a house fire. Be advised, there may be someone in the house according the neighbors. Regular alarm... 6-0's district. House on fire with a possible victim in the house. Not confirmed at this time."

The address was given but I could only hear the street name which I recognized and knew that we were only blocks away.

The rookie driver started the engine. I opened the stall doors and jumped on the back runner of the fire truck, and we pulled out of the station. Knowing that the street was just around the corner, we took a quick left against one-way traffic and another quick left. I could smell the smoke in the air. I thought, "Yep, a working fire! Here we go with the full moon... gonna be busy."

We arrived in less than three minutes and I could see smoke but no flames. The smoke was thick and it was pouring out of all the front and side windows.

I thought to myself as I hopped off, "At least the house is ventilating; that's a good sign."

A gentleman came to us and yelled, "There may be someone inside! It's a vacant house and there is a man that sleeps in there sometimes when it's cold!"

The captain yelled at me, "Conrad, let's go in!"

I yelled back, "Cap, let me put on the BA!" That stands for breathing apparatus.

He yelled back, "No time for that! Let's go inside!"

I said quietly, "Conrad, take a deep breath."

It was just the captain and me. No fire hose, no breathing apparatus, and no way of knowing where this possible victim might be. We entered the house through the front door which was unlocked. We were in a "search and rescue" mode. Today's firefighting techniques require you put on your BA and ensure that you are safe before entering a smoke-filled building or one where you see flames.

I could hear the captain yelling, "Just stay behind me!"

I yelled, "Right behind you, Cap!"

We weren't in there but two or three minutes when we could feel the heat from the flames. In training, we were taught to use the "buddy system" where, in a rescue mode or entering a building you stayed with your buddy so you wouldn't get lost. Well, I stuck with him because I didn't want to get in trouble without a BA! We were yelling for this victim while we were on our knees searching.

I started to gasp and cough. The smoke was not clearing at all. I could hear the captain coughing and spitting also.

I yelled to the captain, "Cap, we need to get out of here! I'm having trouble seeing and breathing!"

He shouted in response, "Good idea!" He was gasping and coughing as well.

I don't know how far we crawled and I thought to myself that we were not going to make it out to the door we came in.

The captain yelled at me, "Where's the front door?"

I yelled, "Cap, we can't make it to the front door!"

He was now crawling behind and next to me as I could feel him brush along the left side of my body. We found the hallway but the smoke was still thick and my lungs and eyes were burning. While we were crawling back, I looked to my right and saw a light in the darkness. It was another room.

I yelled to the Captain, "Cap! There's a light in here! Follow me!"

I felt him grab my boot as we both crawled to the light. When I saw the light getting closer, my head bumped into a wall!

I yelled, "Shit, Cap! It's a wall!"

Then, I stood up on my knees and noticed it was a window. The light I saw was the full moon shining through the window!

"Cap, it's a window!"

We always carried a basic tool belt. On the belt, we carried two steel spanner wrenches to use as tools. While I was coughing and gasping for air, I was able to grab one of my steel spanner wrenches and broke the window!

The window shattered and most of the glass landed outside. I climbed onto the window sill and yelled, "Cap, let's go!"

He replied, "I'm right behind you!"

We both scrambled out the window. The captain fell on top of me as I tumbled onto the ground outside and onto the broken glass. Fortunately, we had on our firefighting gear and suffered no injuries or cuts from the glass.

Smoke inhalation? Yes!

By the time we were outside, the rookie driver had laid the hose, wrapped it around a pole so he could pull away and find and connect to a fire hydrant. With that, the arriving firefighters were able to utilize the hose that was already laid and fight the fire. Smart thinking, rookie.

The captain and I suffered smoke inhalation. And, there was no victim. A bystander saw the homeless man running from the house after he started a small fire in the house to keep warm and unfortunately the fire spread.

The paramedics arrived and gave us oxygen and offered to take us to the hospital. My captain refused, and therefore, I did as well. I didn't say yes because I would have never heard the end of it. Yes, I would have been the laughingstock of the station. I would not have been tough enough!

The fire was extinguished and we headed back to the station.

It was a cold ride standing on the back runner of the fire truck; I had water and sweat dripping down my shirt and bunker pants. Upon returning to the station, I gathered my wet firefighting coat and hung it on the back of the fire truck, took a shower, climbed into bed and said my prayer.

"Please, Lord, keep me safe tonight and let me sleep until daylight."

I soon fell asleep and slept until daylight.

That, my friendly reader, is how a full moon saved my life and the life of my captain. I saw the light, and I continue to appreciate the light from the full moon for that night could have ended tragically for both of us.

Lesson Learned - Don't Get Burned

When it comes to search and rescue, in this case, I should have gone with my gut instinct and put on my breathing apparatus. I took a chance and it almost cost me my life. With only one breathing apparatus on the fire truck, I should have stuck to my guns and said to the captain, "Sorry, Captain, but I will put on a breathing apparatus."

What if we both would have become unconscious from smoke inhalation? What if we were both incapacitated? One or both of us could have perished. My dad would always tell me: "They are giving you some equipment to make sure you don't die from suffocation!"

I should have listened to Dad. Fortunately, no one was hurt and all we had to do was to extinguish the fire.

There are hundreds, if not a few thousand homes, here in San Antonio and surrounding areas that are vacant and a haven for drug users and the homeless. If you happen to live next to a vacant home that you feel may be a threat or danger to your family or the neighborhood, call the city or authorities so they can find a way to either put it on the market, or, in some cases, have the home razed.

If you see homeless people living in vacant homes, they can be directed to other resources in the area where they can have a safe place to stay and a hot meal. The homeless face very difficult times and, they too, need shelter. We can also assist by donating food and clothing to shelters.

A final lesson: Appreciate the full moon - it is a guiding light from above.

Chapter 5
The Full Bloomer

No, the full bloomer is not ladies' underwear! A full bloomer describes a house fire or building that is burning from the foundation up and fully engulfed in flames.

My first shift at the station started on an interesting note. First, I was nervous as hell just driving to the station located on the east side. I always wondered why I was assigned to that station as I asked to be assigned to a station on the south side of town since that is the area I grew up.

I knew the south side of town pretty well. We used to cruise along SW Military Drive, go to the Mission Drive-In, visit South Park Mall, and other eating establishments, like Gyro's, Bud Jones, and many more. I didn't venture anywhere else for I really didn't want to get lost!

Just a few days earlier before graduating from the academy, we were given our station assignments. I was anxiously waiting to read what station I was going to.

"Conrad M. Gonzales, Jr., assigned to Number 9's Fire Station, C Shift."

I asked one of my graduating buddies, "Where the hell is Number 9's Fire Station?" He had no idea. I asked my training officer, "Where is #9's Fire Station, Sir?"

He answered, "At the corner of Mittman and Delmar."

I asked again, "Where is Mittman and Delmar?"

He said, "Off Porter and S. Gevers"

Still puzzled, I asked again, "Where the hell is that?"

"It's on the EAST side close to IH-10 and Walters!" yelled my training officer.

Still in a state of uneasiness, I thought to myself, "What did I do wrong at the academy to not get one of the stations I requested? Oh well, Number 9's Fire Station, here I come!"

Without GPS back then, we had to resort to using a map book. I drove over to the station the day before to make sure I knew where I was going. Why? My dad always told me, "If you don't know where you're going and it's an important meeting or you're reporting for your first day of work, go find it the day before or leave early so you don't arrive late." Those words are still etched in my head today and, yes, I will arrive at least 15 minutes early to my destination. My dad said, "It's called work ethic. That's what employers look for - dedicated individuals!"

The following day, of course, I arrived an hour early.

I pulled into the station and got my bunker gear from my car and proceeded to walk into the fire station. I was met by another firefighter.

He saw me and asked, "Are you the rookie?"

I said, "Yes, sir!"

He took my gear and said, "Here, Rookie, let me help you with that!" He led me inside the station and got on the PA system.

He yelled over the microphone, "Hey, everyone! The rookie is here! His name is "Combat!"

I corrected him, "That's Conrad."

He responded and yelled over the PA system again, "Oh, I'm sorry guys! I stand corrected! It's Conway!"

"It's Conrad." I continued to spell it for him, "C-O-N-R-A-D. Conrad." I repeated.

Pressing down on the mic, he yelled again over the PA system, "Hey, guys! He also knows how to spell his name!"

You could actually hear the other firefighters laughing upstairs and in the kitchen.

I thought to myself, "This is going to be interesting."

That night I thought I was going to bed early but at this station we had ten firefighters; four on the pumper truck, four on the ladder truck, and the district fire chief and his driver. They, of course, didn't all go to bed at 10:00 p.m. or after the news. Being an old fire station, all recreational activities were upstairs in the dorm. So, taking a nap during the day or going to bed early was usually noisy as "the boys" were either playing ping pong or pool, at all hours. Taking a nap was a challenge!

Finally, around 1:00 a.m., I laid down, said my prayers, and went to sleep with two firefighters within two feet on each side of my bed. Yes, another challenge with sleep because they either snored, talked in their sleep, or the bed rattled when they turned on their sides or moved, but all was quiet until 3:00 a.m.

Beep, beep, beep!

"We have a regular alarm, a regular alarm in 6-0's district! Number 9 motor, Number 9 truck, Number 3 motor, and Number 30. Respond to the corner of Martin Luther King and Rio Grande for a house fire. Respond to Martin Luther King and Rio Grande for a house fire."

Suddenly all lights turned on. I woke up turned to my side, put my feet into my boots, stood up and pulled up my pants and my suspenders. (There was no problem with "bumping heads" with the firefighter next to me as we all had our boots "waiting" on the left side of the bed facing the sliding pole.) We all slid the pole and I ran to climb onto the back of the fire truck.

The engineer was already starting the engine, turning on the lights, pulling out and I hadn't even strapped on yet! Holding on to the bar when we pulled out and turned left onto the street, I was able to put on my safety belt without falling off! My first night… my first fire… my first time almost falling off the damn truck!

Whizzing down the street and turning left onto the main street, I could see the "glow" as I was riding on the back of the fire truck. My heart was racing a hundred miles an hour and my knees were clanging against each other with nerves.

As we were getting closer, my heart was beating faster and the "glow" was getting larger. It only took us maybe four minutes to arrive, and there it was - the "Full Bloomer!" The fire had already engulfed the whole house from the foundation up, and flames were shooting at least sixty feet into the sky!

Mesmerized by my first full bloomer, I literally froze standing and watching the fire. Never had I seen a house that was fully engulfed in flames! Yes, I froze. The truck had come to a complete stop and I was just standing there looking at this great phenomenon of flames and the orange glow that lit up the sky and the neighborhood around it.

The captain saw that I was still standing on the back of the fire truck.

He yelled, "Hey, Conrad, whenever you're ready to fight this fire let me know so I can tell the driver to go hook up to the fire hydrant! Are you done looking at the fire? Get your ass off and let's get to work!"

I snapped to it and responded, "OK, Cap! Sorry!"

I got off, took the nozzle and hose, locked in while the fire truck took off to a hydrant. I was still mesmerized as I could now feel the heat from the fire!

The captain yelled, "Don't worry about putting the fire out, we have to protect the exposures! Did they teach that to you in training? They don't teach y'all crap nowadays!"

I couldn't believe he was asking and discussing firefighting techniques while we waited for water! I yelled, "Cap, yes, I know about protecting exposures... put water on the houses next to the house on fire so the others don't catch on fire!"

He yelled, "Shit! Maybe they are teaching you something!" He laughed.

My captain was this old German fellow who was in his 90s, I mean 60s. He really looked old! He was the one that first saw me and quipped, "Wow, I finally got a Mexican on my truck!"

Now I could feel the water charging the hose and the captain yelled, "Open it up, Gonzales! Hit the house to the left!"

We started "wetting down" the house on the left as it was closer to the burning home.

The other trucks showed up and the second pumper did the same to the house on the other side. The third pumper continued to extinguish the "full bloomer".

Finally, after about 30 minutes, we had the fire under control.

I was ready for the agitation and the harassment.

"Conrad is frigid! He froze!"

"What a rookie! He froze!"

For a second there, I thought they were going to give me a nickname like "Ice Cube" or "Frozen Pop." Well, I'm glad I didn't give them any ideas. I'm just glad we made it back safely. Another night... another Full Bloomer.

Lesson Learned - Don't Get Burned

This first fire taught me a lesson. When you get to the fire - fight the fire!

Yes, I froze, but I'm sure there are firefighters reading this story that are thinking "Yep, I remember going through that, too!"

It was my first big fire, and I knew it wouldn't be my last. That same morning, we responded to two more "working fires" and some grass fires. When I went home, I was beat. I showered and went to bed. I slept for twelve long hours. When I woke up that evening, I remember thinking, "Conrad, this is your job now. The Lord put you here for a reason: to save lives and property."

I had a long and rewarding career ahead of me.

Thank you again, Lord, for putting me here to serve Your people.

Chapter 6
First Flight

This is the story of my first night with San Antonio AirLife as a flight paramedic. It was June of 1994. It was hard to believe that I was employed by an air medical rescue helicopter in San Antonio. Many paramedics, nurses, and firefighters dreamed of "flying with AirLife!" And now, I was driving on my way to my first night as a "flight paramedic intern." On the job training, if you will, was going to be something to look forward to! After weeks of training with some of the current flight paramedics and flight nurses, I was now going to be introduced to a world that was the envy of many. The "Elite Few" or "Elite Crew" was the nickname that was given to those who worked with AirLife. Wow, I was one of them!

I arrived at 6:30 p.m. knowing that the shift started at 7:00 p.m. I always made it a habit to arrive early just to make sure I didn't "miss a flight," and of course, Dad always told me to get there early. It was now 6:45 p.m. and both the oncoming flight nurse and paramedic were there. The oncoming shift pilot had just arrived when he motioned and called out to us, "OK, time to take off!"

I said, "Wow! I just got here and we have a call!"

"Well, no," he said. He turned and looked at me and said, "C'mon, Conrad! We're gonna do a check flight. I want to make sure this other guy [another pilot] knows how to fly this helicopter. Want to come?"

What could I say? Then I thought, "He wants to see if this pilot knows how to fly the helicopter? Geez, shouldn't he already know how to do that?"

He said, "Not to worry, Conrad. I'm the lead pilot and I have to watch and monitor the pilots while they fly the chopper."

Suddenly, I felt relieved. I told him unconvincingly, "Of course... I knew that!"

We didn't have to run to the helicopter as I was hoping to and had seen before. I was waiting for the "let's go!" adrenaline rush to kick in; instead we slowly worked our way to the helicopter.

I stepped in and sat on the jump-seat and buckled up as the crew did a "clear left and clear right" check. I put on my headset and plugged in to hear the pilot tell the other pilot, "Let's show Conrad what we can do."

I thought, "Hmmm...."

As the blades turned and whirled to full speed, I realized that I was now a part of the "Elite Crew." We lifted off.

The ground and the downtown area suddenly started to look rather small. We ascended and started to fly west where the sun was setting. With the sun setting off in the distance I couldn't help but look down and see San Antonio from an aerial view of a helicopter.

It was a beautiful evening and the skies were turning a burnt orange because of the sunset. It was somewhat cloudy and I could see the sun peeking through the sky. Because of the "check flight" for the pilot, the lead pilot said over the PA system, "I'm going to have to put you guys on mute so you can't hear when I'm chewing out the pilot!"

The flight nurse said, "No problem!" The look on my face showed her I wasn't sure about that so she said, "He likes to kid around a lot."

I didn't know what to think but what did catch my attention was the extremely sudden turn to the left which

I believe, left my intestines and "family jewels" behind! We were not warned of the sharp left bank turn!

He took us off mute and asked, "What did you think of that?"

I was still pulling my heart and intestines back into my chest and checking to make sure my "family jewels" were back in their place!

The flight paramedic yelled, "That was cool, dude!" I haphazardly smiled at him.

We started flying southeast; the pilot stated we were going toward Stinson Field, a small airport on the southside of town. As we approached the area, I noticed we were descending fast. I looked at the flight paramedic when he told me not to worry. "This is part of his check flight."

We were now flying at 160mph ten feet above the airstrip! What a rush! I just hoped there weren't any ten-foot deer running across or a light pole protruding out of the ground.

Then the helicopter suddenly shot straight up! What a roller coaster ride! Hmmmm….I'm glad they only do this once or twice!

Finally, it was all over. No more sudden bank turns, flying ten feet above the ground or shooting straight up into the sky. The pilot jokingly told us over the PA system, "OK, he passed!"

"Thank God!" I told myself.

Then we started flying west. It was now around 7:45 p.m. As we were flying, I saw that we were ascending, and the pilot said we were going to an altitude of 5,000 feet. There was cloud cover as if a blanket was hovering over the city. Then, all of a sudden, we're flying into the clouds. Not being able to see a thing was creepy. Nothing at all in front of you… just a gray haze.

Then, as if God opened up a hole in the clouds, there in front of us we saw the sun setting! I was in awe! The carpet of clouds beneath us looked as if we could literally step out and stand on it.

I had to pull my clear visor up and pull down my shaded visor to protect myself from the sun. What a beautiful sight! It felt like I could just reach and touch the sun in front of me! I thought to myself, "Thank you Lord for providing such beauty!"

Then I thought, "Geez, this is part of my job. Flying in a helicopter. I could do this forever!" I couldn't help but keep gazing at the sun and the orange sky.

I heard the pilot ask me over the headset, "Conrad, what do you think?"

I responded, "Never have I seen such a beautiful sky as this! Especially from a helicopter!"

I heard him tell the other flight paramedic, "Can you tell Conrad he has to press the button to speak? He's a newbie, you know!"

Yes, a newbie, I was.

After about an hour of flying and heading back to base, I heard Flight Com (the dispatcher) say, "AirLife One, AirLife One." The pilot responded, "AirLife One, go ahead."

The dispatcher said, "You have a call toward Lockhart, Texas. Stand by for your coordinates."

The flight nurse looked at me and said, "This is it. Your first call." I swallowed hard as if swallowing an apple. Lockhart, Texas is about a 45-minute drive east of Austin, Texas. We were making the call because the air medical helicopter in Austin was out on another call. We were the closest.

"AirLife One, here are your coordinates."

She blared out the coordinates while the co-pilot entered them into the system. The co-pilot, who was being checked, had to go with us because, of course, we didn't have time to drop him off at base.

Next thing I knew, the flight nurse and flight paramedic hurriedly reached into drawers pulling out IV solutions, pressure bags, IV catheters, needles and began to prepare everything the patient would need.

Then I heard, "AirLife One, AirLife One...you have a major 10-50 (ten code for a car crash) and may have two patients at scene and two possible DOS." I turned to the flight nurse. She said, "Dead on Scene." I knew what that meant. We also used that term in EMS.

The flight to the scene was a blur as I was watching and doing what the flight nurse and paramedic were asking me to do. By the time I knew it, we were descending and listening to the pilot while he was asking the firefighters on the scene to secure a landing zone.

As we were descending, I could see that we were going to land on a two-lane highway. I could hear the firefighters over the radio telling the pilot "You have some power lines to your right and traffic has been stopped!"

As we circled the scene, we wanted to ensure that all was secure. This is normal when you're getting ready to land. We want to make sure there are no wires going across the highway. Wires can take a helicopter down in a split second, and crews have been killed when striking wires upon descending.

The scene was cluttered with lights from the fire trucks, ambulances, highway patrol, and bystanders were instructed to stay back from the rotor blades. They can cause 90 mph winds and knock someone off their feet.

As we made sure the area was clear, we started to descend. I could hear both the pilot and flight nurse communicating.

"Clear right!" the flight nurse said in calm manner.

"Clear left," responded the pilot.

We landed, and the flight paramedic opened the side door as the flight nurse stepped out the other. Running and being escorted by the firefighters to the scene, I was right behind them when the first responders yelled, "We have four female patients, but the two in the front are dead! The two females in the back seat are very critical. They are conscious, however! We have neck braces on them and we've started two lines in each of them!"

The flight nurse responded, "Great! Thanks!"

Then, we got to the crash. The first things that I recognized were two yellow blankets: one laid over the deceased driver and the other on the passenger, a young female that was on the hood of the car. Next, we found two young patients crumpled in the back seat as if placed in a package on the floor. Surprisingly, both patients were still alive, conscious, and writhing in pain.

Witnesses stated the car, a 1965 red Mustang, was traveling at a high rate of speed. Sixty-five or seventy miles-per-hour is what they said. While entering the curve, the driver lost control because the right wheels were on gravel. The car left the road and hit an oak tree head on. The oak tree had to have been the largest oak tree within miles, with a circumference of maybe six or seven feet. I could not have put my arms around it.

Both the driver and front passenger died instantly. The driver, with no seat belt, was crushed between the seat and the steering wheel with the dashboard on her chest. The front passenger flew through the windshield striking the tree and dropping onto the hood. Her body laid half way on the hood and over the fender.

The roof of the car had already been taken off with the "Jaws of Life," a scissor-like mechanical device that can cut a car in half. I placed myself gingerly and carefully in the back seat to evaluate and examine each patient. Space was limited, but I was able to squeeze myself in there.

I yelled at each of them to get a response, and they both yelled at me "Get me out! Am I gonna die?!"

I told them, "We are gonna get you out right now! It's going to hurt when we pull you out, and you can scream all you want!"

With the help of the firefighters, we placed a backboard behind each of them and teams of two pulled the two young women out. Yelling and screaming, we placed them on two stretchers. Fortunately, they already had IV's in them and that was one less item we had to do on the helicopter. We gave them some pain medication.

As we packaged them to load them onto the helicopter, we radioed to the pilot that we had to take both patients as they were very critical.

He said, "No problem. Brackenridge Hospital is in Austin."

We acknowledged, "10-4."

As the two patients were being wheeled on the stretcher toward the helicopter escorted by firefighters and the flight crew, I turned to the firefighters and yelled, "Thank you and great job!"

Yes, they did an awesome job of getting our patients ready. I knew they now had the gruesome and traumatizing task of piecing everything together and waiting for the arrival of the medical examiner. They had the task of placing the bodies of the two females in hearses to be transported.

We loaded our patients onto the helicopter. The flight nurse and paramedic were moving so fast it was hard to determine who was doing what. The helicopter lifted off and we were on our way. Our ETA was 10-12 minutes.

Blood pressure monitors, ECGs, and pulse oximeters (a device that measures oxygen level in the bloodstream) were placed. I was in awe watching what they were doing.

We landed on the hospital's helipad, and we were met by ER staff and two stretchers. The pilot gave the thumbs up to the ER staff to approach the helicopter after we opened the doors and placed our equipment ready for the transfer to their stretchers. Our patients were still alive.

We loaded the patients and wheeled them into the elevator and down to the emergency room. I went with the flight nurse as she gave the report to the doctors and ER nurses. The flight paramedic went into another ER room and I could hear him give his report. You could also hear another doctor yell, "Chest X-ray! I need a chest tube, stat! Let's get another line! I need blood work, now! What's the blood pressure? Ma'am, can you hear me ok? Where are you hurting?"

I thought "Every damn bone in her body is broken. She's hurting everywhere!"

I walked over to the other room where the other patient was at. Same thing… same orders… same questions… same response… same yelling.

Chaos. That best described the emergency room where the patients were being treated. I heard the flight paramedic give his report to the ER doctor while the ER doctor blared orders to the nurses. The young patient screamed as the doctor inserted a chest tube into the side of her chest. Her lung had collapsed. No anesthesia, no sedative, nothing. Minutes later, she breathed easier and her lung was inflated again.

The flight nurse and flight paramedic walked out of each room after giving their report. The flight paramedic told me, "Thanks, and great job."

I thought, "Geez, what did I do?"

Then I realized I was a part of a team that may have saved the lives of two young females - in a different manner than normal - by air rescue.

I was coming down from my adrenaline rush as both the flight paramedic and flight nurse sat down to write their reports. Their reports reminded me of the reports I wrote after transporting patients to the hospital while in EMS. Sometimes I would take twenty to thirty minutes to document everything I did when treating a patient. From documenting times of IVs started to defibrillating patients that had heart attacks to applying pressure bandages, to documenting times when patients went into cardiac arrest; documenting every detail of the call was tedious and time-consuming, but very important.

The flight back to San Antonio was long, but actually short. When I say long, flashes of the two dead women in the front of the car came back to me. I realized that there was nothing different with this call than any other call I responded to when I worked with EMS. The only difference was we transported by air and not by ground. Another difference was doing procedures that we didn't normally do in EMS.

The "Golden Hour" is the time that a trauma patient needs to improve the chances of survival. In this case, there was no "Golden Hour" for the two front-seat victims. They were killed instantly.

To this day, I don't recall if our two patients we picked up survived. Sometimes, I didn't want to know.

Follow-up on patients was part of our job after taking patients to hospitals. A policy that I wasn't comfortable with. Why? There were times when I really thought patients would survive but didn't. And there were times when I thought "This patient won't make it," but he did.

At least I know we were there, and they were alive when we left. I hope they are alive today. If not, it was God's plan, not ours.

Lesson Learned - Don't Get Burned

Every time I hear or talk about Lockhart, Texas, it reminds me of my first call with AirLife. And, yes, how the crash could have been prevented. Unfortunately, the cause of this crash was attributed to speed, poor judgment, no seat belts, and the sturdy oak tree. The impact of the crash was so great it was a miracle that the two rear seat passengers were not killed instantly.

What is the lifesaving message?

Slow down, buckle up, and think ahead - especially if you don't know the road.

Did the driver of the vehicle know the road? I don't know, and I never will. Mustangs that were built in 1965 did not have seat belts. It's amazing we survived when we were kids because our parents drove cars without seat belts and car seats.

Now that seat belts are standard, I don't know what it'll take to convince occupants to buckle up, slow down, and make better choices. How many of us have been in a car wreck? How many of us did stupid things on the road and now wonder "What the hell was I doing back then? How did I survive?"

At least we're here to ask ourselves that. Some aren't. So please: buckle up, slow down, think ahead, and if you are traveling on a road you don't know, be extra cautious and aware. You just might make it to your destination.

Chapter 7
Dead Man's Curve

How many of you have ever heard of Dead Man's Curve located in west Bexar County close to Helotes, Texas? For that matter, how many Dead Man's Curves are there in our country or around the world?

Dead Man's Curve, off Scenic Loop Road, is northwest of San Antonio just outside Helotes, Texas. It is a winding road that goes for several miles with a small river running parallel and several bridges. Some areas have a sharp drop to the river below. This is a curve where, unfortunately, many people have died in car crashes.

Here's my story.

We were returning from another call in the Geronimo Village area that didn't require transporting the patient to the hospital. My partner and I decided to take the "scenic route" which is Dead Man's Curve. Knowing the "Curve," we knew that we had to be careful as cars sometimes had a tendency to go too fast and there were those that did not know the road well. However, it was the shortest way back to Bandera Road and would take us back to the fire station.

It was lunchtime and we were hungry, so we decided to stop at the Grey Moss Inn to grab something to eat. When we pulled into the parking lot, we saw no vehicles.

I told my partner, "I think they're closed."

Sure enough, the sign said closed for renovation.

"Damn," I said. "Where to now? I guess we'll stop in Helotes to see what we can find there."

The radio blared moments after we pulled out of the parking lot. "841, 841. Respond to the seventeen thousand block of Scenic Loop Road for a major accident. 841, 841. Make the seventeen thousand block of Scenic Loop Road for a major accident."

I told my partner, "Shit, that's around the corner."

He said, "Yep."

As we pulled onto Scenic Loop Road, I said to my partner, "I bet it's Dead Man's Curve."

He said, "I'm not a bettin' man, but I think you're right."

We turned the lights and siren on and continued. Since I was driving, and being familiar with the winding and curvy road, I knew that I couldn't drive too fast. Actually, I was driving about forty miles an hour but slowed down to 25 mph on the curves. That's how "curvy" the road was and didn't want to take any chances with any other vehicles coming around the curves.

After only about four minutes, we arrived on the scene and there it was; a single vehicle on its right side with the driver's side up in the air and the passenger side on the shoulder of the road. The roof of the car was literally leaning up against a tree that kept it from falling into the small river below.

There was no one on the scene yet; the volunteer EMS and fire department were supposedly on the way. With volunteers, it takes a little while for them to arrive, as in that area, some usually respond in their vehicles and someone has to drive to the fire station to pick up the fire truck. So, I imagined they wouldn't get there for another fifteen to twenty minutes.

I got on the radio and told the dispatcher, "841 to Dispatch, 841 to Dispatch. We'll need a truck for extrication and can you send a wrecker ASAP!"

No response from Dispatch.

One more time I yelled into the radio, "841 to Dispatch, 841 to Dispatch! Can you hear me? 841 to Dispatch, 841 to Dispatch! Can you hear me?"

Then, I yelled to my partner, "Shit, we're in a dead spot! They can't hear us!"

Well, sure enough, we were in an area where there were peaks and valleys and, yes, an area where we could not transmit on the radio at all.

I thought, "Dead spot in Dead Man's Curve... not good."

The reason for requesting the wrecker and the ladder truck was the position of the car. The car was on its right side and precariously being held by a small tree. When I walked around to check the car and look for the patient, I saw the patient lying on his back and crumpled at the bottom of the car against the right passenger door. Because the left side of the car was protruding up in the air, the only way to get to the patient was to climb on top of the left side of the car and climb down through the driver's side broken window.

Now, the problem: As mentioned, the roof of the car was leaning precariously against a small tree with a trunk about six inches in diameter. The right front and right rear tires were also slightly off the ground. The tree was the only object keeping the car from falling over into a small river which was about 5 feet below. Any movement or sudden shift could break the tree and the car would then plunge into this river. I really didn't know how deep it was and I wasn't about to find out.

With the car leaning against the tree, I yelled to my partner, "Get on the radio and try again!" He tried and still no response.

I walked to the front of the car not wanting to get near as I didn't want the car to fall and take me with it into the river.

I yelled, "Can you hear me? Sir, can you hear me?"

He barely responded, "Yes."

I yelled, "OK, we're gonna get you out but please do not move at all!" I repeated, "Do not move at all! We have to secure the car, OK?"

No response from the patient.

I had to think, "What can I use to secure the car? A piece of 4x4 lumber? A branch lying around?" Nothing. Securing or "chocking" a vehicle entails placing an object to keep the vehicle from tipping over or moving forward or backwards. This technique is similar to "chocking" a vehicle when you're changing a tire or working under a car.

Then, around the corner, an angel drove up. The tow truck! He pulled up and got out of his vehicle. Before I could even yell instructions, he yelled, "I got you!" He knew exactly what to do.

He immediately turned his tow truck with the rear end facing the "bottom" of the car. Next, he released the mechanism on his tow truck, grabbed the hook at the end of the chain and "hooked" the rear axle. He grabbed a spare chain and hooked the front axle, too. Looking at me he said, "I'm not going to pull the car down! I'm just gonna ask you to hold the chain as I slowly bring the chain to hold it and keep the car stable!"

I knew he'd done this before. How did he arrive so quickly? Well, he just happened to hear the call come in on his scanner and wasn't but a few miles down the road. Thank God!

In the meantime, my partner was grabbing the scoop, trauma kit, and getting the stretcher out. Still, no volunteer firefighters. A scoop is a device similar to a backboard, that is made out of aluminum and comes apart in the middle to enable us to "scoop" a patient up to transport.

Once the car was stable enough, I proceeded to climb onto the top, or left side of the car. Fortunately, the tow truck driver had an extra pair of gloves for me to use so I wouldn't burn myself on the exhaust pipes. I was praying while I was climbing, "Please, Lord, I trust in you and I trust you'll keep me and my patient safe."

I climbed onto the top and lowered myself into the car through the driver's side broken window. Fortunately, there was no movement of the vehicle.

I climbed down through the window being careful not to step on the patient and worked my way to him. I yelled to my partner, "I need a medium C-collar!" That was the cervical collar or neck brace to provide spine immobilization.

I told the male patient, who was approximately 40-years-old, "My name's Conrad. I'm gonna get you out of here, but I really need you to be still. Let me make all the movements, okay?" I asked him, "Are you hurting anywhere?"

He responded, "Just my shoulder!"

I responded, "Did you have your seat belt on?"

I assumed he did not otherwise he'd still be strapped to his seat belt. But, some patients have taken their belts off before EMS arrives and "fall" out of the car.

"No, I did not." He whimpered.

"OK, as I said, we really cannot make any sudden moves."

He said, "OK."

I thought to myself, "This is going to be a very tough extraction. How are we going to get this guy out? We've got to get him out quickly." Fortunately, and thank God, there was no fuel spill. That would have been even worse knowing there was gas leaking with the possibility of ignition. That would not have been good!

I asked him, "Can you move your legs?"

He said, "Yes."

Protocols would warrant no movement of the patient at all due to risk of spine injury. However, in this situation I had to decide. Do I risk spine injury or risk both of us possibly falling into the river and drowning?

As crumpled as he was, I really thought he'd have some serious injuries, but the only complaint was his right shoulder.

I told him, "I'm gonna need your help. We have to get you out quickly and I'm gonna help you try to stand up. It's gonna make it easier for us to get you out. If you feel any pain at all when you move, let me know. OK?"

As we were planning the escape, I heard the volunteers pull up. I yelled to them, "Guys, I have to stand him up so we can slide the scoop into the car! Once we stand him up, I'll secure him to the scoop and then we'll have to pull him out through the driver's side window!"

One of the volunteers asked, "Why don't we take him out through the front windshield?"

I told him, "He's small enough and light enough to get him out through the driver's side window. This would be easier with the wrecker holding the car and the other volunteers assisting. Besides, you're too close to the edge of the river and walking him out through the windshield puts all of us too close to the edge of the river." I didn't want to risk any of the firefighters accidentally slipping and falling into the river.

Meanwhile, the other volunteer firefighters knew exactly what to do. They chocked the car with wooden blocks to keep it from tilting. Now, with two chains and the car being "chocked", I felt "secure" enough to ask two of the lightest volunteers to climb on to the side of the car and lower the scoop into the car.

Fortunately, with only pain to the patient's right shoulder and the cervical collar in place, I was able to assist him to stand up.

The volunteers tied two ropes to the end of the scoop and lowered it down. I secured him to the scoop and also tied the bottom of his feet to the scoop so he wouldn't slide down while they pulled him straight up.

As a paramedic instructor, one of the skills I really enjoyed was extrication and spine immobilization. One has to be rather creative especially when it comes to scenarios like this.

The two firefighters slowly lifted him out and I made sure his feet were "standing" at the end of the scoop. We were finally able to lift him out through the window and lower him off the car to the ground.

With the car still secured, I was able to climb up and out with the help of another firefighter. Getting off the car was easier now as the firefighters placed a small ladder against the car and I climbed down.

Boy, how I wish it would have been that easy if they had arrived earlier. But, sometimes that's not the case. There have been many calls where we, the paramedics, arrived before the firefighters or other first responders.

Fortunately for our patient, the only injury he suffered was a dislocated shoulder and some scratches on his head and arms. He was not wearing a seatbelt and that is why we found him crumpled inside the vehicle. Thankfully, he was safe staying in the vehicle; he could have been thrown out, crushed by the car, or even thrown into the river below.

We loaded him into the ambulance and continued our assessment. We started an IV and told him he was very lucky.

After we stabilized him in the ambulance, I asked my partner, "We ready to go?"

"Yes."

I stepped out of the ambulance and quickly walked over to the volunteer firefighters to give them a big thanks. I looked over toward the tow truck driver and told him, "Thank God you showed up, man!"

He said, "I heard it on the scanner and rushed over. I'm glad I could help."

"You're an angel, brother. We appreciate it!"

I climbed into the front and drove away from the scene. We arrived at the hospital and transferred him to the emergency room staff. Even they told him he was lucky.

After transporting the patient to the hospital and returning to the station, one of the volunteer firefighters called me at the station. He told me that after we left, and the car was finally taken away by the wrecker, he took the six-foot pike pole from the fire truck and inserted it into the river. He wanted to see how deep it was.

He told me, "More than six feet, Conrad...could have been worse."

"You're right." I told him. "Thanks for your help. Great job. I really appreciate you guys being out there."

He replied, "Nah, you guys were awesome! Call us anytime!"

That day, the Lord was with us and Dead Man's Curve did not claim its man.

Lesson Learned - Don't Get Burned

This is another reminder to drive carefully in unfamiliar areas and not to get complacent with areas that you do know. In this particular incident, the driver lived in the area and was familiar with "Dead Man's Curve," however, due to complacency and the dangerous curve, he had an accident.

Here's what you can do to decrease the likelihood of being involved in a wreck in unfamiliar places:

- Slow down! If you are on a highway or road and are unfamiliar with the area, just slow down. Be wary of what's ahead, whether it's other vehicles, pedestrians, bicyclists, sharp curves, or animals. Hey, you may even have an ambulance up ahead!
- Expect the unexpected. You never know what might cause you to brake suddenly.
- I love GPS; however, GPS will not typically inform you of hazards or construction ahead. Remember the old fold up maps that would cover the span of the hood of your car? BUY ONE.
- Preplan your trip. Know where you're going. Mark or highlight your exits on your paper map. Have a backup to your GPS!

Use EXTREME CAUTION when having to pass someone on lonely or winding roads. I would rather be late behind an 18-wheeler than not arrive at all to my destination.

Chapter 8
To The Dedicated Volunteers

Speaking of volunteers…

This chapter is dedicated to the volunteers serving fire and EMS departments all over the country. Well, all over the world for that matter!

In the previous chapter, I mentioned the volunteers that assisted us in the "Dead Man's Curve" call. The volunteer that called me at the station is now a captain with the San Antonio Fire Department.

This was a young volunteer firefighter, about nineteen years old back in the late 80s, who had so much energy he could "outrun" the Energizer Bunny! He was so enthusiastic and so full of energy that he always wanted to be the first on the scene. This kid was great and I knew, one day, he would become one of us, a San Antonio Firefighter and paramedic.

This was a kid who could literally read my mind! When I say read my mind, he knew exactly what we needed when it came to a call. This kid, if he could, would have had a backboard and stretcher in his little Honda Civic! His vehicle could squeeze into any nook and cranny, travel through bushes, meander through rough roads, and he would use his vehicle to help land the helicopter at night! He was great, and I am proud that he is now serving the citizens of San Antonio.

As we responded to many calls in Bexar County and surrounding areas, I always, and I mean ALWAYS, had the utmost respect for the men and women that were volunteer firefighters and paramedics. These men and women were dedicated, sharp, and do the same thing we did, and DID NOT get paid for their service.

It really irked me when some of my partners would make comments that made fun of the volunteers. I would tell them, "Hey, if it weren't for these men and women, we would be extricating, doing CPR, landing the helicopter, getting our own stretcher, getting lost (and that we did!), and lifting patients… all by ourselves!"

So, to all those volunteers that I came across in my years as a paramedic in EMS and AirLife, thank you very much and kudos to you and your families! May God keep you and your families safe! Continue what you are doing because you are making a difference in the lives of those you serve in your area. You definitely made a difference in my life while we saved the lives of others. You are AWESOME!

Chapter 9
Bubbles

As a father and safety advocate, I always made sure my children were safe. I ensured that smoke alarms were installed at home and taught them what to do in the event of a fire or emergency. By the time they were four years old, they knew about calling 9-1-1 in the event Mommy or Daddy were hurt or something happened to us or them. And by the time they were ten years old, they knew how to do the Heimlich Maneuver!

Swimming lessons were a must. Being introduced to water was very important to me since I took swimming lessons at an early age. When my sister and I were four and five years old, my parents enrolled us in swimming classes at the Roosevelt swimming pool. I'll never forget. Saturday mornings during the summer were taken up with getting up at 7:30 a.m. and being at the pool for classes. The pool wasn't heated so we'd step out of the water and sit at the edge of the pool shivering and turning blue from head to toe! I don't think the swimming instructors even knew the definition of "hypothermia!" Can you imagine 40 kids out there shivering from head to toe and we weren't allowed to have our towels until classes were done!

When my daughter, Andrea, was just nine months old, I introduced her to the water. I remember taking her to the pool and just carrying her in my arms and dunking ourselves in the water.

I'd have her in my arms and tell her, "Ok, Mija! On the count of three, we're gonna go underwater! One, two, three, go!"

I would blow into her face and as she inhaled we'd go under and come right back up. She came up wiping the water off her face and laughing! We had a lot of fun. She even learned to hold her breath for a few seconds underwater.

When she was around three years old, we enrolled her in swimming lessons at a local pool. I remember getting her ready: bathing suit, lunch snacks to eat after her one-hour lesson, my chair and a book to read, towels, flip flops, and a snack for me.

When we arrived at the pool, I unloaded everything - plus my daughter! I was used to holding everything in one hand and shoulder so I could hold Andrea's hand as we walked to the pool. Her first swimming lesson! I was excited as she was. By this time, she wasn't afraid of the water. (Beware: children aren't afraid of the water and don't know the dangers!)

I saw the swimming instructor and introduced myself and my daughter. The swimming instructor, a teenager around nineteen years old, stooped down and introduced herself to Andrea.

"Hi, my name is Brittany! What's your name?" she asked my daughter.

My daughter smiled and told her, "Andrea." My daughter was a very sociable little girl and had no problem connecting with the instructor. The instructor told her, "We're gonna have a lot of fun in the water! Do you like the water?"

Andrea replied, "Yes, ma'am."

"Great! We're gonna be great friends, and I am looking forward to teaching you how to swim! It will be a lot of fun! Your Daddy's gonna be right here to watch you, okay?"

Andrea looked up at me and said, "Are you gonna watch me Daddy?"

I told her, "Mija, I'm gonna be right here sitting on my chair and watching you! You'll have fun!"

The instructor took her hand and walked her over to the edge of the pool where there were five other students, around her age, sitting there waiting for their class to start. Andrea turned around one more time to make sure I wasn't leaving.

I called out, "I'll be right here, Mija! See, I'm putting my chair right here close to you!"

Andrea smiled and turned around. I unloaded everything I was carrying and placed my folding chair on the ground. I sat approximately six feet from the edge. I didn't want to be too close, then again, I wanted to be close enough to be there in the event something should happen.

The instructor jumped into the water, turned around, and introduced herself to the children who were all sitting at the edge of the pool. They looked cute all sitting there with their backs to me. I wish I had taken a picture!

The instructor said, "Hi, my name is Brittany, and I'm gonna be teaching you all how to swim."

The children all answered at one time, "OK!"

She said, "Okay, we're gonna start by introducing yourselves. Tell me your names one by one and let's start on this side!" They all took turns yelling out their names. They were all excited. She continued, "Okay, we're gonna start by putting our feet into the water and kicking your feet. We're gonna pretend to be a motor boat! Let's start!"

The kids started kicking and splashing so hard. They were laughing like maniacs; they were kicking and splashing so much I couldn't even see the instructor! They were already having fun! Then she told the kids, "Okay, now I'm gonna pick up each of you one at a time and I'm going to hold you and walk around so you can kick your feet like a boat, OK?"

The kids responded, "OK!"

She said, "Now, when I pick up each one of you, the rest of you stay where you are. You can practice kicking your feet while I go around with one of your classmates."

The instructor went to one end of the line where the kids were sitting and picked up the first child. She had the child by the armpits facing her and told the child to kick her feet. I wanted to see what she was going to do and how far she was going in the pool. She didn't travel more than ten feet away from the children to keep an eye on those sitting at the edge of the pool.

My daughter was in the middle of the line. I watched for a few minutes while she held the first child. She returned to the edge of the pool with the first child to pick up the next. Andrea would be the fourth in line.

Thinking that Andrea wouldn't be up for another ten to fifteen minutes, I settled into my chair and opened my book to read. I had my book right in front of me to ensure that I had Andrea in my view while she was sitting by the edge kicking her feet. All the other kids waiting at the edge were having fun kicking and following Andrea as she kicked her feet. My daughter already had leadership skills!

I don't recall what I was reading but it seemed to grasp my attention. The kids, including Andrea, continued kicking and splashing their feet. I saw the instructor come up to pick up the next child. Andrea would soon be up next.

The instructor dropped off another child at the edge of the pool and picked up Andrea. I was just excited as she was.

"Okay, Andrea! You ready?" the instructor asked her.

"Yes!" she replied.

The instructor picked her up by the armpits and led her around the pool close by. This time, I did take a picture. Andrea kicked so hard it looked as if she would take off on her own!

The instructor told her, "Great job! Keep kicking!"

With more enthusiasm, Andrea complied. After she was done, the instructor came to the edge of the pool and sat her on the edge to pick up another child. Andrea, so excited, turned around to look at me. "Daddy, did you see me?" she asked.

"I sure did! You did great, Mija!" I shouted.

With a big smile, she turned around and continued kicking her feet in the water. She was having a great time! I was having a great time watching her have a great time. Relieved that she was done with the instructor, I delved into the book I was reading.

I must have been intrigued by the book that I realized that I hadn't looked up to check on Andrea. I looked up and suddenly saw that Andrea wasn't there sitting at the edge of the pool.

I looked up and thought, "Ok, she took another turn with the instructor." I thought to myself, "I'm missing this opportunity to see her kicking with the instructor again!" I saw the instructor holding a different child.

Andrea wasn't with the instructor.

I quietly said, "Shit, where is she?"

I bolted to the edge of the pool where Andrea was sitting. I didn't see her.

Then I looked at the bottom of the pool and I was shocked! She was sitting at the bottom of the pool with her legs crossed, looking up and smiling with her eyes wide open and bubbles coming out of her mouth!

I yelled, "Andrea!" I bent over and quickly reached down into the pool with my arm and literally grabbed her by the hair to pull her out! Fortunately, she had long hair to where I could easily snatch her out! I picked her up as she was coughing and gasping for air! I asked her, "Mija, are you ok?"

She said, "Yes, Daddy! That was fun!"

The instructor heard me yell and came over to the edge with the other child.

She nervously told me, "Sorry, sir! I didn't see her jump in!"

I was livid! I told her, "You need to keep an eye on the kids while they're sitting here or hire another instructor to watch them. This is ridiculous!"

I could also see other parents out of the corner of my eye look startled. One parent stood up and grabbed her son and told him, "Son, we're gonna leave now." Her son just looked up at her with this puzzled look not knowing what was going on.

The swimming instructor repeated, "Sir, I'm sorry. You don't have to leave!"

I said, "No thank you. I'll teach her myself."

I picked up everything and left.

Driving away, I was thinking how close my daughter came to drowning right in front of my eyes! Even with the kids kicking and having a good time, I should have never taken my eye off Andrea while she was sitting there. Fortunately, she was in four feet of water where I could reach in and grab her! Thank God.

Even today, when I drive past that pool, I think back to that very same moment that I saw my daughter with her big brown eyes open, smiling, looking up toward the surface, as if it was nothing. Thankfully, I had trained her to hold her breath. I knew she wasn't underwater long Fortunately, she still had some air in her. That's when I saw the bubbles coming out of her closed mouth and nose.

A close call a father will never forget. Thank you, Lord. You helped me save my daughter's life.

Lesson Learned - Don't Get Burned

That day is still etched in my mind. I almost lost my daughter in front of my eyes! Here are a few drowning prevention tips:

- Teach your kids how to swim! If you can introduce your baby to the water, you now have a better chance of making them feel comfortable being around water. But remember, they too can drown when they're "too comfortable" that they may just jump into the water and not be wary of the depth of the pool. They are not afraid!
- If you have a pool at home, ALWAYS be aware of your kids' whereabouts.
- Install a fence around the pool. This may not be aesthetically appealing but it is a lifesaving device! What is more important - your child's life or aesthetics?
- I was always uncomfortable when my children would go to parties where they had a pool. I would go as well just to make sure they were safe.
- Always supervise! Lack of supervision is almost always the cause of accidental drownings. Be there and stay aware.
- Infants can drown in as little as two inches of water. Many infants have drowned while the mother is bathing them. They get distracted and it doesn't take but a few seconds of "answering the phone" when an infant can suddenly turn over face down and drown.
- **Take a CPR class.**

Chapter 10
The Rope

My last day with the San Antonio Fire Department was October 31, 1998. Yep, Halloween! I remember walking out of the building and stepping into my car thinking "Wow, twenty-two years went by pretty quick and now, I'm starting a new life - again!"

Was I thinking of the ideal retired life full of quiet time and hobbies? No, I was thinking about my new job as a safety officer for a company. I retired at only forty-three years old! I knew I was going to continue working.

I remember people telling me, "Conrad, you're retired now! You should be out hunting or fishing every day!"

My response was always "Why go fishing when I can go to my local grocery store and buy any kind of fish I want! Don't have to get dirty, get up early, mess with mosquitos, and I can be in and out of the store in ten minutes! Hey, I even get to park on asphalt!"

(And a note to the avid fisherman: I appreciate fishing, but I relax by playing my guitar!)

In 2005, I worked at a non-profit agency here in San Antonio as an injury prevention educator. I always figured I would continue to save lives because I felt it was still my calling; at this job, I was saving lives indirectly, through education, intervention, and prevention. I guess you can say it was ingrained into me. Seeing people suffer injuries and death, I always thought that I could make a difference by providing safety information to the community, families, and those who might be unaware on the subject.

One day around 2:30 in the afternoon, I was sitting at my desk when my office phone rang. It was one of my colleagues calling my extension.

She whispered to me, "Conrad, can you speak to my brother? He wants to kill himself. I have him on the phone and I told him to please hold on 'cause I wanted someone to speak to him."

I told her, "Get back on the phone with him. I'll be right over."

I quietly got up and walked over and into her office on the other side of the building. I closed the door behind me.

I whispered to her, "Is he on the phone?"
She said, "Yes. Please talk to him."
"What's his name?"
"Ralph."

I took the phone from her and said, "Ralph, this is Conrad. I'm your sister's friend and we work together. Can we talk?"

No response.
I repeated, "Ralph, can we talk?"
He said, "Yes."

I jumped right in. "Your sister says you want to kill yourself, bud. Tell me what's going on. I want to help you."

He responded, "I really don't care about what's going on in my life anymore. My wife is leaving me and taking my kids. I've done everything I could to please her and now she's f---ing leaving me. I don't know what to do. I can't please her. I work my ass off to give her things, try to make her happy. I work two jobs and she does this to me? I figured I might as well just say 'to hell with this shit' and leave this stinking world!" He started to cry. "I don't know what to do!"

I responded, "Ralph, take it easy. Let's talk."

He said, "I really don't think there's anything to talk about. I'm tired of this shit. Why does this happen to me? I don't deserve this!"

I told him, "Ralph, no one deserves to be treated like shit. Believe me, we all have at one time or another been treated like that. You aren't the only one that has gone through this. Yeah, it happened to me, too, and believe me, I felt like shit, too, but it doesn't mean it's the end of the world, dude. You have children to watch grow up."

He responded, "How can I watch them when she's gonna f---king take them away from me?"

I said, "Ralph, you'll be able to see them. It just takes time. Where is she now?"

He replied, "She's went to a friend's house with the kids. She says I'll never see them again!"

I told him, "Ralph, you'll get to see them, you just gotta be patient and all this will boil over. It'll take time and patience and you remembering your love for your kids."

I asked, "Are you by yourself?"

He said, "Yes. But I have some friends outside my house that want to talk to me."

"If they are your friends, they want to help you, too. Why don't you let them in?"

"I don't want to," he said.

His friends had been waiting outside in their vehicles as the front door was locked and Ralph hadn't let them in.

"Ralph, I worked as a firefighter and paramedic here in San Antonio and saw a lot of people die. Children, adults, grandmas and grandpas, small babies, and many more. You are very fortunate that you have your children and they are healthy. Am I right?"

He said, "Yes, but they're going through a lot of shit right now."

"I understand perfectly, Ralph. It's not a pleasant thing to go through, and believe me, I can assure you that someone else is going through the same thing right now and you're not alone." I waited a moment, and asked him, "How do you plan to kill yourself, Ralph?"

He responded, "I'm just gonna hang myself."

"Ralph, before you go and do something, let me go over there and talk to you. I want to sit with you before you do anything. Let's try to take care of this... just you and me. How about it?" But I did have one concern about visiting Ralph. "Ralph, I'm gonna ask you straight up and be honest with me, brother. Do you have a gun or a knife with you or anywhere in the house?"

"No."

"Are you sure, Ralph? I want to come to your house and talk to you but I don't want any surprises if you have a gun or knife and try to do something to me... like kill me. I have children that love me and many friends and family. I would hate for them to have to go to my funeral because you did something crazy. Can I trust you? Do you have a gun or a knife?"

He said, "No."

"Okay, Ralph. I'm gonna hang up and your sister and I are going to drive to your house. It won't take but fifteen minutes to get there. Will you be a man and tell me that you are going to meet me at the door when I get there?"

He said, "Yes."

"Okay, Ralph. Give me fifteen minutes and when I get there I will call you. Your sister will follow me as well.

She's gonna go in her car, and I'll go in mine." No response from Ralph. "Ralph, can you hear me?"

He was crying. "Yes."

"It's gonna be ok, Ralph. Trust me… it's gonna be ok, brother. You can hang up now, Ralph. Give me fifteen minutes." I said.

Ralph replied, "I don't want the police or EMS to come, or I will do it."

I responded, "It will just be myself and your sister. Trust me, Ralph."

"Okay," he said. He hung up.

I turned to my friend, "Let's go. I'll follow you." I jumped in my car and my friend got in hers, and we drove off.

On the way to his house, I was pretty nervous. My mind was on a roll. I thought, "Geez, Conrad, you only did this when you were in EMS. What are you thinking? This guy could be bluffing, have a gun, and shoot you dead then take the gun and kill himself! Are you nuts? Why didn't I just drive to the house and keep him on the phone? No. Don't be on the phone with him while you're driving. The worst thing is to get in a wreck and not be able to help him. I should call EMS and have them on the way. But I told him that it would be just me. He trusted me. I can't break that."

As I worried and wondered about Ralph, many of my thoughts reminded me of my time with EMS; then, we acted on instinct. While driving, it was coming back to me. I was about a block away from the house when my friend called me on my cell.

"We're almost there," she said.

I told her, "Stop in front of the house and don't get out. When I get out of my car, just point to his house."

She said, "Okay."

As I pulled up, I noticed two police cars. I thought, "Who called them? I told him I would be by myself!" It turned out to be two officers from the school district who knew him. I walked up to them and asked, "Has he come out?"

One of the officers, a female, said, "No, he hasn't."

"Okay. I'm gonna go to the door. Please stay close by and, believe me, if you hear anything, come in with your guns drawn."

They walked behind me as I approached the door. I knocked on the door. "Ralph, I'm here. Can you open the door?" Nothing. I repeated, "Ralph, this is Conrad. Can you open the door?"

I could hear footsteps nearing the door. I thought, "Okay, hardwood floors." Not that it mattered, but I learned that when I was with EMS. As paramedics, we had to be cognizant of our surroundings inside and outside homes. What we heard, what we saw, what we felt sometimes could make a difference in saving someone's life, or our own.

The doorknob turned and Ralph slowly opened the door. He stuck his head out slowly.

"It's me, Ralph, I'm Conrad. Can I come in?"

He said, "Yes."

I asked, "Ralph, I'm gonna ask you one more time, brother. Do you have a gun or knife or any weapon with you? Be honest with me, brother, let's not hurt each other because if you do, I'll die fightin' you."

He said, "I'm not lying to you."

I said, "Okay."

He opened the door and saw the two officers behind me. He said, "They can leave."

I replied, "They're your friends, and they're here to protect me, too. I gave them instructions to standby. Trust me, Ralph. It'll only be you and me."

"Okay."

I walked in and, as I closed the door behind me, I saw that he was wearing a T-shirt, some jeans, and some boots. I realized with his untucked t-shirt, there wasn't a visible pistol in his waistband. It also didn't appear that he had a knife on him. His living room was small and the dining area was within twelve feet of the door. This home was built back in the 30s. Small home, small yard.

There was no living room furniture nor frames on the wall. The only thing in view was the dining room table with four chairs. He could tell I was curious and looking around. He looked at me and said, "She took everything but this table and chairs. Everything is gone... the bed, the dressers, the couch, everything that I bought for her."

I asked him, "Do you have clothes?"

"She left my clothes."

I told him, "Let's sit right here and talk, okay?"

He pulled the chair out and sat down. I sat directly across the table from him with my left leg pointing toward the front door; an escape position in the event he would charge at me for some reason or another.

"You're lucky you have clothes, brother, and you're lucky you have a job," I said. "I recall a very good friend of mine went home one day to find his house totally empty. Nothing, zilch, nada... not a damn thing in his home; even all his fishing gear, hunting guns, lawn equipment, and everything he'd accumulated in the eighteen years they were married... all gone. She had, in 24 hours, packed up the kids and everything in the house and left to another country. The only thing she left behind was a letter that said, 'I'm taking the kids. I will write to you someday. Sorry, but I don't love you anymore.' Do you think he was devastated? Uh, yeah!'"

Ralph responded, "I really love my children and don't want them to get hurt. I wanna see them."

"Ralph, if you really love your children and want to see them, you cannot do what you intended to do. You'd only hurt them for the rest of their lives. Killing yourself is not the answer. They would probably think that you gave up on them. Are you giving up on them?" I asked.

"No, I just don't know what I would do without them."

I continued, "How do you think they'd feel if you followed through and killed yourself? What would they do without you? Have you looked at it that way? They'd grow up without a father and you'd never know what it was like to see them grow up and you wouldn't be there to see them graduate from college. You wouldn't see them grow up to be successful and much less see your grandchildren. How do you think they're gonna feel when they're asked, "Where's your father?" And your kids tell 'em, "He killed himself."?"

He looked me in the eyes. For the moment he held his gaze, I thought "Uh-oh… should I get ready to run to the door or be ready to try to fight him?!"

He just responded, "I don't want to do that to them."

I was relieved. I told him, "Then don't do what you intended to do. Let's man up, be the father that you want to be and show your kids that when things are rough you just swallow what happened and move forward. Don't give up on your kids, brother. They love you, and they cannot control what happened. You gotta do what you gotta do. Find an attorney, find friends to talk to. Do you go to church?" I asked.

"No."

"I don't know if you're religious or not. I am Catholic and go to church every Sunday. I'm the children's music director and play every Sunday. You're welcome to come sometime and visit. I play at the 10 a.m. Mass at Holy Family Church. Come join me sometime. There are people that are my friends, and they will welcome you with open arms. They are great people. I know there's a few Catholic churches around here, but it doesn't have to be a Catholic Church, you know. You have to heal, brother, and by praying everyday you'll have your prayers answered. It may not happen too soon, but it will. You gotta have faith and believe in yourself, God, and your children, man."

"Let me tell you something, Ralph," I continued, "You manned up by reaching out to your sister and telling her you needed help. That's why I'm here. That's why your sister and friends are here. Your friends right outside care about you. They want the best for you."

"I want the best for my kids but they can't have it." Ralph replied.

I responded, "They won't have what they need or want if you do something crazy. They want and need *you*, right? They will always want and need you. You just have to be patient and be positive. Shit like this happens to everyone, every day, all over the world, dude. You aren't by yourself, man! The children will know what happened and, most important, they will know that you can pull through anything. They will see the man that you are and the father that you will be to them for the rest of their lives! What more can you ask for?"

"I want my kids."

I said, "Ralph, you will have your kids, but it'll take a little time, patience, perseverance, and a lot of prayer. Dude, you think we have it bad, sometimes? I teach parenting classes at the jail. Those guys in there can only see their children for two hours every two weeks. Do you think they miss their children? You bet they do! And some won't be able to see their kids for a long time!"

Ralph sat and listened quietly.

I continued, "Dude, we both have been through a lot of bullshit. I have… you have… everybody has. But it's how we respond that will determine our future and determine if this is going to make us or break us. If you just stay focused on your children, you will heal and so will your kids. Think about it. I don't want to have to attend a funeral and have your kids and sister there. Let's take care of this right now. Let's kick this in the ass and say, "I'm gonna pull through this 'cause I love my kids." Can you repeat that for me?"

He sat silently.

I tried again. "Ralph, let's say this together: 'I'm gonna pull through this 'cause I love my kids.' Come on… you and me."

We both repeated, "I'm gonna pull through this 'cause I love my kids… I'm gonna pull through this because I love my kids."

I put my hand on his shoulder.

I said, "We're gonna pull through because we love our kids. Ralph, I wish someone would have told me this when I was going through some bad stuff, too. Fortunately, my parents always told me, "Son, pray, be patient, be positive, and you will persevere with God's help."

I told Ralph, "Right now, you have your sister, your friends, me, and the Lord."

He started to cry. "Brother, cry… cry all you want." He cried for about fifteen minutes while I had my hand on his shoulder.

When he stopped crying, I asked him, "Ralph, you said you were going to hang yourself. Where were you going to do it?"

"In the garage," he said.

"Take me to the garage, Ralph, and show me."

"Okay."

We walked to the back door. He opened it and walked ahead of me. As we walked down the steps of a small porch, I noticed a nice, pristine, and well-manicured backyard. It had nicely cut grass with some fresh landscaping and the garage looked like it was just painted. I could tell he was proud of his yard and his home.

I asked him, "Proud of your yard, aren't you?"

He said, "Yes sir."

The garage was an old one-car garage with a side door on the left side. He opened the door and walked in. I walked really slow behind him and left the door open... just in case.

He stopped and turned to look at me, then looked up to the rear of the garage. I looked up and there it was. The rope. It was already hanging from the rafter of the roof with a well knotted noose. It looked as if he'd learned how to tie a noose. I'd seen them before from other hangings I responded to in my career in EMS. I felt my heart skip a beat. I'd seen nooses already tied around those victims that had already given up and hanged themselves. Never had I seen a noose waiting for its victim. I saw a plastic bag on the floor, a receipt, and the stool. He had gone to a local hardware store to purchase the items.

I told him, "Ralph, we're gonna pull through this. I need *you* to go and untie the rope and take it down. This is not going to happen 'cause you're gonna see your kids, and they're gonna see you soon. With you taking the rope down, you're telling your kids that *you* made the decision to pull through this and not give up on them. This is your choice, brother."

I trusted that he was going to do it. He was ready to get on the stool when I told him, "Ralph, use the ladder."

I had seen a folding ladder leaning against the wall. I wanted him to use the ladder so he wouldn't surprise me and "jump" into the noose while up on the stool. He grabbed the ladder, unfolded it, and placed it under the hanging noose.

I said, "Let me place the ladder for you." I did this so he wouldn't try to jump in the noose. I grabbed the ladder and placed it one arm's length so he can barely reach it. He climbed onto the ladder and stopped around the third rung.

"Here's a cutter," I said handing it to him. He cut the rope right above the noose. He climbed down off the ladder and handed me the noose. I asked him, "Ralph, can I have the plastic bag?" He stooped over and picked it up off the garage floor and gave it to me. I placed the rope and cutter in the bag.

I told him, "This is the start of your life with your children. It's gonna be a rough road but we're not giving up. You're not giving up on your kids, and I'm not giving up on you. Let's step back into the house."

We walked out of the garage. He walked out in front of me as I turned around to close the garage door. While I was closing the door, I stopped and took one last look at the rafter where the rope had hung. I breathed a sigh of relief and thought to myself, "Thank you, Lord."

I held the bag in my hand while I walked behind him, and we re-entered the house through the back door. We walked through the kitchen and into the dining area where we had sat before. We both sat down. This time, I sat next to him.

I asked, "Ralph, can we let your sister and friends into the house now?"

He said, "Okay."

"I'm gonna go open the door and let them in," I told him. "Ralph, they're here for you. They love you and want the best for you and your kids. Talk to them like you talked to me."

He nodded his head. "I will."

I went to open the door. His sister, my co-worker, walked in. I said, "Be there for him and thank you for calling me and letting me know about Ralph. He really needs somebody to talk to now and will in the next days, weeks, and possibly months. Keep me posted and call me if anything should come up."

She said, "Thank you, Conrad."

I said, "No, thank God."

His two friends followed behind his sister. I told him, "Ralph, be strong, bud. This is not the end. It's only the beginning of another chapter in your life. It will get better. Believe me, it will get better. Let's keep in touch, Ralph. Take care and I'll see you again sometime soon."

He said, "Okay."

I turned around and told Ralph's sister thanks once again and told Ralph's friends, "Thanks for your patience and being here for him. He really needs you all."

The female officer said, "Thank you, and we will."

I walked out of the house and closed the door behind me. With a sigh of relief, I took a deep breath. I looked toward the street as I was walking down the stairs of the porch. I thought, "Lord, thank you for putting me in Ralph's path. I couldn't have done this without you. He will need your guidance and your strength."

I walked to my car with the plastic bag in hand. I turned and opened the trunk and placed the bag with the rope, cutter, and receipt in the back. I closed the trunk and walked around to the driver's side, opened the door, stepped in and drove off.

It was close to 5 p.m. in the afternoon. I remember thinking to myself, "Why go back to work?" I called my supervisor. She answered the phone right away. "Conrad, is everything okay?"

She knew what was happening. I told her, "Everything's fine. I'm gonna go home. It's almost five anyway.

She said, "No problem."

I pulled onto the highway and continued on my way home. It was hard to describe my drive home. I thought to myself, "Wow, what a way to end my day."

Since I retired from the fire department never did I ever think that I would encounter a situation like this. One thing I knew and remembered was that whenever you came across situations like attempted suicides, you had to think fast, predict what may happen, but most importantly, you have a life to save. You didn't make any sudden moves and didn't tell them anything to make them feel it was their fault because they could try to end it right in front of you and may take you with them.

On my drive home, I felt a sense of relief that I left Ralph and he was still alive and in the hands of people that care about him. I also felt somewhat scared. I thought, "What if something went wrong? What if he did have a weapon and "took me with him?" What if he had hanged himself when I arrived?"

Then I remembered what a very good friend of mine, a priest, told me a while back when I had needed some guidance. It had been a rough month witnessing some bad crashes with some kids being killed.

He said, "Conrad, you can't save everyone. God put you there and gave you His hands to try to save a life, but the ultimate One that can save a life is... God. Yes, you have saved many in your time, and the Lord gave you the knowledge, wisdom, and patience to do that. God blessed you with the ability to talk to people and serve them as the Lord wants us to do - serve our brothers and sisters. You are a public servant for the fire department but, mostly, you are a servant of the Lord. You were chosen by the Lord to serve others in time of need. But remember, whatever life you could not save didn't mean you didn't do your job, it meant it was God's choice. God decides who lives and who doesn't. You are there to assist. I know God has been there for you when there is someone who did not survive and you were there to provide solace and comfort for families by being there for them."

And yes, I remember many times in EMS when we did arrive to a house and found a person already dead and the spouse or children were crying over the body of the loved one. If it was obvious that they had been dead and there was nothing we could do, I would just place my hand on the grieving spouse's shoulders and say, "I am so sorry, ma'am, but he's gone. The only thing we can do now is be here for you and wait. We will have to call the police and the medical examiner, but we will be right here for you."

Then I'd try to escort the family to another room. My partner would get on the radio to let our dispatcher know that we had a "10-29." That was the 10-code for a deceased person that we would not be transporting.

Once I placed them in another room, I would go back to where the deceased was. I would get a sheet or blanket and cover the body only up to their face. The reason I did this was so in the event other family members would arrive; it would make the deceased look like they were sleeping. Of course, this depended on the condition of the deceased. If there was trauma involved, I never let anyone into the room or close to the body.

I wanted the families to at least see them as if they were sleeping. Besides, that's the way they are prepared at the funeral home, right? They're in peace and look as if they just died peacefully.

Now back to my drive home. By the time I knew it, I was already pulling up to the driveway. Driving home, I was preoccupied with thoughts that ran through my head and didn't even realize I had driven almost ten miles. I stopped and parked my car in the driveway in front of the garage. I thought, "Geez, I didn't even want to go into the garage."

I parked my car outside of the garage this time. I took a deep breath and exhaled another sigh of relief. I said in a whisper, "Thank you, Lord, for allowing me to speak with Ralph, for keeping me safe, and please watch over Ralph and his family."

I got out of the car and closed my door. I walked back to the trunk and popped the trunk open and pulled out the bag with the rope, cutter, and receipt. I walked over to the garbage can, opened it, and tossed the bag in the garbage can. I closed the lid. No more rope. No more suicide attempt by Ralph; at least for now.

It was 5:30 in the evening. I walked inside the house and went straight to my bedroom; took my shoes and my shirt off and laid my head down on the pillow. Still light outside, the sun was setting and peeking into my window, I covered my eyes with my shirt. Once more I prayed, "Thank you, Lord, for being with me in time of need, especially in Ralph's time of need."

Emotionally and physically exhausted, I thought to myself, "Tomorrow's another day." I fell asleep and didn't wake up until five the next morning.

Today, I see Ralph's sister every now and then. I ask her, "How's your brother doing?"

She always says, "He's great, thank you!"

I always tell her, "Tell him hello for me."

Then I whisper to the Lord, "Thank you, Lord."

Thank God for helping us cut down that rope and begin a new life for Ralph.

Lesson Learned - Don't Get Burned

If you or someone you love is suffering from depression, anxiety, suicidal thoughts/actions or anything else that could harm you/them, **please stop reading and seek help now**. Call a friend, your doctor, a therapist, see your priest, or check yourself into the ER.

If you are hurting for some reason or another; marital issues, employment or lack of, verbal, emotional or physical abuse, alcohol or drug abuse...there is someone out there who can help. Don't give up!

I didn't give up on Ralph, and I won't give up on you.

Again, as it bears repeating, reach out to someone; a friend, family member, a priest, or someone that will encourage you in a positive way. There are many resources out there to assist you. You just have to go out and find them!

My thoughts and prayers go to those who we lost to suicide, to those considering it, and to those who step out and try to help.

If you ever need assistance or know of someone who may need help:
- Call the National Suicide Prevention Lifeline: 1-800-273-TALK (8255)
- Visit their Website: www.suicidepreventionlifeline.org
- Call 9-1-1. They can help, too.

See Appendix A for a poem from Conrad about finding positivity during hard times.

Chapter 11
The Ice Storm

My friends, how many of you have ever driven in an ice storm? How many of you have been driving and suddenly you hit a patch of ice? Where does your vehicle go? What do you do? Do you panic? Do you take your hands of the wheel and yell, "Lord, take me where you want me to go?" Or, do you just turn in the direction of your skid?

The answer is: turn your wheel in the direction of your skid and slowly pump on your brakes! Your vehicle is now at the mercy of the icy road! And, yes, say a quick prayer!

Icy road conditions can be a challenge. I wish everyone would remember that. When the roads warrant being more careful... then you should BE MORE CAREFUL! It seems that some drivers like a challenge and want to press their luck in dangerous weather conditions. Whether it's rain, fog, or ice, one should exercise extreme caution!

It still boggles my mind when newscasters and police blame weather for crashes. They say, "The crash was due to wet weather conditions." I don't get it! So, when there is a crash in dry weather, do they report "The crash was due to *dry* conditions."?

Please, my friends, be a cautious and courteous driver.

Now, allow me to proceed with the story of the dreaded ice storm.

It was a cold weekday afternoon when it started getting busy all over San Antonio and surrounding areas.

Ice, ice, ice - everywhere! The whole city was going crazy, and the radio was blaring for EMS and the fire department to respond to major accidents all over town. The streets were treacherous, and we knew we were bound to get a call soon. And we did.

We received a call for a major accident not too far from the fire station. I was at Station #41 and my partner, Lee Carrola, was driving that day.

The call came in from Dispatch, "841, 841, respond to the intersection of Grissom Road and Timberhill for a major accident. Please use caution. You may have multiple patients."

I picked up the radio and responded, "10-4, we're 10-96."

Lee and I stepped into the ambulance and pulled out of the station. I told Lee, "Be careful, partner, we wouldn't want to slide into the wreck!"

He responded, "No problem, partner, I'll take care of you."

I replied, "Thanks, brother."

We had to be very careful and pick a safe route to the accident to avoid any curvy or hilly areas. We chose to take a right on Tezel Road which was kind of a straight shot and no curves. If we had gone straight on Mainland Road, the chances were very high that we could skid off the road. Mainland Road was very winding and had many curves as you drove downhill. Sliding into a culvert or someone's home would have warranted a lot of explaining and letter writing!

As we were driving to the scene, Lee was doing his best to drive carefully, and I surely appreciated that! We could see cars ahead of us spinning and sliding. They were going a little too fast for the road. When we saw that, we slowed down even more.

When we arrived at the scene, there was another EMS unit there caring for some patients in another vehicle. We stepped out of the ambulance and were also met by some firefighters that had responded.

One of the firefighters told me, "We have two patients in this car with neck and back pain and no other obvious injuries! Do you want us to get the C-collars and backboard?"

I said, "Yeah, let's get them out of the cold as quickly as we can. Can they walk at all?"

The firefighter replied, "Yeah, the lady was walking around but she got in the car because she was cold. The other gentleman never got out of the vehicle. But he says he can walk."

I said, "OK. Thanks! Oh, can you crank up the heater in the back of the unit?"

"You got it!"

I slowly walked to the lady while my partner, Lee, and another firefighter walked over to the man seated in the passenger side.

I asked the lady, "Ma'am, are you hurting anywhere?"

She answered, "Yes, my lower back hurts and I have some slight pain to my neck."

"Do you hurt anywhere else?"

She said, "No. I don't think so. My chest hurts a little bit, though. I had a heart attack about six months ago and I'm a little scared."

I said, "Okay, ma'am. Is the pain severe?"

She responded, "No, just a little stiffness in my neck."

"What about your chest, ma'am?"

She replied, "My chest hurts but I don't know if it was because of my seat belt or not."

"Okay, when we get in the ambulance, I'm gonna start an IV on you and do an ECG to see if your heart is doing alright. That's just for a precaution."

She said, "That's fine."

I told her, "We're gonna put a neck brace on you and put you on a backboard that's on the stretcher. It's gonna be hard but we need to do this. Okay?"

She said, "Okay."

One of the firefighters placed the cervical collar and brought the stretcher. I told the patient, "Okay, ma'am. Just sit on the stretcher and lay back."

She said, "Thank you."

I could see that some of the firefighters were slipping on the ice. Fortunately, they didn't fall, and we had to roll the stretcher slowly to the unit without slipping and falling on the ice ourselves.

The ambulance wasn't but twenty feet from the wreck, so we didn't have far to roll the stretcher. I opened the back doors to the ambulance and proceeded to load her into the back of the unit. Once inside the unit, I told her, "Ma'am, we're gonna put your friend -"

"That's my husband," she interjected.

"Oh, I'm sorry. I didn't know." I said.

"That's okay."

I continued, "We're gonna put your husband on the bench seat right next to you."

"How is he doing?" she asked.

I told her, "He seems to be doing just fine. He's walking and talking so that's a good thing." Lee was getting another backboard to place on the bench seat so we could lay him next to his wife.

I asked her, "What happened?"

She responded, "Well, I was driving and I hit my brakes because I didn't want to run the red light. I hit this patch of ice on the road and skidded across the intersection. That's when I hit the other car. Are the people in the other car okay?"

I told her, "They're fine, just a little shaken up."

She said, "I feel so bad."

I comforted her by telling her, "Ma'am, they are okay. It could have been worse."

The back doors of the ambulance opened again. Lee assisted the husband as he climbed onto the running board. With his neck brace on, Lee told him to lay on the backboard. I told her husband, "Sir, we'll be on the way shortly, okay? We just have to do a few things before we get going. How are you feeling?"

He replied, "Okay, I guess. My neck hurts a little bit."

I told him, "Not to worry, sir, and your wife is okay, too."

He grabbed her hand after he laid down on the backboard. They seemed very close. They were holding hands while we assessed their condition. Lee and I took vital signs on both of them and secured them to the bench seat and the stretcher. Fortunately, they were both in stable condition, so we could transport both at the same time.

Lee asked me, "Need anything else, partner?"

"Nah, Lee. I'm ready to head out."

Lee stepped out of the ambulance and jumped in the driver's seat. We started to leave the scene. Out of the back window of the ambulance, I could see the police officers stopping traffic so we could work our way out of the intersection. I hoped that other drivers would be careful to not hit the officers. That's another risk first responders take at these types of calls.

"What hospital did you all want to go to?" I asked the couple.

"Well, we don't have insurance and we've been going to University Hospital. We can go there."

I answered, "No problem. We're gonna take it real slow 'cause there's a lot of icy roads out there."

She said jokingly, "I hope we don't get in a wreck going to the hospital!"

I chuckled, "We won't. My partner's a great driver!"

We proceeded slowly down Grissom Road toward Bandera Road which is a major thoroughfare toward the hospital. We knew it would take longer than the typical fifteen-minute drive with the icy roads.

I asked the couple, "How long have you all been married?"

He said, "Twenty years and counting."

What a cool sight to see. Here we were on the way to the hospital, and they're holding hands while they both are laying on backboards asking each other if they're doing alright.

"You okay, honey?" she asked her husband.

"I'm fine, sweetie. I just thank God you're okay." he told her.

"Me, too!" she replied.

After a twenty-five minute ride, which would have taken maybe ten minutes without ice, I could see that we were about a block from the hospital. I took off my seat belt and started to disconnect her oxygen.

I told the husband, "Sir, we're arriving at the hospital. We're going to take your wife down first. We'll get someone from the emergency room to come out and stay with you while we're taking her in. OK?"

He responded, "Okay. Thank you."

"No problem. We'll just be a few minutes." I said. I thought to myself, "Thank God we're here. There was so much ice on the road, and we made it safely."

I could see that we were about half a block from the ER entrance, so I stood up to unhook the IV bag that was hanging on the bar on the ceiling of the ambulance. I unfastened her belts that were holding her onto the stretcher. I was standing, holding on with one hand, when suddenly I heard Lee yell.

"Sit down, Conrad! We're gonna get hit! SIT DOWN!" He saw that a car was skidding right into our lane about to strike us head-on.

As soon as I heard Lee, I threw myself on the jump seat. Just as I sat, we were hit head-on! My head and back crashed into the cushioned jump seat. Simultaneously, the lady on the back board slid straight toward me! The backboard slid over my knees and landed on my lap. Her face was literally inches from my face, and she was looking up straight at me!

She looked up and screamed at me. "AGGGGGGHHHHHHH!"

At the same time, I looked down at her face and yelled, "AGGGGGHHHHHHH!"

(If this had been a movie, it would have been so funny! It kind of reminded me when the kid in the movie *Home Alone* grabbed his cheeks and yelled, "AGGGGHHHH!")

After we both screamed at each other, I quickly lifted her and the backboard off my lap.

I stood up and turned around to see what happened. I looked through the back window between the jump seat and the front cab. I didn't see Lee in the front cab. Then, I looked out the back windows only to see a car sliding sideways toward us!

I yelled to Lee, "Lee, we're gonna get rear-ended! Don't get out!" I really didn't know if Lee had gotten out or not. I just yelled to warn him.

The car was still sliding sideways toward us. I thought the right side of his car was going to actually broadside the back of the ambulance. Then, suddenly the car straightened out and slid right past us to the right.

I yelled, "Lee, Lee! Be careful!" I was hoping Lee hadn't gotten out of the ambulance because the car was going right toward him!

I yelled again, "Lee! Lee!" I told the couple, "Ma'am, sir, I'm gonna get out real quick to check on my partner. I'll be right back!"

She said, "OK, I hope he's alright!"

"Me, too!"

I stepped out of the side of the ambulance. I looked to the rear to make sure there were no other cars coming to hit us from the rear. I then walked gingerly across the sheet of ice toward the front of the ambulance. Lee was nowhere in sight.

I dreaded the thought to look under the ambulance. I hoped I wouldn't see him there! Thankfully, I didn't see Lee there. We were so close to the entrance of the ER that I could see the ER doors from where we were hit.

With Lee nowhere in sight, I wondered if he'd gone into the emergency room to go get some help. I went back to the ambulance, opened the side door and stepped in to check on the couple.

"You all okay?" I asked.

They both replied, "We're fine. What happened? Is your partner okay?"

I said, "Yes, I believe he's fine. I didn't see him anywhere. He must have run into the ER."

I looked out the small side window of the unit. I breathed a sigh of relief! I could see Lee coming with reinforcements from the hospital! He had some techs from the ER behind him pulling some stretchers for the couple.

I told the couple, "My partner's fine and he's coming with some help. He ran into the ER after all."

Lee, along with the techs, began unloading the patients. One of the techs went to the driver of the vehicle that hit us and assisted him onto a wheelchair. He seemed to be fine. We rolled them all into the ER. I followed them, leaving the lights and emergency flashers flashing on the unit. Police were on scene pretty quickly, and they started placing flares on the street.

After some hard effort, we finally got both patients into the ER. I heard one of the staff members in triage. "Hey, one of the ambulances just got hit in front of the ER!" Our wreck seemed to be just another of the many 'exciting' events that happened that day (with many more to come).

We rolled the patients into the trauma room where the physicians were waiting. The driver of the other vehicle that hit us was taken into another room. Lee and I gave our report to the staff. It was rather amusing to them. We had to explain that our patients were involved in two crashes - theirs and ours!

The female patient was listening as I was giving my report to the ER staff. She said, "I think I jinxed us 'cause I told the paramedic that, with the ice, I hope we wouldn't get into a wreck. And look what happened!"

I told her, "Ma'am, it wasn't your fault. We weren't expecting anything to happen either!"

We took them off our stretchers and transferred them with the backboards onto their hospital beds. I told the couple, "Sir, ma'am, good luck! Not a great way to meet but it was a pleasure meeting both of you! God Bless!"

They both replied, "Thank you and be careful out there!"

Lee and I both answered, "We will."

As we walked out of the ER together, I said to Lee, "Hey, dude! Where were you after we hit? I thought you'd gotten run over or something!"

Lee replied, "Well, I got out to see if the guy that hit us was OK. When he got out of his car and was checking the damage, another car came from behind, hit his car, and then his car hit him and threw him across onto the sidewalk and landed on the grass! That car almost hit me too!"

I told him, "I can't believe all that happened after that first hit!"

Lee responded, "Yep, everything happened so fast! It was hit after hit after hit!"

"Wow. It could have been so much worse." He agreed. We were almost to the hospital exit when I said, "Hey, Lee."

"Yeah?"

"Thank you, partner, you saved my life."

"What do you mean?" he asked.

"Well," I said, "When you yelled at me to sit down, I immediately sat down and that's when we got hit. If you wouldn't have yelled at me to sit down, I would have gone crashing into the back of the unit because I was standing up. I was getting ready to unload her and I had just unhooked the IV bag when I heard you."

Lee said "Really, partner?"

I said, "Yep. You saved my life and I owe you, brother."

He said, "Naw, just dinner sometime."

I told him, "You got it, brother!"

We walked out to the street to see the damage on the front of the ambulance. The front grill was caved in about five inches. The damage to the man's car that hit us was pretty bad. The mechanic had already arrived as he wasn't too far when the accident occurred. We had to wait for our EMS officer to come and pick us up.

The story is that he was coming up the hill toward us from the opposite direction when he started to slide back down the small hill. So, he hit the gas and that's what caused him to slide into our lane and hit us head on.

The EMS officer arrived a few minutes after. He'd seen the damage to the ambulance and the other vehicle.

He asked, "How are you guys doing? You hurtin' anywhere?" Funny thing, no one ever asked us how we were except our patients!

I asked Lee, "Hey, how are you?"

He said, "I'm fine. I had my seat belt on."

Then he asked me, "How are you?"

I told him, "You know, Lee, now my back is feeling a little stiff."

I told my officer what happened. "When the impact occurred, I slammed up against the paramedic jumpseat in the back of the unit. I know Lee saved my life when he yelled to tell me to sit down. I could have been severely injured or killed if I would have been standing in the middle by the patient's side. I wouldn't have had enough time to go and sit down as quickly as I did." I told the EMS officer, "I owe my life to Lee."

Lee said, "Yep, you do."

The officer asked, "Do you guys just want to go home?"

I looked at Lee and he looked at me. We both responded, "Yeah, that's a good idea."

The EMS officer replied, "No problem. Let me take you guys back to the station. We'll get some overtime guys to pick up another unit. Best that you guys go home."

We climbed into the officer's van and drove back to the station... very carefully.

Once back at the station, I told Lee again, "I owe you, brother."

"Dinner, right?"

"Yeah, but not tonight. I'm going home," I answered.

Lee replied, "Yeah, me too. Be careful going home."

I said, "I will."

Fortunately, we both made it home safely on the day of the treacherous ice storm.

Today, I still think about that almost fateful day when my partner or I could have been hurt or killed. Many EMTs and paramedics have been injured or killed when struck by other vehicles. I thank God that Lee warned me. I don't know what would have happened if he didn't. I may not be here writing this book or enjoying life with my kids or my wife, Alma.

So, Lee Carrola, thank you. This story is for you, brother!

Lesson Learned - Don't Get Burned

It still boggles my mind when the weather changes here in San Antonio; some drivers want to challenge Mother Nature on the roads. Whether it's ice, snow, sleet, rain - it's all dangerous and I see it all the time.

The driver that struck us head-on wasn't thinking about the consequences of hitting the gas to gain speed, while on ice. Yes, it could have been worse for all of us.

Even today, I know paramedics stand in the back of the ambulance while they treat patients. Sometimes they don't have a choice. They might be trying to reach equipment, start an IV or doing CPR on a patient. They do it; I did it, too. Our lives depend on our driver and those drivers around us.

Please be aware of the dangers of driving on ice! For that matter, be careful when you're driving in dry weather, too!

The lesson I learned that day was... don't stand up in the back of the ambulance until you get to the hospital, but, then again, sometimes there is no choice.

Take care, out there, ladies and gentlemen! Take care.

Chapter 12
Old Habits Die Hard

I mentioned at the beginning of my book that I would be writing about incidents that occurred even after retirement. I retired on October 31, 1998 - yes, Halloween night - and since then, I've worn different "hats" over the years.

In September of 2015, an incident occurred that took me back to the old days. It was exactly 12:30 p.m. on a Thursday afternoon, and I was working in my office (as a parent educator at a local non-profit). I noticed the time on my watch and thought, "Wow, 12:30! Where did the morning go?"

I was concentrating on my notes for the week and working on my weekly report which was due the next day, Friday. It was very quiet in the office but then again, my office was located at the farthest point of the building.

As I realized it was past my lunch time, I went to the bathroom first and placed my work cell phone and personal cell phone on a shelf near the sink. I wanted to make sure I didn't drop my phones in the toilet bowl. Ever have that happen to you? When I was done, I stepped out and walked downstairs.

I asked the administrative secretary if she was going to lunch yet and she said that someone was going to bring her lunch. It was usually customary to ask about lunch to see if she wanted us to bring her anything. Actually, out of courtesy, we asked anyone that hadn't gone to lunch if they wanted us to bring them something.

I told her, "I'll be back in a bit," and I walked out the door.

I got in my car and pulled out of the parking lot when I realized I had forgotten my two phones on the shelf in the bathroom. So, I pulled back into the parking lot and went back to the building and walked in.

I told the secretary, "Can't go anywhere without my phone!" She chuckled. I walked back upstairs and went to the bathroom where my phones were. Yep, left them on the shelf. I grabbed them and worked my way downstairs. I told the secretary again, "See ya in a bit!"

As I pulled out of the parking lot, I took a quick left to make my way to a little park just a couple of miles south of the office. It was a nice, quaint park with a swimming pool and picnic tables, and I would park under the shade, pull my seat back, and take my twenty-minute power naps. Yes, a great way to recharge for the afternoon!

Just as I was pulling up to the intersection which was about 200 feet from the parking lot, I stopped at the red light. Then, I noticed to the right on the street I was going to turn to, a male and female standing in the middle of the street. The man's truck was parked in the middle lane and the woman was on the phone.

I wondered, "What is going on?"

I didn't see any vehicles that had crashed or debris on the street. I pulled up a little closer to the intersection when I saw a woman lying on the street. She had just been hit by a car!

I immediately put my car in park and turned on my emergency flashers. Suddenly, my years of experience in EMS kicked in. I ran to the intersection and approached the woman who was lying on the street. She was on her right side and there was a pool of blood just behind her head.

I thought, "Damn, she's got a head injury."

As I looked to my left, I could see that there was oncoming traffic and we were right in the middle of the southbound lane of the street. My worst fear was all of us getting hit by a car whose driver was distracted, texting, or on the phone, especially if they were turning left onto the lane we were on. The man who had stopped had a white truck and was facing northbound and was parked parallel to the woman that was hit by the car.

I asked him, "Sir, can you move your truck and park it to my left to block traffic? I want to make sure no one comes and hits us!" He was kind of hesitant as he looked at me as if my request was inconvenient but then he jumped in his truck and moved it, blocking all traffic at the intersection. Drivers going southbound were now blocked at the intersection. Drivers going northbound were still able to get by us at the traffic light.

Fortunately, there was a fire station about a half mile from the intersection. Number 7's fire house. A brand new fire house not even a half mile south of us. I was just anticipating the wailing of the sirens to be heard in a few minutes.

I gently placed my hands on each side of the victim's head so I could maintain and stabilize her neck and spine. Although she was on her right side, she needed to stay still. Without any gloves, I could feel the warm blood seeping onto my right hand. I was going to wait until the paramedics arrived to place her on her back and onto their backboard.

I asked her, "Ma'am, where are you hurting? My name's Conrad. I used to be a paramedic with EMS. Let me help you."

She cried, "My ankle hurts! I need to call my job and tell them I'm going to be late!"

I thought of my boss who, if it were me calling to tell him I'd been hit by a car, he would have asked, "Can you turn in your report before they take you to the hospital?" It happens to a lot of us!

I responded to her, "Not to worry, let's take care of you right now! EMS and the firefighters are on the way! Someone will call for you. Just lay still and don't move."

I began to thoroughly question her. "Where else do you hurt? Do you feel any numbness anywhere? Do you feel like throwing up? Do you remember what happened? How old are you? Are you allergic to any medication?"

All of a sudden, I felt like it was all coming back to me. With eighteen years of being a paramedic in EMS, the questions I was asking just came out naturally. I felt I was still on the ambulance. Even being retired for almost two decades, it was second nature that my skills would kick in when they did that very moment.

I asked the female witness that had been on the phone, "Ma'am, did you see anything?"

Still on the phone, she said, "She was on the crosswalk when this lady in the red car turned and hit her. She flew over the car and landed right there! I just called EMS and they are on the way!"

I looked to the crosswalk and saw that she may have landed approximately 20-25 feet from the impact.

I asked, "Was she going fast?"

She answered, "About five miles an hour."

The male witness chimed in, "Nah lady, she couldn't have been going five miles an hour. She got hit pretty hard! She was going about twenty. Look where she landed!"

With the distance from the impact to the area she landed, I thought, "Yeah, I think he's right."

He asked me, "Sir, why don't you put her laptop under her head so she can be comfortable?"

I responded, "No, that's ok. She has her head on her arm and it's helping to keep her from moving her neck and slow the bleeding down."

I thought to myself, "Well, my hand underneath her head is maintaining and keeping her spine in line and also slowing down the bleeding. And, besides, the laptop would be too hard for her head to lie on." I didn't share those thoughts with him, though.

Still without EMS or the firefighters in sight, I asked, "Where is the driver?"

The gentleman in the white truck pointed and said, "She's over there standing by the red car."

I looked over my shoulder to my right and could see a small red car. The driver, who was about seventy years old, looked scared, startled, and confused. I could see some damage on the left side of the hood.

Suddenly, I could hear the sirens coming from down the street. It was the fire truck responding. I told the bystanders, "Okay, as soon as the fire truck pulls up, can you please step aside? They're gonna need some room. Thank you for your help!"

I never got the names of the lady on the phone or the guy with the white pick-up truck who blocked traffic or the gentleman who said the driver was going faster. I always appreciated bystanders. I looked at them as "first responder angels." They were the first ones to stop and help and also played a great role in trying to find out what happened. Many even saved a few lives by controlling bleeding or even just blocking traffic. When working with EMS, I never failed to thank the bystanders who were first on scene.

As the firefighters stepped out of the fire truck, they immediately came to where I was holding the woman's head.

I told the first firefighter, "She was struck by the vehicle behind you. She has no LOC (loss of consciousness) and she's complaining of pain to her right ankle. She has good neuros (ability to move legs and arms) to her extremities. No nausea or vomiting and she's been talking all the time I've been here!"

The firefighter responded, "Very good! Who are you?"

"My name is Conrad Gonzales, retired San Antonio Firefighter...worked with EMS for eighteen years."

He said, "Cool!" As the other firefighters brought a cervical collar.

One firefighter asked, "You got her head?"

I said, "Yes, sir."

We placed the cervical collar while I held her neck to prevent possible further injury.

The firefighter, who I believe was the officer asked, "Where is she bleeding?"

I told him, "It seems like she's bleeding from the right side of her head. I didn't want to check without having the cervical collar on her. I can't feel a hematoma on her head, but I can feel the blood on my right hand which tells me she has a laceration right above her ear somewhere."

As I was kneeling down on the street with my casual slacks on, my name tag from work, and a peach polo shirt, I just realized that I might get blood on my work clothes. But I laughed and remembered how I got blood all over my uniform when I was in EMS. I continued giving the fire fighter the report.

"According to a witness, she was knocked onto the vehicle and flew over the vehicle and this is where she landed. It's about 20-25 feet from the point of impact."

He said, "Perfect! I appreciate your help."

I responded, "No sir. I appreciate you guys getting here!"

Just then, I could hear the wailing of the sirens off in the distance. I told the victim, "Ma'am, EMS is pulling up and they're gonna help you and get you to a hospital!"

She replied, "Can someone call my work, please?"

I told her, "Let's take care of you first and someone will call work for you. The important thing now is to get you taken care of and to get you to the hospital. Okay?"

She replied, "Okay…" She was beginning to cry. Always a good thing! She has a good airway!

The siren stopped as the ambulance came to a stop about twenty feet from where we were. I continued to hold the woman's head. I noticed one of the paramedics was a female and recognized her but I couldn't remember her name. She was a student in my paramedic class and did some "ride outs" with my partner and me when I was in EMS.

A "ride out" was when paramedics in training would tag along with an ambulance crew for on-the-job training. I recalled that she was a very ambitious student and was very eager to join the team of paramedics in EMS.

I remembered telling her that she was going to be an excellent paramedic. She was extremely caring and compassionate, a critical component of being a paramedic; she had the signs of becoming a genuine caregiver in the field. I knew she was going to be a dedicated hard worker.

As she, the female paramedic, knelt at the side of the woman, I gave her my report.

"Hi, I'm Conrad! I happened to come up on the scene and found her lying on the street! She had just gotten hit by a car!"

She asked, "Is that you, Conrad?"

I replied, "Yep!"

She said, "Conrad, how've you been! It's great to see you! I haven't seen you in a long time!"

As I was holding the patient's head, I told her, "I'm just fine."

She told the lady, "Ma'am, you're in good hands! This man is one of the best paramedics I've ever known and worked with! He's an angel!"

I said, "Nah, *now* you're in good hands, ma'am! These paramedics are gonna take care of you and get you to the hospital! You'll be just fine!"

I thought, "Geez, that was a nice compliment."

I wanted to ask the female paramedic her name again but that would be too embarrassing since I had forgotten. Besides, being social was the least of my worries.

She yelled orders to the firefighters, "Can you guys get the backboard and the stretcher?"

The firefighters were now trained as EMTs, they knew exactly what the paramedics needed and the equipment was set aside already.

The female paramedic told them, "Okay, we're gonna place the backboard right next to her, and then we'll roll her over onto the backboard!"

As they placed the backboard next to her, she ordered, "Okay, on the count of three, we're gonna roll her over! Conrad, you ready? It's your call!"

I told her, "Yes!"

"Okay!"

I counted. "One...two...three! Roll!"

Keeping her head in line with her spine, we gently rolled her over and placed her onto the backboard. I kept my hands on her head and now I could see that my hand was full of blood and dripping down my hand and fingers. With her hair matted in blood, I still had a tough time seeing the laceration and where the bleeding was coming from.

Now that she was on the backboard, I waited for the paramedics to place the foam blocks on each side of her head to maintain traction and stabilize her head and spine. The female paramedic, Rosie, (I remembered her name!) told me, "Conrad, thanks for your help! How've you been?"

I told her, "Just fine! I just happened to be going to lunch when I drove up to the intersection and saw what was going on!" Jokingly, I told her, "I still think I have twenty minutes for lunch!"

She chuckled.

The other firefighters had already taken the stretcher out of the ambulance and had it ready by her side so we could place her on the stretcher. As we readied her to lift, one of the firefighters stood to my right to assist in lifting.

Rosie ordered, "OK, on the count of three, let's lift."

The woman was close to 240 pounds. As a rule, I always utilized every bit of manpower, and womanpower, to lift someone that was heavy.

Rosie blared the order, "One... two... three!"

I was at the head of the backboard along with one of the firefighters. We lifted and placed her on the stretcher. Once on the stretcher, Rosie and her partner began to strap her onto the stretcher. I stepped back to get out of the way. I looked again at my hands and saw blood all over my right hand and streaming down to my wrist. I looked down to see if I'd gotten blood on my slacks. How would I explain to my boss the blood on my slacks and shirt?

As I looked up, I was going to ask one of the firefighters if they had any hydrogen peroxide to clean the blood off. Suddenly, standing there, knowingly and already anticipating what I was going to ask, a firefighter, who I think was the officer, had in his hand a spray bottle of hydrogen peroxide and some paper towels.

I told him, "Thanks, Brother, I surely appreciate it."

He responded, "No problem."

He must've sprayed several times before I finally was able to clean the blood off my hands. Just smelling the mix of hydrogen peroxide and blood took me back to the days when I was a paramedic with EMS. I couldn't believe we DIDN'T wear gloves when I first started back in 1980! Those were the days!

As I finished cleaning my hands, I could see that the paramedics and firefighters had loaded up the patient. I started to walk away. I remembered the driver who had struck the lady with her car. I walked up to her as she was now sitting in her car crying, with fear in her eyes.

I asked her, "Ma'am, are you okay?"

She looked at me with the startled look, "I'm sorry, but I didn't see her!"

I told her, "Ma'am, not to worry! It seems like she's gonna be okay. She's talking and awake right now. Don't be afraid! The police officer will be here in a little bit 'cause he's gonna need to get some information from you and ask you some questions. You can sit in your car and he'll be right with you, alright?"

She replied, "Okay."

I introduced myself, "My name is Conrad Gonzales and I used to be a paramedic with the San Antonio Fire Department. I have seen things like this happen before. Just be calm and all will be okay."

I placed my hand out to shake hers. She stuck her hand out the window and said, "Thank you very much. I'm a little scared."

"I know you are, and it's okay to be scared," I replied in a calm and soothing voice.

As I was talking to her, I could see that there was damage on the left side of the bumper and hood. Fortunately for the victim, it was a small vehicle and she was a large woman. If it were a smaller woman and a large vehicle, it could have been much worse.

The female driver was very small in stature and stood probably only about four foot nine inches. A small driver, I figured she didn't even see the woman when she was making her left turn onto the street the victim had been crossing.

With her small stature, she may have just made the left turn and not been focusing on any pedestrians. But, then again, being a short lady, I thought the "post" on the left side by the windshield may have obstructed her view of the pedestrian. I won't ever know but that is what I was thinking. How many times have you made a left or right turn and suddenly there's a pedestrian there? I'm sure it's happened to you because it sure has happened to me!

After reassuring the lady I bid her farewell.

"I will see you, ma'am, be careful and God Bless you! Take care, OK?"

Still afraid, she replied, "Muchas gracias!"

I told her, "De nada! No se preocupe!" (You're welcome. Don't worry!)

As I stepped away and started to walk toward my car, I looked and saw that everything was under control. The police officer was there. Another officer pulled up and started to direct traffic. The ambulance was still there with the patient; they were stabilizing her by starting IVs, giving her oxygen, and doing their physical and neurological assessments.

I saw my car with my emergency flashers on. I realized that I had the engine running the whole time! Oh well - it reminded me of when I was in the ambulance and we always left the engine running!

I got in my car and turned the emergency flashers off and proceeded carefully to make a right turn. The officer directing traffic noticed me as the "guy who stopped to help." He then stopped the other cars so I could proceed forward. While I was passing him, he looked at me and I looked at him. We waved a "thanks" to each other as I drove away from the scene.

As I was driving off, I prayed, "Thank you, Lord, for putting me in Your place. You placed me there for a reason and placed me there to help the woman in need and the lady that hit the woman. I'm glad that I was there to help them both."

The whole incident lasted around twenty minutes, from the time I saw the lady on the phone to the moment I drove off. I had maybe forty more minutes till I had to return back to work. I drove to my parking spot at the park, turned off the car, and put my seat back to take my power nap. I closed my eyes and again told the Lord thank you for putting me at the right place at the right time. I dozed off. After my twenty-minute power nap, I stopped at a taco place for some to-go food and headed back to work.

I wondered if I should mention this to anyone at the office. I answered my own question with a "Nah." I did mention it to the administrative secretary since she was the first one I saw as I came into the office.

If I had mentioned it to the boss, he wouldn't have believed me or I would have been chastised for stopping to help. I could hear him saying, "Conrad, you shouldn't be stopping to help. You don't have any equipment, and you're not a paramedic anymore!"

I won't talk about him… we'll leave it at that! Needless to say, my old habits as an EMT die hard. I loved being in action, and I was so grateful to be there to help.

Lesson Learned - Don't Get Burned

When you're making a turn at a crosswalk…WATCH FOR PEDESTRIANS! You never know if someone is going to suddenly dart or run across the street. You may have a mother with a stroller or a child in hand. Many pedestrians have been killed walking across the street even if they're at a crosswalk and especially when it's dark!

If something should happen and you're involved in an accident or you hit someone, call 9-1-1 and **stay at the scene**. If you feel comfortable, you can render aid. If you leave the scene or don't call for help, you can be arrested for "failure to stop to render aid." This is a crime, and you WILL go to jail with criminal charges brought against you.

I went home that afternoon and told my wife about the call. She said, "The Lord put you there for a reason. The paramedic remembered you when you were a paramedic instructor. If she remembered you, she remembered you for a reason. Why not become an instructor again?"

I resigned three weeks later from the non-profit and decided I would enroll in the paramedic program at the University of Texas Health Center. I got my EMT certification in three months and, lo and behold, I was accepted to the paramedic program to start in the Fall of 2016!

Thanks to my wife, Alma, for believing in what I can do and bringing out the talent in me again!

And, thank you, Rosario Lovelace, the female paramedic who mentioned I was a great paramedic back in the days.

Chapter 13
The Mexican

Working as a paramedic brings many challenges: from patients, to supervisors, to the risks of getting killed on the highway or by some enraged husband, boyfriend, or disgruntled employee. Patients that are dangerous tend to do things that put you and your partner in danger, not to mention themselves. Here's a call that involved a possible suicide.

It was an early Sunday morning. We'd been busy most of the day on Saturday and I had gone to bed around 11 p.m. hoping to get some sleep or a nap before our next call. Saturdays are usually busy, and it is quite uncommon to sleep all night on a Saturday or weekend.

The call came in around 3 a.m.

"841, 841, respond to west Bexar County. Take Culebra Road out toward the county line. We'll provide further details."

I hopped up, walked into the ambulance and entered into the computer that we were 10-96. We knew we had a response time of at least twenty minutes as the call was out in the western part of the county. Culebra Road, back then, was pretty desolate with only a high school and a mobile home park being our last sign of "civilization."

We were about ten minutes in route when the dispatcher told us that we had a psychiatric patient with the sheriff's department at the scene. We didn't get any more details. The dispatcher told us to turn off the lights once we were a block from the scene.

I thought to myself, "Hmmm… not a very good sign."

When we were a block away, we turned off the emergency lights and our headlights. We could see there were two sheriff patrol cars with their parking lights on. Their emergency lights were off, too. One car was on the dirt road in front of the single wide mobile home and the other officer's car was in the driveway.

We parked out on the street.

I knew we had a situation as soon as we pulled up. Before we even stepped out of the ambulance, I could see two officers were at each side of the front door with their backs to the wall. They each had their guns drawn and talking to the patient from outside the door. The patient was inside the mobile home. The mobile home had two doors; a door with a mesh screen and a wooden door behind it. The wooden door, which was half way open, had a small window to where you could look inside. However, I could see the patient, a white male, through the screen door.

The white male, we'll call him David, was sitting at a round table that was up against a wall. He was in a T-shirt and boxer shorts with flip flops on. He was sitting facing the door. Behind him was the countertop. So, I figured with his size at about 300 pounds and maybe six feet tall, he would have to struggle a little to try to lunge at us. Then I noticed in his right hand, he held a kitchen knife, around eight inches long, against the right side of his throat.

I asked the officers, "What's going on?"

One of the officers replied, "His wife filed for divorce and left him a note when he got home telling him that she was done with him and going to her mom's house. She's got the kids."

I said, "Okay."

I turned and spoke to David through the screen door.

I asked, "David, my name is Conrad. I'm a paramedic with San Antonio EMS, and I want to help you. Can we talk?"

He yelled, "No! I don't want to talk to anyone! So, get the f--- outta here!"

I responded, "David, we're here to help you and not hurt you. I'm sorry that you're going through this but we really want to help you. Can we talk?"

He said, "If you wanna talk, the sheriffs have to leave!"

I told him, "David, they are here for my protection and yours. They will have to stay but they will be right outside the door. You have to trust me and the officers."

He sat there just looking at me as I was standing outside the screen door.

My partner said, "David, talk to us. We want to help you."

Then I heard him say, "Okay, but I want to talk to the Mexican!"

I looked to my left... a white sheriff. I looked to my right, another white sheriff. I looked at my paramedic partner. He looked white, too. One of the sheriffs smiled at me and said, "That must be you 'cause you're the only Mexican here!" He grinned from ear to ear. Well, what can I say? He was right. I was the only Mexican!

I told him, "David, I will come in, but I need you to stand up and get rid of the knife. Stand up and throw the knife toward the door."

I wanted him to stand up to make sure he didn't have anything like a gun on his lap. Since he was only in a T-shirt and boxer shorts, I figured he didn't have too many places on him to hide anything.

I asked him, "David, do you have any weapons on you like a gun or any guns in the house?"

He said, "No, I don't like to have guns in the house 'cause I got kids."

I told him, "That's very smart to think of your kids' safety, David. I appreciate that and I'm sure your kids do, too. Now, I can see you through this screen door. I can see every move you make. Don't do anything foolish 'cause the officers will do what they have to do to protect me and themselves. If you want to see your kids again, just be smart and let us help you. If you do anything dumb, you won't see your kids. I can assure you of that."

He sat silently and slowly stood up. He was a large guy. My mere 160 pounds would have been no match for David. He would have tossed me around like a piece of Samsonite luggage! He threw the knife toward the door.

I said, "Okay, David, now have a seat and don't move." I opened the screen door. I softly told the officers, "Back me up, guys. Do what you gotta do if he does something crazy."

One of them said, "We got your back."

David had thrown the knife right at the door and sat down at the table again. Keeping my eye on him, I had to get down on my knee and reach around the door to get the knife. Fortunately, I had my gloves on. Although, there wasn't any blood on the knife, who knows what he could have done prior to our arrival and I didn't want any fingerprints on the knife. It was standard protocol to wear gloves anyway. I grabbed the knife and laid it on the front porch behind me. The officers also kept their eyes on him.

I told him, "Thank you, David. Now, I'm coming in and I will have my emergency box with me in case I need to take any bandages out and also take your blood pressure. Is that OK?"

He said, "Yeah, come in." I really wanted to take the trauma kit in so in the event he would lunge at me, I would have something to throw at him to slow him down.

"Before I come in David, I have one more question. Did you take any drugs or have you been drinking?

"No, I don't drink and I only take medication for high blood pressure. That's it."

I asked, "Did you take your medication today or any other drugs?"

"No."

"Is there anyone else in the house, David?"

"No," he replied, "I'm by myself."

I slowly started to open the screen door. I looked at him and I said, "David, the officers are right outside the door and they're gonna be looking in. As I told you, they will do what they have to if you do anything foolish. And, I don't want to be in the middle of this. Do you understand?"

He sat on the chair at the table and was "cornered" in a way that he would have to lift the table to get to me in the event he started something. I slowly walked to the table and sat down. I put the trauma kit right at my feet to my right so I could grab it with my right hand and throw it at him… just in case. I looked on the countertop to see if there was any weapon. I looked around, keeping my eye on him, to see if there was any other thing that he could use as a weapon. It looked clear. I quickly glanced down under the table and on the floor. Nothing. We began to talk.

"So, David, tell me how all this started tonight."

He began in a trembling voice, "I came home from work and found this note that said my wife was done with me and she was moving in with her mom. She wanted a divorce. I can't take this shit. She's pulled this before and I thought we had worked things out. I don't know what happened."

"How long has this been going on?"

He said, "About a year, maybe longer. I thought that we had made up and we were gonna patch things up and make it better for the kids."

I asked him, "What about making things better for both of you? You've got to work things out between you both. Once that happens, the kids can and will see how you both can resolve issues and problems. Setting a good example for them is important. But constantly fighting and arguing only make things worse for you and the kids."

He said, "I try so hard to make things work. I work my ass off for her. I wanted to buy a house and get outta this stinkin' trailer shithole. I work two jobs so I can save for a house and she does this shit to me! I don't understand!" He began to cry. "I wish I could do more for her and the kids but I can't take her moving back and forth to her Mom's house and then back here! Why does she do this to me?"

I told him, "David, sometimes people do strange things when times are desperate and there's a lot of tension and it's really hard sometimes to understand why people do things. There are people that can change and those that don't want to. How long have you been married?"

He said, "Four years, but we've been together seven years."

"How old are your kids?"

"Seven and four. My son just celebrated a birthday last week. We had his party here, and we all had a blast. We had my family and her family here too. I wasn't expecting this."

"Things got worse during the week?" I asked.

"Yes, I had to work a lot this week. Overtime and I do odd jobs, too."

"What else do you do, Dave?" I asked.

He said, "I'm a handyman. I paint, do concrete, foundation work, framing, sheetrock, and anything else I can do. I like doing things with my hands and I like showing my son how to do things."

David seemed more relaxed now after he cried.

I said, "David, you are a very talented man. Boy, I wish I had your talent and was able to do all that you do. I'm not a plumber but I can put a washer on the water hose!"

He smirked a little, so I continued, "Electrical work is not for me. Well, maybe I do some electrical work. I'm proud to change a light bulb!"

He smiled. I even heard the officers and my partner smirk in the background. One of the officers, speaking through the screen door, said, "Hey, David, I know a lot of people that could use your talent. I work part time with a builder, and they're always looking for contractors to do small jobs. Maybe we can get you some work."

"You see, David, you are needed. But most important, your children need you. Trying to kill yourself only tells the children that you gave up on them." I said, "Hey, dude, I went through the same thing. I didn't get to see my kids as often as I could. Man, I had to call the cops many times 'cause my ex-wife wouldn't let me see my kids when I went to pick them up on my weekends. But I made sure I spent as much time as I could with them and I know you do the same thing, don't you?"

"I do. I want to be a great Dad but how can I when she wants to leave me and take the kids?"

"David," I said, "Whatever happens, do what you can to spend time with the kids. They'll remember you being there. But right now, let's move forward and make sure you're around for them. Don't quit, brother. I didn't quit and you know that they're a lot of other fathers that have gone through what you and I have gone through. Let's prove to your kids that we are not quitters, man."

"Okay," said David. "What do we do now?"

"What we do now, David, is I'm gonna ask you if you'd like to go with us in the ambulance to the hospital or you can go with the officers. It's up to you. Your choice, brother. Now, I must tell you that whether you go with us or with the officers, we'll have to put the handcuffs on you. And, that, again, is for your protection and our protection. We don't want anyone to get hurt. Is that cool with you?"

"That's cool," he said quietly.

"Okay, David," I said, "What would you like to do?"

"I don't want to go in the ambulance."

I told him, "OK, David. If you want to go with the officers, can they come in now?" He nodded. "They'll put the handcuffs on you and take you to the hospital so they can at least get you some help. They'll get a doctor to sit down and talk with you just like we did now. What they'll do is make appointments for you so you can go see a private doctor as well. They'll take care of you, man, don't worry. Hey, these officers and my partner care about you. I care about you, and I care about what happens to you and your children."

Dave sat there quietly listening.

"OK, Dave, the officers will come in now."

I looked at the officers and nodded to them to come in. They came in along with my partner. David turned around and let the officers put on the handcuffs.

"David," I said, "Thank you for being a great dad and you always will be. Thank you for letting us help you and thank you for being cooperative and letting the officers put the cuffs on you."

The officers escorted David to the door and onto the porch. I picked up my trauma kit and headed to the door.

I asked David, "Do you have the keys to the house?"

He said, "Naw, but that's okay. Just lock the door behind you."

I said, "Okay."

As I was getting ready to turn the key knob to lock the door, I looked at the table where we sat. I thought to myself, "This could have turned for the worse." I looked around his living room and kitchen. This was his home and his family's home. I said a quick prayer, "Lord, help David and his family."

I closed the door.

I proceeded to the squad car that the officer was placing David into. Handcuffed, David permitted the officer to open the door to the car. David stepped into the back seat. The other officer entered the back seat from the other side and fastened David's seat belt. Before the officer closed the back door, David looked up at me and said, "Thank you, man, and I didn't mean to call you a Mexican."

I smiled, "Not to worry, I've been called worse. Take care and I'm gonna keep you and your family in my prayers."

He said, "Thanks."

The officer closed the door and got in the front seat. He started the car and pulled out of the driveway. As they drove off I could see David looking at my partner and me. I waved at him.

My partner looked at me and asked, "You ready, Mexican?"

I said, "Si, gringo!" We laughed, got in the ambulance and drove off.

My partner said, "Another day at the office, huh?

"Yeah, another night in San Antonio."

I reached over and grabbed the radio. I told the dispatcher, "Dispatch, this is 841. We're 10-98 and back in service. We're headed to the station."

The dispatcher responded, "Good to hear from ya."

I responded, "Yeah, good to be back."

We drove back to the station, and I went to bed. I put my head down on the pillow and closed my eyes. Once again, I said a quick prayer, "Thank you, Lord, for keeping me safe. And please, look over David and his family." I took a deep breath and fell asleep.

David, wherever you are today, thanks for your patience. I hope you got some help. I was honored to be your token "Mexican."

Now, fast forward twenty-three years to August 27, 2018. I wanted to take a before and after picture of my partner, Lee Carrola, and I standing in front of the ambulance at Station 41. I thought it would be cool to put this before and after picture in the book, so I gave him a call to set it up.

Lee had recently seen a segment on the news where I was featured promoting my book, specifically talking about suicides. I had mentioned the story of "The Mexican" in the television interview. Lee told me he was so moved with the interview that he called his family and friends to tell them to watch it. Lee's picture also appeared on the news . He was so proud that he'd been on television.

Lee told me when we chatted, "Conrad, when you mentioned the guy with the knife and you going inside by yourself, it dawned on me that I was with you on that call!"

"Are you sure, Lee?" I asked him.

He said, "Of course, I'm sure! I'll never forget you going in there all by yourself and thinking how brave you were to go in and talk to the guy. I remember the officers telling me, "He's sure in there a long time!" and I told them, "Not to worry, Conrad's got it. If there's anyone that can handle this situation, it's my partner, Conrad."

After Lee told me that he was my partner on that call, I had to apologize to him for not even remembering that he was with me.

He said, "Partner, don't worry. I was just glad and honored to be there and be included in your book!"

Well, there you have it. My partner, Lee Carrola, was on that call with me. I wouldn't have known it if it wouldn't have been for the interview that Lee saw on TV. Now I know, and now you know. A night to remember for all. Thanks, partner!

And, by the way, Lee is Mexican! He just doesn't look it!

See Appendix C for photos of the author throughout his career.

Lesson Learned - Don't Get Burned

The lifesaving messages that I want to get across here are two-fold: about suicide and the risks in trying to prevent one like in David's case.

We don't need to see statistics on suicides to know this is an all too tragic issue that has affected many people far too many times. We all know someone, whether a friend, family member, or co-worker who talked about suicide or committed suicide.

I can assure you that we all have been through all kinds of trials and tribulations and wondered how we would get through life. Has suicide ever crossed our thoughts? Maybe... but we all have a reason for living. Our mission here on earth, no matter what goes on in our lives, is to live and reach out to others in time of their crisis. And, when WE are going through troubled times, WE should reach out to others and seek help.

Now, in David's case, I do not recommend trying to "disarm" or try to talk someone out of hurting themselves, especially if there is a weapon involved. Leave situations like this up to the professionals like EMS and the police. I had training and protection. Did I take a chance? Yes, but I had the officers there, and I had a plan. Would it have been different if I was by myself with David? Yes, I would have stepped out and called 9-1-1. So, please do not take it upon yourself to try to diffuse the situation if you have no one there. Don't risk your life if you don't have anyone there to assist you.

If there is an emergency, again, **call 9-1-1**. If you think of hurting yourself or have suicidal tendencies, call 9-1-1 or the suicide hotline. Every city and state has a suicide hotline and you can talk to someone 24/7. They are there to assist and talk to you. Also, please share this with someone that may be having problems. Help me by helping yourself and others save a life.

If you ever need assistance or know of someone who may need help:
-    Call the National Suicide Prevention Lifeline: 1-800-273-TALK (8255)
-    Visit their Website: www.suicidepreventionlifeline.org
-    Call 9-1-1. They can help, too.

Chapter 14
She Looked Like My Daughter

This call was rather difficult for me. I also found it difficult to write. I knew that eventually I would write about it, but I just couldn't because it reminded me of my daughter. It took me nine years to finally sit down and put my thoughts together. I had to do it. It could save the lives of others.

I submitted this story to the local newspaper and I have to thank the columnist, Susan Yerkes, who published it in her column on July 10, 2005. Thank you, Susan.

It was an early summer morning in 1996.

I was working part time as a flight paramedic with San Antonio AirLife, an air medical rescue helicopter based in San Antonio. Having just returned from a flight, I laid out my sleeping bag to try to hunker down and get some sleep. It was about 2 a.m. when I was awakened to the tones alerting us for a flight.

The dispatcher called over the radio, "AirLife One, AirLife One, respond to a major accident to Pearsall, Texas, for a one-vehicle rollover on IH-35. Your ETA is fifteen minutes. Stand by for your coordinates."

I stumbled out of my sleeping bag, slipped into my flight suit, grabbed the radio and darted out the door with the flight nurse and pilot behind me.

As we were lifting off, the dispatcher advised over the radio that the sheriff's department said we may have multiple patients. Knowing that it was out in a rural area and on the highway, my gut instinct was to go ahead and launch the second helicopter as we didn't want to get overwhelmed and we might as well send the second chopper just in case. I thought we could always cancel them if not needed.

I replied, "Launch AirLife 2!" AirLife 2 was the second helicopter based at University Hospital, our local Level I trauma center in San Antonio.

Our flight was going to be a short distance, around fifteen minutes. Pearsall is about 30 miles south of San Antonio. The highway, IH-35, is the main highway that runs between San Antonio and Laredo.

As we were flying from the downtown area and AirLife 2 was launching from the northwest part of town, I knew we would probably see each other in flight, and minutes later, we did. AirLife 2 was flying actually off to our right side and behind us. It would have made a great photo with both helicopters airborne and flying together.

AirLife 1, the chopper I was in, was going to be the first to land. AirLife 2 would circle around and locate a second landing zone. It was the firefighters and troopers on the ground that were responsible for locating a safe landing zone for us. We depended on them to find a safe landing zone that was free of wires and trees. Wires and trees could easily take down a helicopter and kill us all. We always instructed the ground crew to stop traffic on all lanes in both directions to ensure the safety of the flight crew. They were and are the key factors in landing a helicopter safely! (Thanks, guys and ladies!)

One of the ground crew firefighters gave us a report when we were about two minutes from the scene. I could hear the desperation in his voice, "AirLife 1 and AirLife 2, we have nine patients! We have three DOS (dead on scene) and six needing help!"

I responded, "10-4! We'll be landing in 2 minutes!"

The first responder replied, "10-4! AirLife 1, you will be landing in the first landing zone 200 feet south of the scene. AirLife 2, we have a landing zone on the northbound lane of 35 just north of the scene! You are clear of wires! We'll guide AirLife 1 first and then AirLife 2!"

As we arrived we began to circle looking for the designated landing zone. I could see chaos on the ground. Several ambulances and firetrucks had converged on a van that had rolled over. There were firefighters and EMTs tending to patients. I could see three yellow blankets draped over three bodies with rocks on the corners to keep from flying off with the wind created by the helicopter rotors. We saw our landing zone.

The pilot said over the radio, "I see our landing zone. How do I look?" He was asking if we could see any hazards while we started to descend.

I responded, "You're clear on the left."

The flight nurse repeated, "You're clear on the right."

We slowly descended and touched down. I opened the door to the helicopter and stepped out. A firefighter came up to me and yelled into my helmet, "We have two patients in our ambulance! Come with me!"

My partner, the flight nurse, ran off with another first responder to another ambulance. The other helicopter landed and the flight crew was met by other firefighters and EMTs.

I asked as we walked to the scene, "What's the story?"

I didn't want to run since we were on the grassy median and one never knew if there were any holes or anything to trip on. The last thing I needed was to sprain or break an ankle at the scene!

The firefighter yelled, "Witnesses said that the van went off the road and the driver overcorrected as soon as the van hit the gravel on the side of the road! Everyone was ejected! They were all over the place when we got here. We triaged and found 3 patients with no pulse so we didn't work them!"

I yelled, "That's OK! That's what triage is all about!"

We arrived at the ambulance with two patients inside. I opened the back door of the ambulance to find two first responders doing CPR on an adult female on the stretcher. On the bench seat, I also saw two other first responders doing CPR. I couldn't see the patient on the bench seat. It was crowded in the ambulance.

I leaned over to the team doing CPR on the adult and told them to go ahead and stop CPR. The patient had just gone into traumatic arrest. Her heart stopped. I could see that her abdomen was severely distended which was indicative of internal bleeding. She would not survive. They stopped.

Unfortunately, 99.99% of patients in traumatic arrest out in the field do not survive. Being thirty-five miles from a trauma center only decreased the chance of survival. We had too many viable patients that we needed to work on.

I turned around and still couldn't see the patient on the bench but I could see they were doing CPR. I asked the first responder, a female, doing CPR to stop so I could take a look. She stepped aside as I told her thank you only to see tears streaming down her cheeks. I looked at the patient and that's when my heart stopped.

I froze. I was stunned… speechless. She looked just like my daughter. Here was the most beautiful little girl with long jet-black hair with the most dark and beautiful eyes and smooth bronze skin and she was in a traumatic arrest, too. No pulse. Not breathing. Her pupils were blown. No oxygen to her brain. No heartbeat. No signs of life. She was ejected from the van. No seat belt or booster seat.

It took me a few seconds to "snap to" and I told the crew, "Stop CPR. She's gone. We have other patients to work on."

The first responders stopped. They were in shock as well. I could see they were heartbroken and didn't really want to stop.

I took a deep breath and whispered a quick prayer, "God bless you, Mija."

I asked one of the EMTs as we stepped out of the ambulance, "Okay, what other patients do we have?"

I had to recoup quickly as I knew we had more patients. We went to a female. She turned out to be the mother. She was already packaged and ready to go. This means her spine was immobilized with a cervical collar and strapped to a backboard, IV started and ready to be placed in the helicopter. She was semi-conscious, going in and out.

I asked her, "Ma'am, can you hear me?" All I heard was groaning. At this point she was still with us. I yelled to the EMT, "Okay! Let's get her in the helicopter! As soon as the pilot gives us the thumbs up, we'll move forward to load her up, OK?"

The helicopter never stops the engine unless we're going to be there for a while. We always waited for the pilot's thumbs up indicating it was safe to approach the chopper.

I looked at the pilot and waited for the thumbs up. When we got the thumbs up from the pilot to proceed forward, I, along with four other EMTs, carried the backboard over the grassy area to the helicopter. I opened the door and yelled to them, "On the count of three we'll lift the backboard and place her feet first and swing her head to the front! Ready? One, two, three!"

We lifted and loaded her in. I yelled to them, "Thanks, guys! Great job!" Yes, they always did a great job. I deeply respect and appreciate what first responders do.

I closed the door, turned around and saw my partner, the flight nurse, with another patient that was talking and seemed stable. I asked my partner, "You okay?"

She yelled into the mic piece in her helmet, "Yeah! Her vitals are stable! How about you?"

I yelled, "I've got the mom here. She was ejected. She's groaning a bit and responds to pain stimuli! I'll holler at you if I need your help!"

She said over her helmet microphone, "OK!"

I strapped in and told the pilot, "OK! We're strapped in! Let's go!"

The pilot replied, "10-4. Two patients, correct?"

I answered, "Yes, two patients going to UH!" (University Hospital, the trauma center) We lifted off. I told the flight nurse, "I'll call the report for my patient first, OK?"

She replied, "Sounds good!"

I was getting ready to turn in my report to the hospital when I heard the mother scream, "My baby! Where's my baby?!" She screamed so loud I could hear her even with my helmet on.

I asked her, "You had a baby in the van?"

She yelled, "Yes, where's my baby?!"

"Where was your baby?"

"She was in the front seat! Where is she?!" She started to cry.

"Was the baby in a car seat?"

She yelled, "No! She was asleep on my husband's lap!"

I asked, "Where was your husband sitting?"

She yelled, "In the front seat!"

I asked her, "Are you sure you had the baby in the van?"

"Yes! Where is she?!"

I asked my partner, the flight nurse, "Did anybody tell you anything about a baby?"

She replied, "No! Nothing about a baby!"

I answered, "OK!" I was thinking, "Shit, the baby was ejected. But where was the baby ?"

Then it hit me. Rollover. Baby in father's arms. Father ejected, too. Then I remembered, while we were circling to land, I noticed the van was upside down. I thought, "Oh, no. Maybe the baby's under the van." I told the pilot to patch me in with one of the first responders at the scene.

I got on the radio, "AirLife 1 to Company 4. AirLife 1 to Company 4!"

I heard one of the volunteers, "AirLife 1, this is Company 4! Go ahead!"

I asked him, "Have you seen a baby that might have been ejected?"

He replied, "No, sir! I think those are all the patients!"

I told him, "We have the mother, and she's sure her baby was in the van!"

The first responder replied, "We haven't come across one yet! The Sheriff's Office thinks that's it!"

I told him, "Do me a favor and turn the van over! Has anyone checked under the van?"

He said, "No!"

"Please check and get back with me!"

"OK!"

Minutes later, I heard him on the radio, "AirLife 1, this is Company 4!"

"Yes, go ahead, this is AirLife 1!" I said.

"You were right, sir, we found the baby... DOS, sir."

I took a deep breath. "Damn. Okay, thanks."

That was my gut feeling. It wouldn't have made any difference. The baby was crushed. I yelled to the mother, "Ma'am! Ma'am!" She was slipping in and out of consciousness. I had to tell her.

"Ma'am, your baby did not survive."

She did not hear me. She slipped into unconsciousness and stopped breathing. I started to get my equipment to intubate her. I yelled to my partner, "She crashed! I'm gonna intubate her! She still had a pulse."

I intubated her and ventilated her until we arrived at the hospital. The ER staff met us at the helipad and we rushed her to the ER. She was rushed into surgery.

It was a rather solemn flight back to our downtown base. It was quiet in the helicopter. We did not say a word. It was around 5 a.m. when I finally laid down to sleep again, however, I couldn't relax as the little girl's dark brown eyes kept looking at me. An innocent little life taken in a matter of seconds. Unfortunately, the mother died the following day.

This is what happened as told by one of the survivors to the deputies at the scene.

This family was coming from a city in South Texas. It was two in the morning. The father was driving and started getting fatigued so he woke up his wife, the mother, to drive for him because he was dozing off. She had the baby asleep on her lap on the front seat. They pulled over on the highway so they could switch drivers. The husband climbed into the front passenger seat and put the baby in his arms. The mother then got into the driver's seat and drove off.

The mother, after about thirty minutes on the road, fell asleep at the wheel. She was startled and woke up when she realized that the right wheels were on the shoulder of the road. She quickly jerked the wheel to the left, overcorrected, and that's when witnesses stated that the van rolled at least 5 or 6 times. All the passengers were ejected.

Total in the van: ten
Survivors: three

That morning, when I got off, I called my daughter at her mother's house. She was asleep. I told her mother to give her a big hug and a kiss for me. I also told her to please hug and kiss my son.

When I saw my daughter a few days later, I hugged her and kissed her and was grateful she was safe. I grabbed my son and gave him the biggest hug, too.

God Bless the little girl that looked like my daughter. She's now an angel in heaven.

Lesson Learned - Don't Get Burned

It amazes me today how many people still don't restrain their children, much less themselves. With the leading cause of death for children being car crashes, you would think that parents would take heed and restrain their children every time they get in the car. Do you restrain your kids? Do you buckle up yourself? Remember, children do what they see and they say what they hear. If they see that you do not use your seat belt, they too, will follow "mommy or daddy's" example. If they hear you say, "I'm just going to the store," they will use that same lame excuse!

Do your research about infant, convertible, and booster seats for your children. You are responsible for their health and safety. Don't be a victim or let your children be victims of your negligence.

You can call your local United Way or SafeKids Coalition to find out how to install your baby's or child's seats correctly. Some police and fire stations can help install or check seats, too.

Don't make the mistake. Remember, your child's life is at stake. Buckle them up! Tell your adults passengers to buckle up and BUCKLE YOURSELF UP, TOO.

If you are tired and exhausted, please DON'T DRIVE!

Chapter 15
Holiday Pains

The holidays are a time for laughter and fun; there are office parties, family gatherings, and eating endless amounts of turkey, dressing, cakes, pies, and Mom's famous fruit salad with pecans! Yes, a time to relish and a time I look forward to! And, also a time when people are most likely to choke to death! I would know. Read on!

It was about fifteen years ago. We were all at my sister's house on Thanksgiving Day. Everyone was already in "sleep mode" from the turkey (some people say there is no chemical in turkey that brings you to drowsiness and thus passing out on the couch with a piece of pie on your lap, but dispelling the myth is not my focus). My brother-in-law and I were standing and chatting by the kitchen island. I was watching my sister, the infamous and exceptional host, make sure that everyone was comfortable. She was running around asking, "Are you ok? Would you like some more to drink? Can I get you anything else? Can I refill your coffee? More pie for you?" You get the picture!

I was exhausted watching her run around from the kitchen to the living room to the back patio! I'm glad I didn't have to go to the bathroom. I could hear her now! "Conrad, do you need some more toilet paper or soap in there?" Knowing her, should would have just opened the door and thrown the toilet paper onto the floor! Then she would have told me, "Don't forget to wash your hands, little brother!"

All this with food in her mouth!

She'd take a bite of food, get up, and start walking around seeing if everyone was okay. She'd come back to the table, take another bite of food, and get up just to see if maybe she'd missed someone that she didn't ask if they were okay. Wow! Yes, a great hostess!

That's my sister. Love her to death. Needless to say, I'm glad I was there to keep her from that!

A few minutes later, after taking a few bites and running around, she sat down to finish eating. Of course, she's the last one to finish eating because all this time she's been in marathon hostess mode.

I had to catch my breath from just watching her. I was still standing by the kitchen island talking to my brother-in-law. He had a beer in one hand, and I was drinking a glass of wine. I don't recall what the conversation was about but we both were having a peaceful and not too stressful chat about something.

Then I looked at my sister as she was sitting at the table. She turned around and looked at me with her eyes wide open. Then, she turned back around facing the table. I kind of thought, "What was that all about?" Then, again, she looked at me and turned around again. My brother-in-law noticed that, too.

He asked me, "Hey, what's up with your sister?"

I looked at him and shrugged my shoulders.

She suddenly got up from the table and walked over to me with eyes wide open. Then she turned around and started hitting her stomach like a gorilla pounds on his chest. She turned around looking at me like she's trying to tell me something.

I said, "Shit, she's choking!"

I quickly turned her around, wrapped my arms around her and placed my fists over her navel area and started giving her abdominal thrusts! After four or five attempts, I screamed at her, "Is it out yet?"

She just shook her head with a no.

Her head was bent over. I thought she was going to pass out. I continued with the abdominal thrusts but even harder. I must have done around three or four more when, suddenly, all the food came out. I mean, ALL the food. Turkey, mashed potatoes, green beans. I may have even seen a piece of pie there, too!

She turned around and looked at me. "Didn't you see that I was choking?!" she yelled.

I responded, "You were looking at me like you were surprised I was your brother! That is not the way to tell someone that you're choking! This is the universal sign of a choking victim! This is it!" I was demonstrating by placing my hands around my throat. "You have to place your hands around your throat, Marina! I thought you knew that!"

I turned around to my brother-in-law and asked him, "Jeff, do you know how to recognize when someone is choking?"

He looked at me and nonchalantly said, "No, that's why we invite you just in case this happens. You're a paramedic, right?"

I said, "No, no, no, no, Jeff!"

I looked at my sister and I finally asked her if she was OK.

She responded, "Oh, now you ask if I'm okay, little brother!"

I looked at my brother-in-law and said, "Geez, can't win for losing!"

He said, "I know how you feel. Your sister's my wife." I love my brother-in-law, Jeff; he's so cool, calm, and collected.

Then I thought to myself, "What would have happened if I wasn't here?"

So, I yelled to everybody in the kitchen and living room, "OK, everybody! We're gonna have a quick in-service training on the Heimlich Maneuver! Everybody in the living room now!"

On Thanksgiving Day, in the middle of a Dallas Cowboys football game, I turned the TV off and gave a quick class on how to save a choking victim. I had to make sure my sister didn't go back to the kitchen to finish eating. I needed to keep an eye on her just in case.

This was a Thanksgiving to remember. At least now she knows the universal sign of a choking victim. Now we can avoid more holiday pains - until the next time, anyway!

Lesson Learned - Don't Get Burned

Take a CPR class!

Do you know that over 3,000 people choke to death every year? Did you know that an adult choking victim's heart will stop in six minutes from lack of oxygen?

You have two pipes in your throat. One pipe, the esophagus, is where food travels into the stomach, and the other, the trachea or windpipe, is the pipe that goes directly into your lungs and allows you to breathe. When we're eating and start to choke, both pipes are blocked at the base of the throat. When we have a complete airway obstruction, we cannot breathe at all. There is no airway exchange whatsoever.

In three minutes, if no one has successfully done the Heimlich Maneuver, you will go unconscious. In the next three minutes, your heart will stop and you will go into a cardiac arrest and your brain will suffer irreversible damage.

This is how people choke to death!

The average response time for an ambulance or fire truck in the country is around seven minutes. Now you can see the importance of knowing what to do in the event of a choking emergency.

So, PLEASE, PLEASE, PLEASE, set up a time to take a CPR class!

Chapter 16
"Hey, Gonzales, Happy New Year!"

Working with EMS was always challenging, but I really enjoyed it. Tough days were the norm, but the holidays presented other challenges. This particular New Year's Eve was interesting but rewarding.

I believe it was New Year's Eve of 1995. In EMS, our shift started at 7 a.m. until 7 a.m. the following morning. Yes, we worked 24-hour shifts. Fortunately, I worked at #41 fire station which, back then, was one of the slowest stations located on the Northwest part of town. However, it being New Year's Eve, I knew we'd be busy because once the downtown units started picking up, we'd eventually get sucked in to the downtown area.

The morning was quiet.

I thought, "Hmmm, okay, everyone's resting for tonight so they're all taking naps or sleeping late. It won't be too long before things start to pick up."

After checking, restocking, and cleaning the ambulance, we went for breakfast at our favorite taco place not far from the station. By the way, you can always tell when a restaurant has great food. If there's an ambulance, fire truck, or police officers parked outside, they have great food!

That evening, around 7 p.m., things started to stir around town. People getting drunk and fighting was the norm on New Year's Eve. Grass fires started to light up with sparklers and bottle rockets landing in dry fields and peoples' yards. Firefighters and paramedics were responding to calls all over town.

We finally got back to the station around 9:30 p.m. We had dinner on the road as the firefighters didn't have any time to cook knowing that we all were going to be busy. We were all on our own. I decided to lay down and try to take a little nap. I dozed off.

I woke up to the radio tone. It was 11:25 p.m.... New Year's Eve, thirty-five minutes before the stroke of midnight. I heard, "841, 841, respond to the area of Prue Rd and Babcock for a possible MI (heart attack). Will give you the address shortly."

I stumbled out of bed and put on my boots and shirt. I grabbed the radio and responded, "10-4." Still half asleep, I almost ran into my partner, Val Castaneda, and our rider, Eddie Casias. I'd worked with Val several times and I always enjoyed working with him. Eddie was going through the paramedic program and was assigned to ride out with us to get some in-service training. As a former paramedic instructor and preceptor, students were sent to my station to ride out with me so I could evaluate their performance. Back in the 80's I used to be an instructor at the University of Texas Health Science Center (now The University of Texas Health Center) where we trained future EMTs and paramedics.

As we were walking to the ambulance, Eddie, the trainee, asked, "What we got?"

I told him, "We have an MI. So far, he's conscious, let's hope. Don't forget to buckle up."

Eddie answered, "Cool. I won't."

Eddie climbed into the side door and in the back of the ambulance. Val and I hopped in the front seat. Val was driving and I was the "doctor" who would provide care and ride in the back of the ambulance with the patient. We drove off. As partners, we took turns as to who would be driving and who was going to ride in the back with the patient on the way to the hospital. I directed Val how to get to the address since he wasn't quite familiar with the area.

I picked up the radio and told our dispatcher, "We're 10-96. Waiting for the address."

"10-4," The dispatcher responded.

As we were on the way, I wrote down the street and address. I asked the dispatcher, "Any more details? Is he conscious?"

The dispatcher responded, "None yet. We haven't received a call-back with any changes."

I responded, "10-4, thanks."

Fortunately, I recognized the street. It was the same street my nephew lived on and I knew exactly where it was. The location wasn't but maybe ten minutes away. Our station was on the Northwest side of town which has a higher elevation. There are areas where we could see the skyline of San Antonio at night. Of course, being New Year's Eve and with all the fireworks, you could actually see the smoky haze that hovered over the city from all the fireworks and rockets shot into the air.

On our way to the call, I thought, "Someone at the address may have been drinking too much or got into an argument while celebrating. Now, they may be having a heart attack. We'll know when we get there."

We pulled up to the house which was on the left side of the street. Val got on the radio and told dispatch, "841, 10-97." (at the scene.)

Dispatch responded, "10-4. 841 is 10-97."

Val got out the driver's side and I got off the passenger side and told Eddie, "Hey, Eddie, grab the heart kit and the heart monitor."

He said, "Got it, Conrad."

As we're walking toward the house, I could see the house was decorated with Christmas lights and had a very nice curb appeal. We could hear fireworks in the neighborhood. We walked up to the front porch and rang the doorbell.

The door opened and we were met by an Asian woman.

I said to her, "Hello, Ma'am, we're EMS. What seems to be the problem?"

She nervously responded, "My husband! He's not feeling well!"

"OK, where is he at?"

Right after I asked, I saw him walking up to us from the living room and into the hallway. When I saw him, I thought to myself, "Shit, he doesn't look good." He was pale and very sweaty. He looked as white as the wall in the hallway. His shirt was soaking wet, indicative of a major heart attack or shock.

I told him, "Sir, stop right there. Don't move, sir. We're gonna get the stretcher and bring it to you. Don't move!" I thought if he moved any further he would crash on us and go into a cardiac arrest.

I asked the patient, "Sir, what's your name?"

"Benson, Winthrop Benson," he replied.

I turned to Eddie and Val and calmly told them, "Guys, get the stretcher, quick." I didn't want to look or sound too excited so as not to excite Mr. Benson; however, Eddie and Val could tell by the look on my face and the tone of my voice that this was bad and could turn worse.

As they grabbed the stretcher, I placed Mr. Benson on oxygen. I checked his radial pulse and felt that it was very irregular. I put him on the cardiac monitor and found that he was having a massive heart attack, ST-elevation to be exact.

I asked him, "Mr. Benson, what were you doing when you started having this problem?"

"I was walking back from a neighbor's house. We were celebrating New Year's and my neighbor wanted to go home by the stroke of midnight, so I decided to walk her home. I didn't want her to walk home by herself." He continued, "It wasn't too far."

"Did you feel anything on your way back?" I asked.

He said, "Well, I was feeling tired and short of breath. I had to walk uphill a little bit."

"How far did you walk?" I asked.

He said, "I walked about a block."

"Has this ever happened to you before, sir?"

He replied, "Not that I can recall. I've never had a heart attack before."

"Okay," I said, "I just have to ask questions, so we can tell the doctor at the hospital."

When Val and Eddie returned with the stretcher, I quietly said to them, "ST-elevation, guys. We need to get going quick. We don't have too much time." ST-elevation is indicative of a major heart attack.

They both said, "Got it."

I told Eddie, "Eddie, go to the ambulance and spike an IV bag."

Eddie said, "You got it," and hurried back to the unit while Val and I stayed with Mr. Benson.

I told Mr. Benson, "Mr. Benson, let's get you on the stretcher, OK? We need to get going to the hospital."

He responded, "Okay. I want to go to BAMC." BAMC, Brooke Army Medical Center, is a military hospital in San Antonio. Being a retired serviceman, that's where he wanted to go. Unfortunately, it was much further than the local Methodist Hospital. It was twenty-two miles to BAMC which would take us thirty minutes. It was six miles to Methodist Hospital or about twelve to fifteen minutes. With his condition, I knew we'd be there in ten.

As we assisted him onto the stretcher, I said, "Mr. Benson, we're gonna have to go to a closer hospital. You are having a major heart attack, and we're only about ten to twelve minutes away. It would take us thirty minutes or more to get to BAMC and that is too far at this point."

His wife, who walked alongside the stretcher, looked at me and said, "But he has all his paperwork at BAMC."

I looked right into her eyes and responded, "I understand that, ma'am, but he's in critical condition, and we have no choice at this time. The hospital that we're going to will get his paperwork from BAMC. Not to worry. Can you meet us at the Methodist Hospital? We need to get your husband to the hospital as soon as possible. You can have someone drive you there."

Mr. Benson asked, "Why can't she go along?"

"Mr. Benson, it's best that she goes with your family. We are going with lights and sirens and we'll be going through red lights. I don't want your wife to get too excited or nervous. We have to go now."

He replied, "No problem." He told his wife, "Honey, have the kids take you to the hospital. I'll see you there."

With his condition, I didn't want to have his wife in the ambulance. I was afraid he would go into a cardiac arrest and my fear was, if he did, things would turn for the worse if we got to the hospital and we're doing CPR on her husband as we're getting out of the back of the ambulance. I would not have his wife be a witness to that.

Believe me, I learned my lesson. That happened once. The wife was in the front seat. I was in the back with the patient who was conscious and talking when he crashed on me and I was the only one in the back of the ambulance. We had to stop and call for a back-up. She witnessed her husband die. It didn't turn out well.

Before we loaded Mr. Benson into the ambulance, he asked me, "Is it bad?"

"Mr. Benson," I said, "You're having a heart attack. And we need to get moving. Are you having any chest pain right now?"

He said, "You know, now I'm feeling some pressure in my chest. I just don't feel well."

We hurriedly loaded Mr. Benson into the ambulance. Eddie, the trainee, jumped into the back of the unit followed by Val and myself. As Val and Eddie secured the stretcher and the oxygen tank, Mr. Benson looked at me and then at my name tag and said, "Hey, Gonzales."

"Yes, sir?"

"Hey, if I don't make it, Happy New Year to you."

"Mr. Benson, you're gonna make it, sir. We'll get you to the hospital, and they'll take care of you. Trust me."

He said, "Okay, but just in case, Happy New Year to you guys."

"Happy New Year to you, sir. You'll be fine."

I thought to myself, "You're not dying on me on New Year's Eve! I will not let that happen. Not on my shift!"

It was 11:45 p.m., fifteen minutes before the stroke of midnight and ringing in the new year. Moments later, Val looked at me and said, "Conrad, since he's got some pressure in his chest, I'm gonna check his blood pressure and if the blood pressure is okay I'll give him some nitroglycerin for the pain."

I told Val, "Yeah, perfect. A baby aspirin first, then the nitro."

Val replied, "Got it. I'll get Eddie to start the IV on the way. This'll be his first IV with the ambulance moving." Val looked at Eddie, "You can do it, brother!"

Eddie said, "No problem!"

I had confidence in Eddie. I believe it may have been his first or second ride out with EMS as a paramedic student. I knew he was going to be a great paramedic.

Knowing that Val was unfamiliar with the area, I decided to drive to the hospital instead of riding in the back with Mr. Benson. I closed the doors to the back of the ambulance and got into the driver's seat. I buckled up, put it in drive and we took off. I knew Eddie was going to start the IV so I tried to drive as gently as I could. Fortunately, the roads in route to the hospital were free from bumps. I got on the radio.

"841 to Dispatch. 841 to Dispatch," I said.

The dispatcher responded, "841, this is Dispatch. Go ahead."

"We're 10-96 to Methodist ER. Code 3. ETA around ten minutes."

"10-4." The dispatcher said.

I turned around to my right and yelled through the back window behind me.

"Hey, Val, Eddie!"

Val answered, "What's up?"

"Okay, whenever you're ready for the report. Make sure you tell them he's got ST-elevation so they'll be ready! They may have to take him right up to the cath lab when we get there!"

"You got it! Eddie's got the IV already. I'm gonna turn in the report right now!"

"ETA of eight minutes now!" I yelled.

"10-4!" Val responded.

I knew that if we told the ER staff that he had ST-elevation, it would prompt them to be ready at the ER entrance, look at Mr. Benson, and see what he's showing on the heart monitor. They would determine if he'll bypass the emergency room and go straight up to the cath lab for catheterization of his arteries. The ER staff would then notify the cath lab and any heart surgeon that an emergency open heart surgery is possible.

I could hear Val turning in the report as I was driving to the hospital. Fortunately, there wasn't too much traffic. Everyone was out getting ready to celebrate the New Year in just about ten minutes. I could see the hazy smoke all over the city. It actually looked like fog.

Shortly, we arrived at the hospital. Thank God!

"We're here, Val!" I yelled through the back window.

"841 to Dispatch, we're 10-97 at Methodist," I said over the radio.

I stepped out of the ambulance so fast I didn't even hear the dispatcher acknowledge that we arrived at the hospital. I ran and opened the back doors of the ambulance. I looked at Mr. Benson. He still looked pretty bad.

"Okay, Mr. Benson, we're here," I told him. "How you doin', sir?"

"So far, so good." Mr. Benson replied.

"That's good, Mr. Benson. We're gonna take you inside and they're gonna take a quick look at you. They're gonna ask you the same questions we did, so be patient, alright?"

He replied, "No problem."

I reached to pull the stretcher out as Val and Eddie stepped out to help me unload the stretcher. Val and Eddie had already put him on oxygen, placed the IV bag between his legs, and had him on the heart monitor. We rolled him out, made sure the stretcher was locked in place, and ran to the ER entrance. As we entered the emergency room, we were met by the ER doctor and nurses.

The doctor asked me, "Is he still having ST-elevation?"

I said, "Yes, sir."

We stopped right inside the ER doors when the doctor looked at our heart monitor and said, "Yep, still in ST." He told the nurse, "Let's go to the cath lab."

The doctor told Mr. Benson, "Mr. Benson, you're having a severe heart attack. We are gonna take you straight up to the cath lab and see what we need to do, okay? Nurse, call the cath lab and tell them we're going straight up. We'll need all the lab work we can get from him."

The doctor asked me, "Can you guys keep him on your stretcher and we'll all take him up?"

"No problem."

We didn't want to waste any time moving Mr. Benson onto another stretcher and cause him to exert himself any more than he had to. Thanks to security, the elevator was already waiting for us to take him upstairs. We all stepped in and pressed the button to go upstairs.

On our way up, I asked Mr. Benson, "How ya doin'?"

He said, "Still good. We got here pretty fast. How fast were you driving?"

I responded, "I have no idea. Traffic wasn't bad at all, though."

The elevator doors opened and the staff met us and escorted all of us to the cath lab. Once in the door of the cath lab, we prepared to get him off our stretcher and onto their bed. Everyone was prepped and ready. We took off the electrodes, unhooked our heart monitor, and placed the IV on the IV pole as the cath lab nurses took over. We placed our stretcher next to theirs.

"OK," one of the nurses said. "On the count of three we'll grab him and place him on our bed. Ready? One, two, three!" We all lifted Mr. Benson onto the hospital bed.

After we placed Mr. Benson on the bed, one of the staff members standing in the back said, "Hey, Happy New Year everybody."

It was 12:02 a.m. on New Year's Day.

As we were stepping out the door with our stretcher and out the door of the cath lab, I told Mr. Benson, "Mr. Benson, it was a pleasure meeting you, sir. You're in good hands now."

He said, "Hey, thank you guys. You all were great. I hope to see you all again and Happy New Year. Have a great night!"

"Thank you. We will, Sir."

The cath lab staff was already prepping to do the catheterization on Mr. Benson. One of the doctors told us as we were stepping out the door. "Great job, guys."

Val, Eddie, and I turned around and told him, "Thanks, and Happy New Year."

As we walked to the elevator to go back down to the ER, I looked at Val and Eddie and said, "Well, Happy New Year guys, and I'm glad we got him here alive. This was a touch-and-go call."

Eddie responded, "Yeah, glad I got the IV."

I said, "Great job. There's more to come tonight. It's still early and everybody's still partying. I hope we make it back to the station. I hope he makes it okay."

Val replied, "Yeah, me too."

We got down to the ER, restocked the ambulance, loaded the stretcher into the unit and headed back to the station. Surprisingly, we didn't get a call while heading back. Once we got to the station, I went straight to the EMS dorm and went to bed. We celebrated the rest of New Year's night asleep. Thank God.

The following day, I wondered what had happened to Mr. Benson. I wondered if his catheterization had gone well. After two weeks, we still hadn't transported a patient to Methodist Hospital. I wanted to ask some of the nurses if they could find out the outcome of his visit, but I couldn't call the hospital because of privacy regulations. I didn't want to go by his house either. My fear was visiting his house and getting bad news. So, I thought, "Well, if the Lord meant him to be here, that's His will."

About a month later, I received a call at the fire station. One of the guys answered the phone and called me on the PA system, "Hey, Conrad! Back phone!"

I asked the firefighter who answered the phone. "Who is it?"

He said, "I have no idea."

I picked it up and said, "Hello?"

I heard, "Gonzales! How are you?"

"Fine, sir! Who do I have the pleasure of speaking with?"

He asked, "You don't recognize me?"

I replied, "Hmm, your voice sounds familiar, sir. But I can't pinpoint it."

He said, "You picked me up on New Year's Eve at my house right before midnight. Remember?"

I was shocked. "Mr. Benson?!"

He said, "Yep! I made it!"

I replied, "Well, I'm glad to hear from you, sir! I was wondering if everything turned out okay!"

He said, "Well, they decided that catheterization wasn't going to cut it. So I had a quadruple bypass! They told me another thirty minutes, and I could have been dead."

I asked, "A quadruple bypass? Wow, how did it go?"

"Well, I'm talking to ya, so I think it went okay!" he said jokingly.

I told him, "Mr. Benson, you don't know how happy I am to hear that! It was quite a scare for us. I'm glad we got there in time and if it weren't for your family, yeah, it could've been worse."

He said, "Yeah, I'm glad they called. It was a scare for me and my family!"

I asked him, "So how's the family?"

He responded, "Everybody's fine. They were just a little scared." Mr. Benson continued, "Hey, I just wanted to tell you and your partners thank you very much for saving my life!"

I said, "No, Mr. Benson, thank you for not crashing on us! I knew we were going to get you to the hospital in time. I'm just glad you didn't get worse on us!"

"Yeah, well, I'm fine now and wanted to get your name and your address to send you a thank you card."

"Mr. Benson, you don't have to do that. We're just glad you are alive and well. That is your gift to us."

He proceeded, "What's your first name anyway? I knew your last name was Gonzales but I never got your first name. I also need the names of the other two gentlemen that were there, too."

"My first name is Conrad. The other two were Val Castaneda and Eddie Casias. Eddie was a paramedic in training. He started the IV on you and Val was in the back with you."

"Okay. Now I need your home address," he said.

"Mr. Benson, you don't have to do this. Val, Eddie, and I are just grateful that you are okay. That was a New Year's gift to us. Really, you don't have to."

Mr. Benson insisted, "I really need your address. I will not hang up this phone until I have your home address."

"Okay, sir," I obliged.

He said, "Expect to get something in the mail in the next few days. It's just a show of appreciation from myself and my family. You guys saved my life and I surely appreciate it. You may have given me a few more years."

"Thank you, Mr. Benson. Just to let you know it is against our policy to receive any gifts from patients," I said.

He quickly replied, "Don't worry. If anybody tells you anything, you tell them to call me. I'll take care of them."

I said, "Okay, sir."

Well, a week later, I received 3 gift cards in the mail to a restaurant for myself, Val, and Eddie. I called each of them up and told them, "Hey, guys, we got a gift card from Mr. Benson. I'll get these to you guys."

Val said, "That was nice of him. How is he?"

I told him, "He had open heart surgery. Remember we thought he was just going to have a catheterization done? Well, it was worse than we thought."

"Wow, that bad, huh?" Val said.

"Yep," I replied. "I'll mail these to you and Eddie. I'm glad he called."

Mr. Benson apparently had been looking for us. He had obtained some information when he called the fire chief's office asking for the station and number of the station. He was determined to find us, and he did.

From then on, New Year's Eve of 1995 till 2013, Mr. Benson sent us gift cards every year until he passed. I had visited him a few times throughout the years. Before my last visit he had a small stroke but was doing fairly well when I saw him. He didn't have any speech impairment, but you could tell he was a little slow with words. His wife was in the living room sitting with us as we spoke about that evening that we picked him up. I read about his death when his daughter posted it on Facebook. They had buried him that day.

Today, I still think about Mr. Benson on New Year's Eve. I think about him when I pass the street that he lived on. As mentioned earlier, my nephew lives on the same street that Mr. Benson did. Today, I still recall vividly him looking at me and calling out my last name, "Hey, Gonzales! If I don't make it, Happy New Year!"

It certainly was the start of a good year considering he survived the heart attack that night.

Mr. Benson, I'm glad to have met you, known you, and most important, I'm grateful that everything went smoothly that evening on New Year's Eve. And, even most important, Val, Eddie and I are happy to have given you a few more years on this earth with your family and friends. Val, Eddie, and I consider ourselves your friends. God Bless and Rest in Peace.

Lesson Learned - Don't Get Burned

What lesson did I learn, or can we learn from this? I really don't know where to start but I will begin by saying that the Lord placed us in the right place and the right time to save Mr. Benson's life.

Regarding medical care, here are some thoughts. If it weren't for his family, who recognized that Mr. Benson wasn't feeling well, he could have gone into cardiac arrest or died at home. This was a classic textbook call where everything went smoothly, from the time we received the call, our timely response, three paramedics, communication between us, EMS, and the ER and communication between the ER and the heart team.

Here are signs and symptoms of someone having a heart attack: chest pain; chest pressure; nausea or vomiting; shortness of breath; pale, cool, and clammy skin; diaphoresis (cold sweat); general weakness, dizziness, or unsteady gait; feeling of impending doom; and possible denial.

Some patients may exhibit all the signs, one sign or symptom, or no symptoms at all. They may just clutch their chest and then collapse. This is called a "Sudden Cardiac Arrest" where there are no signs or symptoms.

But if someone starts complaining of these signs or symptoms, it is best to call EMS immediately. Don't wait - the heart is being deprived of oxygen and blood!

And of course, please take a CPR class. If EMS takes too long to respond, you may need to attempt rescue breathing and chest compressions for the victim. Everyone should know basic life-saving techniques!

Chapter 17
The Mirror

When I first got into the San Antonio Fire Department in 1976, I was a firefighter assigned to Station #9 which was on the east side of town. When I arrived at the station one day, my officer told me, "Hey, Conrad! You're detailed to #18's!"

Someone was either sick or on vacation and I was "selected" or now "detailed" to that station, so I packed up my gear, boots, coat, helmet, and drove to Station 18.

Station 18 is located on the east side of town and was actually a pretty busy station. It was a single station with one fire engine and only four personnel. However, that day, we were only going to ride with three men, the officer, engineer (driver), and the firefighter... me.

Yes, only three firefighters, and I would be riding on the back of the old International fire truck. This is the same one that you rode on the tailboard standing up and had a safety belt to tie yourself on (and pray you didn't fly off when you hit a huge bump on the road!). It was the kind of fire truck that you had only your helmet and coat to protect you from rain, sun, and even hail! Sometimes I had to cover myself with the tarp that was draped over the fire house to keep the fire hose from getting wet or me getting plummeted by hail!

It was around two or three in the afternoon when we received a call for an apartment on fire. I ran to the back of the fire truck, put my coat and helmet on, and jumped on the tailboard. I made sure I was strapped in before we took off. The driver, at times, didn't care to look back if you were on the back. It was your responsibility to make sure you WERE on the back before the motor started otherwise you were either left behind, or if you weren't strapped in, take the chance of being thrown off. Fortunately, I always beat the driver and was able to strap in.

It was a clear afternoon and as we turned the corner on E. Southcross, a major thoroughfare, I could see light smoke in the horizon. We pulled up to the apartment complex and followed the smoke.

When we arrived, we saw smoke billowing out of the front window and door of a second story apartment. I jumped off the back of the tailboard and saw my officer jump out of the front seat of the cab.

He yelled, "Get the inch and a half and take it up the stairs!"

I yelled back, "Let me get the BA on first!"

He looked at me and yelled, "Don't be a sissy! You don't need to put that thing on! Let's go!"

Unfortunately, back then, you were called *worse* than a sissy if you put on a breathing apparatus. I always told the officer, "They're my lungs, not yours!" I put it on anyway.

The officer grabbed the hose and stretched it toward the stairs leading to the upstairs apartment. I had just put on my breathing apparatus and followed him up the stairs dragging the hose behind me.

He yelled, "Stay behind me and feed me some line!"

We entered the smoky apartment. The smoke wasn't as thick anymore, and we could see our way through the living room. We advanced the hose. We weren't but ten feet inside the apartment when he yelled, "I see the fire!"

Up ahead, I looked over his shoulder and saw flames to the right at about two o'clock. My officer started coughing without his breathing apparatus. I, fortunately, had no problem breathing (I actually sounded like Darth Vader with the oxygen tank on!). As he opened the nozzle, we noticed that the water didn't even make a dent in extinguishing the fire!

Coughing and gasping for air, my officer yelled, "Conrad, take over! I have to get out! I can't breathe!"

I shouted, "OK!"

He crawled past me to go outside almost knocking me on my ass! I continued to try to extinguish the fire but to no avail! I saw the flames and thought to myself, "What the hell is burning?! Is it gasoline or oil?"

I inched closer, still on my knees with hose in hand and still nothing. The water had no effect on the fire at all. I was alone with no success. Then, I felt heat from behind me and to the right. I thought, "Shit, there's fire behind me too!" I turned around and saw more fire behind me, realizing there were flames in the kitchen; I turned the nozzle to the flames.

I quickly turned around and saw a glimpse of my reflection on a mirror that was hanging on the wall in the dining room! That's what we were shooting water at... a damn mirror! The flames from the kitchen were reflecting on the mirror on the opposite wall!

I felt like such a fool!

Fortunately, I knocked the fire down and, fortunately, I had my breathing apparatus on. All that happened in a matter of about three minutes after entering the apartment. Finally, the truck crew arrived. The came in with tarps to place over the furniture and smoke ejectors to get the smoke out of the apartment.

My officer? He was outside smoking a cigarette.

I walked out of the apartment, looked at him and told him, "I got it, Cap!"

He responded, "Great job, Gonzales. I just needed some air."

I told him, "No, you needed a breathing apparatus. Don't be such a sissy!"

He laughed.

I couldn't believe we were fooled by a mirror. And water damage? Yeah, all because of a damn mirror! I sat on the running board of the fire truck and took off my breathing apparatus.

I told the officer as I laid the breathing apparatus on the pavement, "Hey, Cap! You have dark stuff coming out of your nose. Next time put a BA on."

He responded, "To hell with you." But... not quite in those words.

Enough said.

Lesson Learned - Don't Get Burned

To all my firefighting colleagues: ALWAYS USE A BREATHING APPARATUS! And, if you shoot water and it don't go out, it's either a flammable liquid or a DAMN MIRROR!

Be safe out there. A very good friend of mine, Jesse Bricker, died hours later after a fire consumed a hotel east of the downtown area. He was probably 300 feet from the building, however, he was being exposed to the smoke that was carried by the wind toward his direction. He was not wearing his breathing apparatus. He had a heart attack hours later at the fire station. You never would have expected it with how far the smoke traveled.

To my readers: Smoke will kill you before the flames do. Take my warning and install smoke alarms in your home. They will warn you of smoke in the home and give you time to exit your home. PLEASE! With a smoke alarm, you have a better chance of getting out alive. Why not stay alive?

Make sure you do the following:
- Install smoke alarms in each bedroom and hallway.
- Have an escape plan. Talk to your children about an exit plan and practice it!
- Check the battery ONCE A MONTH!
- Change the batteries twice a year. Usually, the best time to change the batteries will be around Daylight Savings time. When you Spring forward and Fall backward, change the batteries!

Chapter 18
The Toaster

"The Toaster" is a story that, again, highlights the importance of installing smoke alarms and that even the slightest error or oversight can cause a fire at home.

Back in the early 90s, my mom was the caregiver for my grandmother who was bedridden and confined to a hospital bed. I must hand it to Mom; she had the difficult task of watching Grandma 24/7. She had to turn my grandma on her side every three or four hours to keep her from developing pneumonia. She had a history of congestive heart failure and it could prove fatal if she wasn't repositioned every few hours.

Every now and then, Mom had to hire someone to come and watch Grandma so Mom could go out and run some errands. Dad was usually working. If you have ever been a caregiver, you know what it's like having to hire someone to take even a short break. It can be physically and emotionally exhausting.

One afternoon, Mom hired a lady to come and watch Grandma for a few hours. When the lady arrived, Mom gave her specific instructions. Mom was only going to be gone for a couple of hours so the lady did not have to worry about turning grandma over on her side. Mom left and the lady and Grandma were by themselves. Again, with Grandma bedridden, the lady had only to sit and watch. Grandma would usually sleep.

Not too long after Mom left to run her errands, the lady got a little hungry and decided to go to the kitchen and make some toast. She put the bread in the toaster, pushed the lever down, and went back into Grandma's room which was about twenty feet away.

After a few minutes, the lady was startled when the smoke alarm activated! She ran out of the room toward the kitchen and could see smoke in the kitchen and fire coming out of the toaster. She immediately ran to unplug the toaster (smart!), threw a towel over the toaster which smothered the fire, and removed the burnt toast. Fortunately, she did not burn herself.

There was smoke in the kitchen and she had to open the windows and doors to ventilate the house. Thankfully, it wasn't a lot of smoke, but there was enough to activate the smoke alarm!

Mom's toaster was a little old and wasn't working well. By that, I mean that you had to monitor the toaster and manually "push" the lever up to eject the toast. There was no automatic ejector function on the toaster.

Well, the lady didn't know that and that's how the toast burned. If the smoke alarm would not have activated, the toaster fire could have spread to the cabinet above. By the way, is your toaster also placed under a cabinet? I'm sure your toaster isn't one that has to be manually operated!

Well, when Mom told me what had happened, the first thing I did was go to the nearest Montgomery Ward (remember that store?) and buy her a brand-spanking new toaster! Problem solved!

This could have been devastating because, if there would have been a fire, there was no way this lady could have carried my Grandma out of the house! The toaster - a simple electrical appliance - could have taken possibly two lives, the caregiver and my grandmother.

Lesson Learned - Don't Get Burned

Okay, how many of us have burnt the toast, had a fire in the oven, or even turned around and gone back to the house after realizing you'd forgotten to turn of the coffee pot, iron, or unplugged the curling iron? I believe we all have! (Hey, guys, I don't use a curling iron!)

It doesn't take but a few seconds to think to yourself before you leave the house, "Did I turn everything off?" Even the Christmas tree lights during the holidays...

Electrical appliances, frayed electrical cords, old lamps and heaters that are plugged in, etc. can certainly pose a great danger to those in the home and to firefighters as well. Remember, when there's a fire in the house or any other building for that matter, when you run out, firefighters run in. As first responders and rescuers, they are now in danger of suffering severe injuries or death. Mentioned earlier, a firefighter's job is to save lives and property, however, they now are at risk of losing their lives and not going home to their loved ones.

Some simple reminders for fire safety:
- Turn off appliances when not in use.
- Install smoke detectors.
- Clean your chimney annually, and make sure every single ember is burned out before bedtime.
- Don't cook with long sleeves or a robe on.
- Remove any flammable liquids from the house.
- Have any gas heating systems or portable heaters serviced seasonally.

COMMON SENSE WILL KEEP YOU AND YOUR FAMILY ALIVE!

Chapter 19
Fifty Feet

It was around 11 a.m. when we were called for a cardiac arrest. I was a firefighter and assigned to Ladder #6 which was located just north of the downtown area. It would only take us about seven minutes to arrive to the corner of Broadway and W. Hildebrand, which was a very busy intersection.

When we arrived at the intersection, we got off the truck and asked the police officer who arrived first where the patient was. He just pointed up to the air where we saw a billboard and a worker doing CPR on the catwalk of the billboard!

My officer whispered, "Oh shit."

I thought the same.

Here was a billboard installer that was doing CPR on his co-worker fifty feet off the ground! The co-worker doing CPR, fortunately, was strapped on to a safety belt as was his buddy who had the heart attack!

The police officer told us, "Good luck."

I thought, "Yeah, thanks."

My officer told me, "OK, Conrad. You're it!" I knew what he was telling me.

I breathed a big sigh and said, "Okay."

First, we had to extend the ladder up toward the catwalk. It only took about five minutes to get the ladder up the fifty feet to the catwalk; I started to climb the ladder to reach the heart attack victim. A paramedic followed me. While climbing up, we dragged a Stokes litter (a long-wire basket) to place the victim in once we were up there.

166

Together, we gingerly climbed the ladder until we reached the top, basket included.

We knew we didn't have much time, and the best thing to do for the patient, and for our safety, was to place the victim in the basket and get him to the ground as soon as possible. I knew it wouldn't turn out well as he had been unconscious and without a pulse for at least twenty minutes.

I was the first to reach the victim on the catwalk. I yelled to the co-worker performing CPR, "What happened?"

He yelled back, "I was on the other side of the catwalk when I heard him yell that he felt faint. I told him to sit down. When he sat down, he just fell back and he became unconscious!" Then he added, "Here! Put this safety belt on and hook up to this wire so you don't fall!"

He handed me the belt then I hooked onto a wire that was draped along the catwalk. The catwalk was approximately three feet wide and ran the length of the billboard, about thirty feet. The safety wire was used so the workers could hook on to the wire and work safely along the length of the billboard.

Fortunately, the patient had his safety belt on and fell back from a sitting position onto his back. If he had fallen off the catwalk, he'd be dangling from the wire, which would have made a rescue difficult and challenging. We would have had to pull him up onto the catwalk and begin CPR.

The paramedic behind me climbed onto the catwalk and told the co-worker, "Okay, you'll have to stop CPR while we load him onto this basket!"

The co-worker yelled back, "OK! Is he going to make it?"

I looked at the paramedic and he answered, "We're gonna do the best that we can. We just have to get him down!"

The co-worker responded, "OK!"

Normally, with a cardiac arrest patient, we'd try to revive the patient at the scene by starting IVs, shocking the patient, establishing an airway for the patient to breathe, and administering heart drugs. In this case, our utmost priority was to get the patient down safely, not to mention ourselves and the co-worker.

With the co-worker, myself, and the paramedic secured to the wire, we stopped CPR and lifted the patient onto and inside the Stokes litter basket. The paramedic and I knew it was futile because of the time that he was unconscious and without a pulse. But, we knew we had to get him down.

Once we got him on the basket, I turned the basket toward the tip of the ladder which was just two or three inches off the catwalk. My weight would have brought the ladder to lie on the catwalk itself. I proceeded to climb onto the ladder and work the basket to the tip of the ladder. We were bringing him down feet first.

I first placed my feet on the ladder and, as I got to the bottom end of the basket on the ladder, I proceeded to climb down one rung at a time. We were able to get the basket on the ladder. The ladder was at a 45-degree angle. We descended very slowly. Fortunately, he weighed about 160 pounds which I was thankful for, as I was carrying the bulk of the weight at my end. It was easy. I just slid the basket down the ladder one rung at a time.

When we were at about forty feet, I felt something very peculiar but frightening. It was a warm morning and I was sweating, not just from the heat but from nerves! I heard a humming sound right around the back of my head. I wondered, "What the hell is that?"

The paramedic yelled at me, "Duck your head! You're close to the wires! Duck your head!"

He didn't have to tell me twice! I ducked so quick I just about knocked my teeth into the victim's work shoes and the wire basket!

The paramedic yelled again, "Keep your head down and don't look up!"

Apparently, throughout the catwalk ordeal, the ladder was moved to where it was only two feet from the electric wires! So, while climbing down, I had no idea the wires were behind and above my head. That was the humming I heard. Fortunately, I had my helmet on. If not, I could have been electrocuted as sweat was dripping down the front and back of my head! Water and live wires do NOT mix well.

That paramedic saved my ass!

I was grateful (and then a little pissed off that the engineer of the truck didn't yell at me to warn me about the wires).

Once we got to the base of the ladder truck, the other firefighters took over and grabbed the Stokes basket, placed him on the ground where the stretcher was waiting. They continued CPR and finally transported him to the hospital. The co-worker had climbed down the ladder of the billboard and met us on the ground.

He said to us, "Thank you, guys. Doesn't look good, does it?"

I told him, "No. Sorry sir, but thank you for trying. You did a brave thing by doing CPR up there. Took a lot of guts."

He said, "That's my buddy. I had to do something. I didn't have a choice."

I replied, "His family will appreciate your efforts to try to save his life. At least you tried."

He said, "Thank you, sir."

I told him, "No, thank you for thinking about our safety, too. Those safety belts saved us from falling."

He hopped in his truck and headed to the hospital.

Still rattled from almost getting electrocuted, I walked over to the engineer (driver) of the ladder truck and yelled, "Didn't you see my head close to the wires?"

His response: "Nope, sorry man!"

I walked off, took my helmet off and threw it on the ground. I was livid. We loaded up and drove back to the fire station. It was now almost one o'clock. We usually got relieved at noon. That's when we worked from noon to noon the following day. The call came in at 11 a.m. This was a two-hour ordeal.

Once we got to the station, I just picked up all my gear and left without taking a shower. I just wanted to go home. While driving home, I was thinking about the call and the man who suffered a heart attack. This man really didn't have a chance considering the time we spent trying to get him off the billboard. This gentleman was someone's husband or father, someone's son, someone's brother, uncle or nephew, or someone's best friend. Who knows if this could have turned out differently if he had any signs or symptoms before climbing up to the billboard. We'll never know.

I thought about what would have happened if the paramedic didn't see the wires and couldn't warn me. I would have been electrocuted forty feet up on the ladder truck. I could have fallen off the ladder and plummeted to the ground. That would not have been good. My son, Christopher, then only about two years old, would have been without a father.

I looked back and thought, "What could we have done differently to save this gentleman's life? Could we have gotten him down differently to somehow expedite his transport to the hospital?" Well... no. We did all that we could have done considering the circumstances.

It was his time... not mine. Once again, the Lord was with me in this call - fifty feet off the ground. Thank you, Lord, for keeping me safe. And, thanks to the paramedic who yelled at me to duck! To this day, I don't know who that paramedic was. He saved my life, too.

Lesson Learned - Don't Get Burned

What did I learn from this call?

When I think back, I should have been more cautious about the hazards that existed; the height, the wires, the possibility of falling. And I think about the lack of communication between the engineer and myself. I could have said, "Please let me know about any hazards I can't see." Or maybe I could have turned to look back before I took each step down the ladder.

So, to my fellow firefighters, paramedics, police officers, and first responders... COMMUNICATE WITH EACH OTHER AND WATCH EACH OTHER'S BACKS!

I was very fortunate to have survived this call. Take care brother and sister firefighters and paramedics!

Chapter 20
One Lucky Guy

When I first got promoted to the rank of Engineer, I knew I was going to be "drafted" to EMS. This was not out of the ordinary. Anyone that made the rank was sure to join the ranks in EMS. That's exactly where I wound up. However, I had no worries because I was going to volunteer for EMS anyway. As a matter of fact, as soon as I found out I was getting promoted, I went to the Fire Chief's office and placed my name on the list to go to EMS. That was on a Monday morning in the Fall of 1979. I was the first on the list of volunteers.

The station that I was assigned to was #805. That was Fire Station #5, located just east of the downtown area. I was told this station was very busy. I was not surprised that we responded to over fourteen calls on my first shift. Our shifts consisted of twenty-four hours at a time. Yes, we took a beating!

That part of town was quite "interesting" if you will. There were bars on just about every corner. It was an area that you wouldn't want to cruise around in after dark, perhaps even during the day. Fort Sam Houston was just north of the station, and fortunately, a Level I Trauma center was just four miles away. That was definitely a plus for us.

One afternoon, we were returning from a call around 5 p.m. I was driving and my partner, Bob, was riding passenger. We were at the intersection waiting to make a left turn onto Mason Street and could literally see the station as we were waiting to make the turn.

As I was watching traffic to make a left turn, suddenly we saw people running out of a bar 100 feet to our left. One, two, three, then six to eight people ran out of the bar scattering in all directions.

Next thing we see is a young Hispanic male running out of the bar with a gun in his hand!

I yelled, "Shit, Bob, there's a shooting and there goes the shooter!" The shooter ran right by us and headed west toward our fire station. There were other patrons chasing the shooter!

I picked up the radio and called Dispatch, "805 to Dispatch! 805 to Dispatch! We have a shooting at the corner of Mason and New Braunfels right by the fire station. Advise PD that the shooter is headed west toward the fire station and is being chased by the patrons of the bar! We are going to the bar to see if anyone has been hit."

Dispatch responded, "10-4, 805, proceed with caution."

"10-4" I responded.

We traveled only 100 feet to the front of the bar and pulled up. We both stepped out of the ambulance and carefully walked into the bar.

I carefully opened the front door to the bar. "Is anybody hit in here?" I was expecting to see a body or two on the floor of the bar.

A patron yelled, "No, nobody got hurt. He shot twice but didn't hit anybody. He just ran out the door. Did you see him?"

"Yes, we did! Are you sure nobody's hit?"

The manager answered, "I'm sure!"

"OK!" I yelled.

Bob and I both ran out and got into the ambulance to head toward the station. When we took a quick right, we could see five or six people surrounding someone on the ground. They were actually kicking the living crap out of someone! And it was the shooter they were pounding on! They chased him down and had him on the ground!

The firefighters were just coming out to see what the ruckus was all about. We stopped right in front of the mob and witnessed them drag the shooter onto the street and kept kicking him! Someone had taken the gun away from the shooter during the assault.

Now the shooter was "disarmed" and wasn't going anywhere, so we told them to stop. They obliged. We had our patient now.

The police had just pulled up.

I asked the bar patrons who chased him down, "Is everybody okay, here?"

A young male raised his hand and said, "Sir, sir, I got shot."

"You got shot?!" I asked.

"Yes sir," he said.

I asked him, "Where did you get shot?"

He opened his shirt. I saw a small caliber bullet hole in his chest. The bullet hole was just about an inch to the left of his sternum (breastbone).

I thought, "Shit." But I calmly told him, "Don't move." I took his shirt off. His buddies saw the bullet hole and they seemed to react in unison. "Wow, bro! You got a bullet to your chest, man! Cool!" I quickly looked at his back to see if there was an exit wound. No exit wound.

I told my partner, "Bob, get the stretcher. Also, tell Dispatch to get another unit out here and tell them we are taking the first patient ASAP."

Bob replied, "Got it."

One of the firefighters told the patient, "Dude, you are one lucky guy!"

I told the firefighters, "Hey, get some vital signs on the shooter. He got pretty beat up. We have another unit on the way."

They responded, "Got it."

One of his buddies who was also involved in taking down the shooter told him, "Hey, you're one tough motherf---er, man!"

I asked the victim, "Are you having any pain or shortness of breath?"

He responded, "No, sir."

I told him, "We're gonna get you on the stretcher and take you to the hospital right away."

He said, "I'm OK, sir. I feel alright."

I told him, "You don't understand. You have a bullet in your chest. You're lucky to be standing right now. There's a hospital just five minutes away."

The hospital was BAMC (Brooke Army Medical Center), a military hospital that was a Level I Trauma Center. Fortunately, we were only four miles away.

Bob, along with a couple of firefighters, pulled the stretcher up to the patient.

I told the patient, "Okay, just have a seat on the stretcher. Let me know if you feel any different. We're gonna start an IV and get you to the hospital right away.

He said, "Okay, sir."

I told my partner, "Bob, set up an IV for me. I'll start the IV on the way to BAMC."

He said, "Got it." We loaded him into the ambulance.

I heard the buddy tell the victim again before we shut the doors to the ambulance, "Hey, bro! You're a tough motherf---er! See ya later, man!"

I thought, "Boy, his bro is really proud of him."

As I climbed into the back of the ambulance, I closed the doors behind me. I saw that Bob had already set me up to start an IV. He already had the electrodes set up so I could get an ECG on him.

I said, "OK, Bob, let's go!"

Bob stepped out of the back, got in the driver's seat, and we drove off. Knowing that we were very close to the hospital, I knew I had just a minute or so to start the IV. Fortunately, he had some huge veins.

I told him, "Listen, I'm gonna start an IV on you. You need this in case they have to give you blood."

He said, "But I'm not bleeding, sir. And I hate needles!"

I said, "Dude, you've been shot in the chest. I wouldn't worry about a small needle, and we don't know if the bullet nicked an artery or not. Your blood pressure and heart rate are fine now, but it could get worse. Trust me."

He said, "Okay."

The road to the hospital was pretty smooth. We were traveling Code 3 with lights and sirens (nowadays it's called "Priority One"). I was able to get a large bore IV on his left arm. "Thank God!" I thought to myself.

I told the patient, "We're almost there! When we get to the hospital, they are going to start another IV on you. They are also gonna take some X-rays to see where the bullet is located. They may also take you up to surgery. So, be ready to be poked everywhere, OK?"

He said, "Okay, sir."

I thought to myself, "Even though he got shot in the chest, this kid is very courteous. He was polite and answered with a 'yes, sir' or 'no, sir' each time."

I quickly got on the phone and turned in my report to the ER at BAMC. We were about a half block away when I heard Bob yell through the little window between the cab of the ambulance and the back.

"Hey, Conrad, we're pulling up now!"

I yelled back, "OK!"

I quickly unfastened my seatbelt and started disconnecting the ECG wires and placed the IV bag between his legs.

I told the patient, "Okay, we're here now."

As soon as we came to a stop in the ER entrance, suddenly the back doors of the ambulance flew open. There they were. Five doctors anxiously waiting to see what was coming.

One of the doctor's asked the patient, "How ya' doing?"

The patient answered, "I feel fine, sir."

With the patient's shirt off, they could see the bullet hole in his chest. One of the doctors said, "Looks like a .22 caliber."

Another doctor replied, "Yep, that's a good thing."

Then, another doctor added, "Hmmm… maybe not."

Bob came around and we started to unload the patient. We rolled the stretcher into the ER where a slew of staff was waiting.

I gave my report: "We have a 23-year-old male with a gunshot to his anterior chest approximately one inch to the left of his sternum. As you can see, there is minimal bleeding. There is no exit wound; he denies any shortness of breath or pain at all. When we got to the scene, he was standing up and just raised his hand after I asked if anyone had been shot. He has no allergies and takes no medication. He's been conscious and alert since we got to him. His vital signs are stable and there are no abnormalities on his ECG. He is not tachy (tachycardia, which means a fast heart rate) and no other visible signs of any other gunshot wounds. He's been talking all this time. We have a 16 gauge IV on his left arm and we are running Lactated Ringers, KVO (keep vein open)."

Since there was no obvious bleeding and his vital signs were stable, we didn't have to give him a lot of fluids so we just kept his vein open by not emptying the whole bag of IV fluids in him. Orders from the ER doctors were barked:

"I need a chest X-Ray! Let's start another large bore IV! Where is respiratory? They were supposed to be here by now!" A nurse replied, "They're on the way!" More instructions: "Let's get a Foley in him and get some lab work also!" There must have been eight doctors and nurses working on him.

I told my partner, "Hey, Bob, let's stick around. I wanna see the X-ray."

He said, "Okay."

Well, we stuck around for an extra thirty minutes. It took that long to get the X-rays back then. When the X-rays returned, they showed that the .22 caliber bullet had passed just three centimeters from his aorta and lodged one inch from his back.

One of the doctors said, "He needs to buy a lotto ticket."

I thought, "Yeah, and not go to that bar again."

Bob and I picked up, stocked the ambulance and drove back to the station. Of course, the bar was still open for business. I told Bob as we were driving past the bar, "Hey, Bob, if we ever go for a beer, let's not come here."

Bob replied, "I won't. I don't drink anyway."

Today, that bar has been razed and there is a new building there. No bar... no chance of another shooting. Let's hope, anyway!

Lesson Learned - Don't Get Burned

Two lessons I learned from this call.

1. I learned that we have to appreciate each and every day we wake up and we can't take life for granted. This kid was very fortunate.
2. I'm not drinking at that bar! I never planned to anyway.

Chapter 21
Get Out

Before I go on with this story, I would like to warn that this story is about domestic violence, but I feel it must be told. Domestic violence or spousal abuse, whether the victim is female or male, is rampant all over the world. It must be addressed or more people will be severely injured or killed.

When I first got into EMS, I was assigned to an area of town that was busy, not only with fires, but many calls from stabbings, shootings, arson, overdoses, and assaults. Domestic abuse calls were not out of the norm.

It was a hot summer night in the early 80s, and we were called to respond to a house on the east side. We heard the dispatcher call over the radio.

"EMS to 805, 805, respond to Eastway Homes for an assault. PD is on the way."

I responded, "10-4. 805 is 10-96. We're on the way."

About three blocks from the scene, I got on the radio, "805 to Dispatch. Is PD on the scene?"

Dispatch responded, "10-4, they just arrived. You have a male patient with burns."

I thought, "Burns? Hmm… How could that have happened?"

I told the dispatcher, "10-4. We're 10-97." (We arrived.)

Fortunately, the police were already there. With assault calls, PD was always dispatched. Unfortunately, whenever we received a call to go into this area, we had to have a police escort for our safety. As a firefighter, we were shot at a couple of times, and we were very lucky we didn't get hit. There were other parts of town where we also needed a police escort.

As we pulled up to the parking lot, we recognized the apartment complex. We all responded to this complex quite a bit. There must have been ten to twenty people standing outside. Neighbors were curious to see what happened.

As my partner and I were getting out of the ambulance, I could see that the police had a woman in custody. She was standing outside next to the police car. A police officer stood next to her asking questions. She had her hands handcuffed behind her back. I walked up in front of her and saw that she had lacerations on her face, swollen lips, a broken nose, and her right eye was almost swollen shut. Her T-shirt was just about torn off. She had no shoes on and was just in her underwear. One of the officers had put a sheet around her.

From the apartment, which was on the first floor, I could hear a male screaming his lungs out. I could hear him yelling, "I'm gonna kill that f---ing bitch!" in between his agonizing screams.

I asked an officer, "Is that the burn patient inside?"

He said, "Yeah, he's the perpetrator. He's doesn't look good. You better check him out first."

I said, "Okay. Let me call another unit to take care of her." I turned to the female victim, "Ma'am, are you OK?"

She just nodded her head, sniffling through her broken nose. Her nose was so swollen it was hard for her to breathe. I told her, "We're gonna call for another ambulance to come and take you to the hospital, okay?"

She quietly responded, "Okay."

I called for another unit. "805 to Dispatch, 805."

"Go ahead, 805," Dispatch replied.

"Can you send me another unit? We have two patients here."

"10-4, we'll send another unit."

My partner and I started walking toward the apartment. We could still hear the perpetrator screaming "That f---ing bitch!" repeatedly from inside. I heard a female in the crowd yell, "That motherf---er deserves it! She shouldn't put up with that motherf---er. They need to take his ass to jail!" Others joined in. "Yeah, take his ass to jail and hang his ass!" The neighbors were really upset.

My partner and I opened the door and walked into the apartment. There were four police officers standing in the living room in front of the patient. I really couldn't see the patient with the officers in front of him. I could only see his feet. His screaming was deafening. It was ear piercing. I felt like covering my ears. One of the officers was wincing every time he screamed. We walked up to the patient and the police officers moved out of the way. I could see him now.

The patient, a male, was sitting naked on the couch. With his hands handcuffed behind his back, I could see he had deep second degree burns on his chest and abdomen. It was so deep the skin had starting to slough (peel). He had a towel over his genitals. The officers had also tied his feet together so he wouldn't kick them.

His screaming could have burst my eardrums.

One of the officers looked at me and said, "He has no penis or testicles."

I responded, "Pardon me?"

The officer said, "She poured boiling cooking oil over his penis and testicles. As I said, he has none."

184

I said, "Okay..." and turned to the patient. I yelled, "Let me take a look! I'm gonna take the towel off! Okay?"

He yelled, "Goddammit! Just take me to the f---ing hospital! I'm gonna kill the bitch! Take me to the f---ing hospital!"

I took the towel off. Shit. The officer was right. There wasn't much left.

I heard my partner say, "We need to go to BAMC." Brooke Army Medical Center was the trauma hospital that also had a burn unit.

I told him, "Yeah."

Over the guy's screaming, I yelled to him, "We're gonna take you right now. We're gonna go get the stretcher."

He kept screaming his expletives. My partner and I both turned around to get the stretcher. I asked one of the police officers to follow us out.

I asked him, "Boy, what did he do to piss her off?"

"She used cooking oil, brother. She told us that he came home drunk and started beating her. He raped her several times and passed out on the couch. While he was passed out, she boiled some cooking oil and poured it on his penis and testicles. Then she threw the rest on his belly and chest. She ran outside and went to a neighbor's house to call us. We've been here a few times already. We kept trying to tell her to press charges but she always refused."

That sounded familiar. I asked him, "Was that Barbara?"

He said, "Yep."

I remembered her. We had seen her a couple of times when she was beaten up. She was at a different apartment not too far from where we were. I recall that each and every time we treated her, she would tell the officers, who had her boyfriend in handcuffs, "Don't take him to jail! He didn't mean it!"

The police officers would tell her, "Ma'am, you need to press charges. He's gonna kill you someday!"

She'd respond, "No, he won't! We just had a fight!"

They had no choice but to take the handcuffs off and release him. Unfortunately, back in the 80s, if the victim didn't want to press charges, the officers would uncuff the assailant and release him; a practice that I didn't understand. It's different today. The assailant goes straight to jail.

This time, he'd be going to the hospital and then jail.

We placed him on the stretcher and covered him with a burn sheet. We rolled the stretcher out of the apartment and toward the ambulance in the parking lot.

The neighbors started yelling, "Hey you motherf---er! You deserve it! Hope you hang, you asshole!" I thought that if they could get a hand on him, they would kill him, too.

Screaming in pain, the patient yelled back, "Shut up y'all motherf---ers! F--- you!"

We hurriedly loaded him into the ambulance. I could see the other EMS unit that arrived was tending to Barbara, the patient. I could see she was still in the police car as the paramedics were treating her. We could still hear the neighbors cursing and yelling at our patient. I couldn't blame them.

As much as he was hurting, we didn't have any medication to administer for pain. I told him, "Sir, we're gonna have to start an IV on you, give you some oxygen, and do an ECG."

He writhed in pain, "I don't like needles! Can't you give me anything for pain?!" He kept cursing. "Why can't you give me something?! It f---ing hurts!"

I said, "I'm sorry, but we don't have anything for the pain!"

I was able to get a large bore IV on his left arm to administer some fluids. Because of the burns, he would eventually need a lot of fluids in his body. I grabbed some large sterile dressings and placed them on his "almost gone" genitals. I also placed some dressings on his chest and abdomen. He was definitely in excruciating pain.

I told my partner, "Let's go Code 3." Code 3 meant traveling in route to the hospital with lights and sirens.

He said, "Got it."

He climbed into the driver's seat, and we took off to the hospital. I also noticed one police car traveling behind us with lights. I figured he was going to ask the patient more questions.

In route to the hospital, he yelled and screamed. My ears hurt so badly that I was already hearing some ringing in my ears. I stuffed some ear plugs in my ears to muffle his screaming.

We arrived at the emergency room at BAMC where the physicians were waiting outside of the ER. They opened the doors while the patient continued to scream and yell.

One of the physicians yelled at him, "You need to stop yelling and cussing. It's not doing you or us any good!"

The patient yelled back, "F--- you! Just give me something for the pain!"

We transferred him from our stretcher to theirs. The ER staff started barking orders. One of the physicians took the burn sheet off his genitals. He just stared and took a deep sigh. He turned and looked at his ER colleague and whispered, "Nothing we can do. It's almost gone." The other physician looked, as well as the nurses. Their eyes just opened wide. One nurse shook her head and turned away.

We stepped out of the trauma room with our stretcher and went toward the ER exit. We were met by the police officer when we stepped toward the ambulance. He told us, "I believe this is the last time he'll be beating her like this."

My partner and I said, "Yep, sure looks like it."

As my partner and I were cleaning the back of the unit, my partner told me, "Boy, that really sucks."

I responded, "Well, seems like she just got tired of it. But you know, she may have saved someone else's life."

We drove off.

Lesson Learned - Don't Get Burned

Simply stated: Domestic violence, as is child abuse, is 100% preventable! How? By not hurting people you love.

By the time you finish this story, current statistics show that over 24 people will suffer from domestic violence, rape, or physical abuse. That's per minute. So, if it took you 20 minutes to read this chapter, that's 480 victims. That's one terrible statistic!

My message to the males: Did your father ever tell you *to never hit a woman* no matter what? If a woman hit you, what were you supposed to do? Hit back? No, you turn and walk (or run!) away unless you have to defend yourself from being injured or killed. Did you learn how to treat a woman with respect, love, warmth, and gentleness? That's where the word comes from, guys! G-E-N-T-L-E-M-A-N! Yes, a "Gentle MAN" is what you should be!

Whether it is physical, emotional, or verbal abuse, it must stop! If your children see this on a daily basis, I can assure you they will have an open door to the criminal system which means jail or prison time. Is that what you want for your children?

Whether you are a victim, male or female, my message is the same: get out now.

You do not deserve to be treated with disrespect. You deserve a better life. Your children deserve a better life. There are many resources out there to assist you and your family. If you continue to make excuses for your abuser, you and your children will suffer, get injured, or take the risk of being killed.

Please do not take matters into your own hands. Retaliation will only worsen the situation and can cause even more danger to yourself, your children, or your future.

If you or anyone you know is involved in an abusive relationship, here's the number to call.
The National Domestic Violence Hotline
(available 24/7/365): 1-800-799-7233
1-800-787-3224 (TTY for deaf/hard of hearing)

Please, let's do what we can to help save a life. Call the Hotline or call anyone you trust. Even if you have to call 9-1-1, let them know what's going on and leave.

Just get out.

Chapter 22
The Crying Baby

In the early 80s, I was assigned to the dispatch office for almost two years while I recuperated from a back injury that I sustained in EMS. We lifted a patient that weighed almost 600 pounds! It took ten firefighters and paramedics to lift him. In the process, three of us hurt our backs. One of the paramedics ruptured three discs in his back. The other paramedic ruptured two discs in his neck. I, fortunately, only suffered a severe strain to my lower back muscles that would require no surgery but rehabilitation for two years. So, being assigned to the dispatch office was considered my light duty.

Working at the dispatch office was not a piece of cake. We literally worked twenty-four hours straight except for a four-hour break. During this break, we had a choice of going home, sleeping or just hanging out. Believe me, as much as I treasured my sleep, I only took my sleep breaks when no one was in the bunk room. We had some snorers that could wake up the dead!

I remember one early morning. It was around 3 a.m. when the phone rang. Another dispatcher and I were the only ones awake at the time.

I told him, "Go to bed, I'll get this."

He said, "Okay, thanks," and stepped into the other room and closed the door.

I answered the phone. "EMS, can I help you?"

Suddenly I heard a screaming lady on the line.

"Sir! My baby is crying! My baby is crying! Please help me! I can't make it stop! Please help me! I don't know what to do! Please!"

Competing with her screaming at me, I could hear the deafening sound of a baby screaming and crying. "WAAAAAAH! WAAAAAH! WAAAAAAH!"

I had to move the phone away from my ear! I spoke loudly to the mother. "Ma'am, please settle down! I can't hear you! Is the baby sick or hurt?"

She screamed, "No! No! No! I just can't make the baby stop crying! I don't know what to do! Please help me!" Then she yelled, "I just want to throw her against the wall! Help me please!"

When she said that, I knew I had to calm her down. I lowered my voice, "Ma'am, Ma'am." No response. I said a little louder, "Ma'am? Are you there?"

With the baby still crying in her arms, I could hear she got a little quieter.

I asked again, "Ma'am?"

She said through tears, "Yes?" I could hear her sniffling.

"Ma'am, what's your name?"

She replied crying, "Sheila."

I told her, "Sheila, my name is Conrad. I'm gonna help you. Is the baby hurt?"

Crying softly, she answered, "No, I just (sniffles)... can't make her stop crying!"

I asked, "Sheila, are you close to the baby's crib?"

She said, "Yes." She was still sobbing and sniffling but much calmer.

I calmly told her, "Sheila, I want you to put the baby in the crib. Just lay the baby down softly. Okay?"

Sniffling, she said, "Okay." The baby was still screaming.

After a few seconds, I asked, "Sheila, did you put the baby down?"

She replied, "Yes. The baby's in the crib. What do I do now?"

"Sheila, again, my name is Conrad. Please, just step out of the room for a second. You've got to control yourself. Go to the door, step out of the room and keep the door open just a little bit so you can see her. Is anyone in the house with you?" I asked.

She quietly replied, "No. I called my mother but there was no answer. I called my husband but he didn't answer either. He's out of town, that a--hole!"

I told her, "OK, Sheila. Just calm down. You'll be okay. Did you feed the baby last night or do you think the baby's hungry?"

She said, "I woke up to feed her. I thought she was hungry."

"Is his diaper dirty?" I asked.

"It's a baby girl." she replied.

"Oh, yes, I'm sorry, Sheila. Have you changed her diaper?"

She said, "Yes."

I said, "Ok, Sheila. How old is she?"

"She's six months today."

"Well, congratulations on your new baby! Is this your first?"

"Yes." Her voice sounded much calmer.

"That's great, Sheila." I asked her, "Can you see the baby from the door?"

"Yes," she replied. "She's not crying as much."

"Yes, I can hear that. Did you check to see if she had any bites or anything on her body?"

Sheila answered, "I checked but I didn't see anything. I thought that maybe something bit her, too."

"Have you ever seen any bugs like scorpions or spiders in the house?"

She replied, "No, I've never seen any."

"Okay, Sheila." I added, "I want to thank you for calling 9-1-1."

She started crying softly. "Well, I didn't know who else I could call so I called 9-1-1 because I was getting ready to lose it. I'm sorry but I didn't know what to do."

"Sheila," I said, "You did the right thing. You called EMS and I'm glad I was here to answer the phone. How's the baby? I don't hear her crying anymore. Can you go in and check on her, please?"

She said, "I'm walking in now."

There was a short silence.

"Sheila?" I asked.

"She's asleep now. Thank God." she said.

I told her, "Sheila, you never know. She may have had a bad dream or something. Has she been sick lately?"

She answered, "No, she's been fine."

"Sheila, I have a son. I am a young dad and I know things like this happen. You just have to be patient and try to figure out what the problem may be. You fed her, you changed her diaper and you checked to see if anything bit her. You did the right thing. Calling 9-1-1 was the right thing to do, especially if no one was there to help you. You almost lost it, didn't you?"

She said, "Yes."

I told her, "It's normal to get frustrated when a baby cries and cries and cries. Now, it's abnormal to hurt the baby. Some people do lose their temper and hurt the baby by shaking the baby or doing something worse. When you felt that you were gonna lose it, you called EMS and that's OK. You needed someone to talk to. How does your baby look now?"

She said quietly, "She's sleeping so peacefully now. She's beautiful. I can't believe I said what I said."

"I'll bet she's beautiful, Sheila. Remember this. Listen, Sheila. This won't be the first or the last time that she cries like that. However, remember that crying is a form of communication for babies. Babies will cry if they want something. Now, let me ask you. If she was hungry, do you think she's gonna stop, jump out of her crib, walk up to you and tell you "Uh, Mom, can you please fix me a bottle of milk? Make that about six ounces and please don't use the microwave! It's not good for me. I'll be waiting in my crib. Thanks, Mom!" Wouldn't that freak you out, Sheila?"

I could hear Sheila chuckle a little. "Yeah, and no, she's not gonna do that."

I continued to ask, "Do you think she's gonna tell your husband while standing on her crib holding herself up on the rail, "Say, Dad! Dad! Where are you? Can you come over here and change my diaper? I seem to have poo-poo in my diaper and I'd really hate to get diaper rash. While you're at it, can you bring the baby powder, too? Oh, might as well bring the Desitin while you're at it!""

Sheila laughed a little.

"Sheila, believe me, we all have rough times like that. Remember, your daughter is just trying to tell you something. And, sometimes we just don't know what they want. We just have to be there for them. Next time this happens, just check all those things that we mentioned; change her diaper, feed her, pick her up and sing to her, try to soothe her with some music or just distract her somehow. It works, Sheila, but it may take a little time and a lot of patience!"

"I'm sorry I lost it," she said.

I told her, "Sheila, if you had lost it, I'd be sending an ambulance, a fire truck, and a police officer to your house. You did the best thing for your daughter by calling us. You don't have to apologize. Now, I have one thing to ask you." She replied, "What's that?"

"You just saved your daughter's life. Every day and on her birthday, just appreciate the fact that she's alive. Can you do that? Things could have turned out worse today. And, if this ever happens again, and you have no one to call, call us. We're here twenty-four hours a day. Okay?"

"OK, thank you, sir. I am glad you were there to answer the phone."

I told her, "Sheila, I'm glad you called. She still asleep?"

She said, "Oh yeah. Sound asleep. I'm gonna go to bed now."

"Get some rest, Sheila. And congratulations for being a great mom. Take care of yourself and your baby, alright?"

She said, "I will."

We both hung up. I took a deep sigh and leaned back on my chair staring at the phone. Strange, no other calls came in during our conversation. We must have talked for almost twenty minutes. I knew that if a call came in, I would have put her on hold hoping she'd still be on the phone when I returned.

I wondered, "What if I wouldn't have been the one to answer the call? Would the other dispatcher handle the call as I did? What if the dispatcher was busy with another call? What if the dispatcher didn't have any kids?"

Thank God I answered the call. The Lord put me there for a reason. Sheila and I both saved her child's life.

I reached over to get my cup of coffee. Another call came in.

The Crying Baby

I picked up the phone. "EMS, can I help you?"

Lesson Learned - Don't Get Burned

This is a quick and very important message to parents, caregivers, babysitters, daycare providers, boyfriends, aunts, grandparents and anyone that takes care of infants and children: Please, please, be PATIENT when caring for infants and children!

When I heard Sheila say that she felt like throwing the baby against the wall, it reminded me of a call that I responded to where a baby was thrown against the wall by the mother's boyfriend. It brought back vivid memories of that call. The baby died of fractures from the right side of her head all the way down to her right lower leg. This was a call that was 100% preventable.

How many of you have ever felt that way? How many of you felt helpless when the baby was crying and crying? Did you feel like you were about to lose it? Did the baby cry so hard that you wondered about taking the baby to the emergency room?

It happens to all of us. And we figure out what to do through practice and time. Give yourself some grace and know that your baby needs you, especially in those challenging moments, to be there for him.

Here are some tips if you are caring for a baby that continues to cry:
- Sing softly to the baby
- Play some soft music
- Try the "shushing" technique. While carrying the baby, place your mouth close to the baby's ear and go "Shhhhh, Shhhhh, Shhhhh, Shhhhh."

Keep doing this repeatedly, but don't pass out from hyperventilating!

- Try carrying the baby in a different position and make sure you always support his or her head.
- Call someone!
- Now, if you've just about come to the end of your rope, PUT THE BABY DOWN IN THE CRIB AND STEP OUT OF THE ROOM! Remember, the baby will not die from crying! Take a short break and breathe.

It takes a lot of patience. Children are innocent. They are fragile. They are human just as we are. They have a different way of communicating with us and the world. If you teach them patience, they will learn patience. They will learn from you. Are you a good example or a poor example?

Now my final message to you: go hug and kiss your babies, now. I don't care how old they are.

See Appendix B for personal stories about new babies.

Chapter 23
The Guitar

Well, here we go again! Another New Year's Eve to remember. This was a close call... I mean really close!

It was around 9 p.m. when we received a call to respond to the deep southwest side of town. I was working overtime that evening just east of the downtown area. The call came in over the radio.

"805, 805. Respond to IH-35 South and Loop 410 for a major accident. PD's on the way."

I got on the radio. "10-4. 805 is 10-96."

I was working with another paramedic, Ruben Sanchez. I recall that we grew up together in elementary school. He was a couple of years younger; I was probably in the 7th grade and he in the 5th grade. Small world! We reminisced about the teachers and priests that were there.

We jumped in the ambulance and headed out. The scene was quite a distance away from us, so we had at least a twenty-five-minute response time. I drove. When we pulled out of the fire station, I told Ruben, "We got a long way to go."

He said, "Yeah, it's gonna start picking up, too. Of course, everybody's probably all primed up for the stroke of midnight."

We got on the highway and headed south on IH-37. We could see the downtown area to our right. The Tower of the Americas was lit up like a Christmas tree in red, green, and blue. Off in the distance and all around us, we saw fireworks exploding in the air. The sky was smoky from the fireworks bombarding the San Antonio sky. New Year's Eve was gonna get busy.

We passed the downtown area and took the exit ramp to go west onto Highway 90. As we turned onto the exit ramp from IH-37 to Highway 90, I started to slow down to take the curve. I looked ahead and saw a huge "object" in the middle of the ramp.

I told Ruben, "Shit! It's a truck upside down!"

He said, "Yeah, there's people standing around, too!"

I slowed down and stopped approximately fifty feet from the upside-down truck. It was literally in the middle of the ramp. There was room on both sides for other vehicles to get by. People were standing around the truck.

I got on the radio and told the dispatcher, "805 to Dispatch. 805 to Dispatch! We came across another accident here at the entrance ramp to 90 West. You need to get someone else to respond to 35 and 410. We have some people standing, and we have traffic coming from behind us! Get PD out here right away! We don't want these people to get hit!"

Dispatch responded, "10-4! Any injuries out there?"

I answered, "Everybody's walking around. We'll let you know!"

We both got out and walked over to the people standing by the truck.

"Is everybody OK?" I asked.

"Yes, we're OK! We had our seat belts on and we just crawled out!"

"Okay! Get off the road! We're blocking the truck with the ambulance. We're gonna stay here until the police arrive. You all need to move off to the side or you'll get hit by a car!"

They complied. They moved over toward the guardrail.

I yelled to Ruben, "Ruben, let's get some flares out and put them behind the unit! Be careful with the cars coming on the exit ramp!"

He replied, "Okay!"

I told dispatch, "Everybody's alright. We're gonna stay here before they get hit by a car. It's too dangerous out here for them!"

Dispatch replied, "10-4. Be careful out there!"

I answered, "10-4. Thanks!"

I walked over to the compartment where we kept the flares. I gave Ruben around six flares. With the emergency lights on, I figured the oncoming cars could hopefully see the ambulance and slow down.

I yelled to Ruben, "Ruben, I'll start putting flares here! You can work your way up and place some up there. Just be careful and watch for the cars!"

Ruben went behind the ambulance and started placing the flares. I was closer to the ambulance and was placing the flares at least 20 feet apart. I could see some cars coming so I looked up to ensure that they saw Ruben and myself. Fortunately, the few cars that we saw slowed down and drove by us safely.

We had placed around eight flares and I saw that Ruben was up the ramp placing his last flare. I looked up and saw a car coming around the curve toward Ruben. I could see the car wasn't slowing down. I kept watching. The car was not slowing down!

I yelled, "Ruben, watch out! He's not stopping! Watch out!" I yelled again, "Ruben, jump over the guardrail, now! He's not stopping!"

I saw Ruben scurry toward the guardrail and jump over. The car was coming right at him! I jumped over the guardrail as the car was barreling toward me!

I yelled over to the occupants of the truck. "Get over the guardrail! Now! Now!" They jumped over the guardrail.

I looked at the car and thought, "Shit! He's gonna hit the ambulance!" Then, without even braking, the car slammed into the back of the ambulance! BAM!

The impact knocked the ambulance at least forty feet and stopped only ten feet from the upside-down truck! The car had to have been traveling fifty miles per hour! And they didn't even hit their brakes!

After the impact, I looked over to the occupants of the upside-down truck and yelled, "Stay put! Don't move!" The police hadn't arrived yet.

I yelled at Ruben, "You OK?!"

He said, "Yeah! How 'bout you?"

"I'm fine!"

I walked over to the car that hit us. It was an SUV. I took my pen light and directed it into the front seat of the SUV. I could see there were two male occupants in the SUV. The driver was slumped over on the steering wheel and unconscious. The passenger was slumped onto the side of the door. Both had hit the windshield and were not restrained. I could smell beer. I shone my pen light to the floor. Beer cans on the floor. They'd been drinking.

I called dispatch, "805 to Dispatch! 805 to Dispatch! Send me two units! We just got hit, and we have two patients that were unrestrained! They're unconscious!"

Dispatch responded, "10-4, 805! Do you need fire out there?"

I responded, "10-4! Tell PD to hurry! We don't want to get hit again!"

"10-4, we'll call them again and let them know the situation!"

"Thanks!" I replied.

I yelled to Ruben, "Let's get some C-collars on them! They're out, but they're breathing!"

The driver's door was jammed so I reached in the window, pulled the driver back, and placed a cervical collar on him. As soon as I pulled him back off the steering wheel and placed the collar, I could hear him whimpering. Fortunately, he was coming around a little. He smelled like beer. I looked across to the passenger. I could see a guitar that was between his legs. The neck of the guitar had impaled his seat!

Ruben saw the guitar. I told him, "Damn lucky guy! Almost had the guitar in his chest!"

He said, "Yep! That would not have been good!"

Upon impact, it appeared the passenger was probably passed out and leaning to his right and on the door. He was holding his guitar with the base on the floor and the neck of the guitar between his legs. As he flew forward, the guitar flew back causing the neck of the guitar to narrowly miss his chest and impale the front passenger seat. Ruben reached in through the window, pulled him back and placed a cervical collar on him. He, too, was breathing but unconscious!

Ruben said while placing his cervical collar on, "Boy, he smells like a brewery!"

I agreed, "Yeah, they both do."

I was pissed. I was so mad that they hit our ambulance! But I had to put that aside because we had work to do. The only thing we could do for them was put cervical collars on them. There was no way to get the stretcher out of the ambulance because the impact was so great that the back doors could not be opened. The rear doors were caved in close to a foot. The running board was destroyed and under the ambulance and the impact also knocked out the power. We had no lights except for one on the right side of the unit; the side that we needed. It seemed that the Lord decided to keep this light on so we could see! And, fortunately, we could still get to the flares that were in a compartment toward the front of the ambulance.

While we were tending to the patients, one of the male occupants from the original upside-down truck came over to us.

"Hey guys, are you all OK?"

I said, "Yeah, we're fine! We're lucky we weren't inside the ambulance or loading a patient!"

The guy from the overturned truck was the driver. He apologized. "I'm sorry to have caused this accident. I guess I was going too fast around the curve and lost control."

I responded, "Don't worry about it. At least you all weren't hurt. Thank you for asking, though. We have two other ambulances coming to get these two guys. They're hurt pretty bad. If you don't mind just waiting with the rest of your friends, I'd appreciate it. I don't want you to get hit again."

The police officers arrived and the other two ambulances pulled up.

One of the paramedics stepped out of his ambulance, looked at our ambulance and asked, "Dude, what the hell happened here?"

"Well, take a look at the back of our unit! What do you think happened?"

He responded, "You got rear-ended pretty bad!"

I said, "Yep, we did. Here are the two patients. One of them almost got impaled by his guitar!"

The paramedic responded, "No shit?"

"Yeah, it's impaled into the front passenger seat. It could've gone right through his chest."

I walked him over to the car. The two patients were still breathing. One of them started moaning and barely talking. The paramedic saw the guitar impaled into the seat.

He said, "Wow... nice guitar. Looks like an Ovation."

I told him, "Sure does." We were both guitar players. I continued, "We couldn't put them on backboards 'cause we couldn't get them out of the back of the ambulance."

The paramedic said, "Okay, we got it! Looks like they're both going to University." University Hospital was the Level I trauma center in town.

I said, "Yeah, the windshield is shattered on both sides, so I would take them Code 3."

He replied, "Yeah... Good luck the rest of the night!"

"Thanks, partner! I hope it gets better than this!"

One of the EMS supervisors pulled up to take us to the maintenance shop to pick up another spare ambulance. The back of our unit was pretty much totaled.

I said "Yeah, a passenger almost got impaled by a guitar. Wanna look at it?"

He asked, "What?! Yeah."

I walked him over to the car. The paramedics had already removed the patients to transport them. The guitar was still impaled into the seat. The police officer was taking pictures of the guitar.

The EMS supervisor looked at the seat. His eyes opened really wide.

"DAMN! Never seen this before!"

I replied, "I've seen the guitar, but never impaled into a seat! Hey, we better get out of the street so PD can do their job and direct traffic."

Fortunately, PD had arrived and started placing flares out, too. I told them, "Be careful guys! We were putting flares out when we got hit!"

One of the officers responded, "Thanks! Your ambulance looks like shit!"

"Yeah, it could have been us that looked like shit, too!"

He said, "You're right!" and continued to place flares on the road.

I looked over to the area where the occupants of the overturned truck were standing. I could see they were gone. They had been picked up by a family member according to a police officer on scene.

Ruben and I climbed into the EMS Supervisor's vehicle and drove away from the scene. It was now around 10 p.m. Two more hours until the stroke of midnight on New Year's Eve. I thought, "What's next?"

The two male patients survived the ride to University, but the driver suffered a severe head injury and a partial tear to his aorta. He was slowly bleeding out. He also apparently had a seizure on the way to the hospital. Not good. The passenger, I was told later, also survived but suffered head and abdominal injuries.

We arrived at the maintenance shop to pick up another ambulance. By the time we left the shops, it was close to midnight. I could smell the smoke from the fireworks.

We were on the south side of town when the clock struck twelve.

I looked at my partner, "Happy New Year, partner."

He replied, "Happy New Year. This is one I'll remember."

We finished the overtime shift at 3 a.m.

On my way home, I was hoping I wouldn't encounter another drunk driver. When I pulled up to the driveway, I said, "Thank you, Lord, for saving my life tonight." I knew the Lord heard me and I knew His reply was, "I got your back, son. I still need you here on this earth to save more lives."

I know the Lord's got my back, and I know He's got the back of many of my fellow firefighters, paramedics, law enforcement officers, first responders, and volunteers that risk their lives every day when they go to work. Even when they're off duty, many continue to serve. Many have been injured or killed when stopping to assist at car wrecks or other incidents. It's in our blood to continue to help people in time of need even when we're not on duty.

To my colleagues: Keep up the great work, ladies and gentlemen. Be safe out there, take care of each other and watch each other's backs.

Lesson Learned - Don't Get Burned

In this particular case, I learned that we have to make life-saving decisions even if it means saving our own lives. I always knew that, as first responders, we have to expect the worst. I had to learn to develop a "sixth sense," if you will. There were many times we responded to calls where patients didn't seem very injured or ill, however, my gut feeling always told me, "Hmmm... this patient needs to be evaluated at the hospital." Usually, my gut feeling and "sixth sense" proved correct.

When Ruben and I were placing flares out that evening, we had a few things against us: 1) it was New Year's Eve; 2) it was dark; 3) the time was ripe for drunk drivers and party revelers to be out on the roads; 4) the curved exit ramp created an obstructed view for the drivers coming our way; 5) we were the first on the scene and didn't have protection from PD.

The only thing we had going for us? My gut feeling and "sixth sense" that someone would hit us.

Today, I still thank God that we didn't get hit. We could have been killed if we were loading a patient into the back of the ambulance. Fortunately, there was a grassy embankment over the guardrail. I think back and ask myself, "What if there was no grassy embankment? What if we would have jumped over the guardrail only to fall 50 feet to the highway below?"

It was either jump over the guardrail or take the chance of the car hitting both Ruben and me, and whoever might have been in the ambulance.

To my readers and colleagues: if you feel that something isn't quite right, make the decision to err on the safe side whether it involves your children, your family, or your colleagues at work. That night, my "sixth sense" kicked in and saved us, with the help of God.

Chapter 24
I Lost It... But I Was Saved

It was a late Saturday evening in the mid-90s. I was either working overtime or was detailed to a station where someone called in sick or was on vacation. The fire station was located on San Antonio's west side of town. It was pretty busy that evening. I'd say it was around 10 p.m. when the call came in from dispatch.

"833, 833. Respond to Callaghan and West Commerce for a major accident. That's West Commerce and Callaghan for a major accident."

I responded, "10-4, 833's 10-96."

We weren't very far from the accident location since we were returning to the station from another call. I knew it wouldn't take us but two or three minutes. I don't remember who I was working with that evening but the rest of the details, I recall vividly.

When we arrived at the intersection, we found nothing.

I told the dispatcher, "833 to Dispatch, we're 10-97 and we don't have anything here. Do you have a better location?"

"No sir; the caller called from a pay phone somewhere near the area."

I said, "10-4. We'll look around."

Then, I looked west on Commerce Street and saw the tail lights of a vehicle. I told my partner, "That's gotta be it."

My partner, who was driving, said, "I bet it is." We drove toward the lights. We had found the collision. No

211

one was around. We were out there by ourselves with two vehicles that had collided head on.

I told dispatch, "833, we're 10-97! We have a head-on collision! Looks bad! Can you send me a backup? Better yet, send me two backup units! Now!"

The dispatcher asked, "Did you say two backup units, 833?"

"That's correct, sir; we need two backup units and PD ASAP! We have no traffic control. Send fire as well. We smell gas!"

That part of the road was very dark. As we pulled up to the side of the crash, I could see the front driver and passenger. The driver was draped over the steering wheel and had hit the windshield. The passenger, a female, had also gone through the windshield and was draped over the dashboard with half her body on the hood of the car.

I stepped out and told my partner, "I'll check the driver! You check the female passenger!"

He said, "OK!"

As I walked toward the first vehicle with the male and female, I could hear crying that was coming from the back seat. I looked in the back seat to find two small children, probably around eight and ten years old. They were on the floor crying and screaming.

I yelled at them, "We're the paramedics! We're gonna help you!"

They continued to cry. They were yelling, "Mommy! Mommy! Daddy! Daddy!"

I quickly reached into the front seat to check for a carotid pulse on the driver's neck, the dad. My partner checked the pulse on the female, the mother.

I looked at my partner, "I've got no pulse."

He replied as he checked the pulse on the mother, "I have no pulse either."

I quickly told him, "They're gone. Stay with the kids. I'm gonna go check the driver of the other car."

"Sounds good."

As I went past the back seat, I could hear the children screaming and yelling, "Mommy! Daddy! Mommy! Daddy!" I told them as I put my head through the window, "We're gonna take care of you!" They continued to scream, "Mommy! Daddy!"

I walked toward the other vehicle. I was thinking and shaking my head, "Damn, the kids' parents are dead!"

I found the driver of the other vehicle. I couldn't believe what I saw and heard. The driver was laughing and throwing his hands up in the air. His speech was slurred. He asked while laughing, "Hey man! What did I hit? Did I hit a tree or what? What the f--k is going on? Haha!"

He was still laughing. Not a scratch on his body. Maybe a cut on his head but that was it.

In that split second, I lost it. I grabbed him from his shirt and started pulling him out of the car through the window.

"You f---ing idiot! You just killed a mom and dad! What the f--k were you doing, you stupid little shit! I'm gonna kick your ass!"

I had him halfway out the window. My adrenalin was in overload; he weighed almost 200 pounds. As I pulled him out, he continued laughing. I was going to beat him to a pulp. I was furious!

He started yelling, "Let me go! Let me go!"

He was pretty much draped over the door window when suddenly I felt someone grab me. I thought it was my partner. The driver I had in my hands fell. He didn't fall onto the street. He was still hanging over the window of the door. I didn't know who was holding onto me as I was trying to get away.

I yelled, "Let me go! Let me go! I'm gonna kick his ass!"

Then I heard, "Conrad, stop it, dude. It ain't worth it, man. Stop it!" As he kept holding onto me, I struggled to get free. "It ain't worth it, brother! You're gonna lose your job, man!"

I finally settled down. I was still being held back by the person I thought was my partner.

I heard his voice, "OK, man. Settle down. It's cool, brother. Settle down."

He let go of me. I turned around. I saw who was holding me. It was Hector, a police officer. My friend.

He looked at me, "Conrad, take it easy, brother. It ain't worth it. I'd have to take you in for assault, dude. I don't want to have to do that, hermano. Chill out, OK?"

I took a deep sigh as I looked at Hector. I was sweating. My heart was racing. I turned around and looked at the driver, who was still laughing. Hector grabbed my shoulder anticipating that I would grab him again and beat him.

"I'll take care of him," Hector said. "Go take care of the kids. I'll cuff him. If he's not hurt, he's going to jail. I got this. C'mon, brother. Let it go."

I took another deep sigh.

I told Hector, "Thanks, brother. I'm good." I walked toward the children in the back seat. I stopped huffing and puffing.

The children were still crying. My partner had already retrieved some cervical collars and had them ready to apply to the children. I could see that they were both unrestrained, flew forward, and struck the back of the front seats. Fortunately, they were not ejected.

The other two EMS units arrived as did additional police officers. I had to refocus and get my head straight for the sake of these kids.

I told one of the newly-arrived paramedics, "Hey, brother, get two yellow blankets and cover the parents. I don't want the kids to see this."

He said, "Okay. We'll take the kids to University Hospital. We'll take them separately, though. They're in bad shape."

"Yeah," I replied. "Best not to take them together."

My partner and I focused on the ten-year-old girl and the other unit was going to transport the eight-year-old boy. They both had fractured legs with possible fractured arms. Fortunately, they were both crying which indicated they had good airways and they were breathing okay.

As we were placing the boy on a backboard, I turned and looked over to where Hector had the driver in handcuffs. Hector looked at me.

I said, "Thanks, brother."

He replied, "You're welcome, man. We'll see you again."

"You got it," I answered. "Be careful out there."

"I will," Hector replied.

The children survived the crash. The daughter suffered a fractured skull and had some abdominal contusions (bruising in the abdomen). The son had two fractured legs and a fractured arm. They were going to be in the hospital for a while. The parents, I heard, were buried a week later.

Hector and I were good friends. He worked on the west side of town. I worked at #41 fire station which was also on the west side of town. We met at a call one time and I remember, somehow or another, we started talking about high schools.

I recall asking Hector, "Hector, what high school did you go to?"

He answered, "Central Catholic."

I told him, "Oh no! The Buttons?"

He asked me, "Well, where did you go?"

I told him, "Holy Cross High School, brother! On the west side!"

I'll never forget he said, "Holy Cross sucks, man!"

"No, brother, Central does!" I'd reply.

Holy Cross High School, where I attended, was rivals with Central Catholic. Central Catholic High School was located in the downtown area. They were both all-male Catholic schools back then. When Hector and I were both on duty, sometimes I'd see him at a call or accident. We'd look at each other and whisper to each other.

"Hey, Conrad! Holy Cross sucks!"

I'd respond, "Central sucks tambien!"

That went on for a few years.

It was funny. My EMS partners would always ask me, "What was that all about?" I'd tell them that we went to rival high schools, and we always would agitate each other about it.

I asked Hector one time. "Hey, dude! Who would call a high school mascot the Buttons? That's like los Botónes?!"

He'd answer, "The Knights?! C'mon. Y'all could have done better than that!"

I always enjoyed seeing Hector. He was a great guy. He saved my career. I wish I could have saved him.

Lesson Learned - Don't Get Burned

This incident taught me a great lesson. No, Hector taught me a great lesson. His lesson to me was, "Do your job no matter what you come across."

When Hector pulled me off the driver, he literally saved my butt from being suspended or being terminated for assaulting this guy. We, as professionals, take an oath to act as professionals and maintain that mentality no matter the situation. Maintaining our professionalism is the key to maintaining our integrity as a public servant. Because we are hired to serve others and help others.

I'm glad Hector was there.

I retired in 1998, and I never saw Hector after that. Until one day I saw him on TV. I was packing to go out of town to conduct some training and was watching the 10 p.m. news. The newscaster announced, "A sad day here in San Antonio. Police officer Hector Garza was killed this morning while responding to a domestic call on the west side of town. He was shot while trying to break up a fight between a husband and wife."

Hector's picture was on the TV screen. I stood there in front of my suitcase staring at his picture and began to cry. I sobbed while listening to the story. The male gunman had also killed his wife and wounded his brother-in-law.

I still think back to the day that Hector pulled me back from beating that guy to a pulp. I still think about Hector when I go down West Commerce Street and Callaghan.

Sometimes when I'm in the downtown area and drive by Central Catholic High School, I think about Hector. I think about him when other police officers are injured or killed answering disturbance or domestic violence calls.

I will never forget Hector and I agitating each other for being at rival high schools. But I know one day, when I meet Hector up in Heaven, we'll make sure God doesn't hear us when Hector and I, with wings on our backs, whisper to each other, "Hey, Hector, Pssssst! Central sucks!" He'll respond, "Shhhh! Conrad, yeah, Holy Cross sucks, too!"

God Bless you and your family, Hector, and your family of law enforcement.

Rest in peace, brother.

Chapter 25
The Rock

One early afternoon, my partner and I were just pulling into the station after transporting to the hospital. It had been pretty busy most of the morning, and we didn't get a chance to eat breakfast. So, we had to settle for lunch, a late lunch for that matter. We had pulled over and stopped at our favorite barbeque place, ordered, and jumped back in the ambulance. We had our food on the front seat.

The aroma of BBQ and three sides filled the cab of the ambulance. My mouth was watering when we arrived at the station and pulled into the bay area to park.

I told my partner as I turned off the engine, "Era tiempo!" (It's about time!)

He said, "I know. I'm starving!"

I picked up my plate from the front seat and stepped out of the unit. I was getting ready to place my plate on the running board to plug in the unit. My partner was almost inside the door of the station ready to put his plate down on the table. He was fast!

Then the tones on our radio went off.

I said, "Damn! Can't even eat!"

I heard the dispatcher: "841, 841, respond to Braun Road and 1604, that's Braun Road and 1604 for a major accident. You have a nurse on the scene who said you have a patient with head trauma."

I responded, "10-4. We're 10-96. Put AirLife on standby."

AirLife is the air medical rescue that was located at University Hospital and Baptist Medical Center. I requested they be put on standby because of the distance from the location to the trauma center. I wanted to be on the safe side and have them ready to launch. I had this gut feeling we'd be needing them.

Fortunately, since I was working part time as a flight paramedic, I knew that it would take the pilot, flight nurse, and flight paramedic about 5 minutes to step out of the office, run to the helicopter, start it up and launch.

I unplugged the ambulance, opened the door and placed my BBQ plate on the front seat. I quickly looked to see if maybe there was a roll I could eat on the way to the call! No luck, though - no roll! My partner jumped in. I didn't even ask him if he'd gotten a bite of his plate.

We drove onto the ramp and quickly took a right and then left to get to Braun Road. I heard the dispatcher.

"841, 841," the dispatcher said.

"Go ahead, Dispatch, this is 841," I replied.

The dispatcher answered, "841, we just received another call that the patient has severe head trauma and is incoherent."

I responded, "10-4. Go ahead and launch AirLife. We'll need the motor out there to set up a landing zone, too!"

Dispatch replied, "10-4."

I knew that we'd get to the crash in less than seven minutes. I also knew that it wouldn't take but 10 minutes for AirLife to arrive. Back then, there wasn't much traffic out that way. Loop 1604, back in the 80's, was only one lane going west and one lane coming east. It was out in the country.

We arrived at the intersection. Nothing there. I looked to my left and saw a lady waving at us about 100 yards from the intersection. I took a left and drove to the scene. As we pulled up, I could see that a car had driven off the road and hit a barbed wire fence. The car was at least 100 feet from the road. There was a male and female at the scene tending to the patient.

Noticing that the county sheriffs hadn't arrived, I knew we'd need to stop traffic for AirLife to land on the road. I parked the ambulance perpendicular to the flow of traffic to stop any traffic coming from the south, but there was no one blocking traffic coming from the north. I stopped a vehicle that was coming from that direction.

I yelled at the driver, "Can you block traffic for me, sir? We have a helicopter that will be landing in a few minutes! We really need your help. We have a major emergency!"

The driver said, "OK!"

"Turn your car sideways so no one gets through! Thank you! The helicopter will be landing shortly so stay in your car and don't open the window. The wind from the helicopter will blow very hard!"

My partner had gotten out with the trauma kit and was already working his way to the car. Walking to the car was a little treacherous. The grass was knee high and we really couldn't see if there were any holes or a ditch in front of us.

I don't know how I did it, but I beat my partner to the car. I went toward the driver's seat where I met the man and woman who stopped to assist. They had the patient's head wrapped and were trying to calm her down.

The man yelled at me, "She has a head injury, and she's asking for her baby! I don't see a baby at all!"

I told him, "Thank you for stopping! Do you know what happened?"

He yelled, "Yes! I was behind her and a rock flew out of a truck in front of her and crashed through her windshield!"

The driver, a female, kept fighting and flailing her arms. "Where's my baby? Where's my baby?" she yelled.

I noticed blood on the front and side of her head. I was shocked. She had small pieces of brain matter on the front part of her head!

I thought, "Oh shit!" Then I looked down at the floorboard. There it was! There was a rock about the size of a cantaloupe that had crashed through her windshield.

I saw the windshield was shattered but I thought it was her head that shattered the windshield. No! It was the rock that came through the windshield and struck her head. I looked up at the roof above her and saw that the rock had ricocheted off her head and hit the roof causing and indention on the roof. The dent was protruding from the top of the car. That's how hard the rock hit her head.

I radioed for AirLife.

"841 to AirLife! 841 to AirLife!"

I knew AirLife was monitoring the radio. It was customary that AirLife would get on a channel to speak with the ground paramedics or a fire crew. I yelled into the radio, "Get the Succs ready! She has a severe head injury, and she'll need to be intubated! She's very combative now!" ("Succs" is short for succinylcholine, a medication used to facilitate intubating a patient.)

AirLife responded, "10-4! Do we have a landing zone?"

I responded, "I have blocked traffic from the south and a private vehicle has blocked traffic from the north! Fire is not here yet!"

They responded, "10-4! We'll look out for the cars!"

I yelled to my partner, "Go get the backboard and a C-collar! We gotta get her out so we can load her into the helicopter!"

He said, "OK!"

Then I heard the sound of the helicopter rotors. AirLife had arrived. I looked up as they were circling and aiming for the landing zone. I looked around and the fire crew wasn't here yet. There was no one to help land the helicopter.

I yelled to my partner, "Go get the C-collar on her! I'm gonna land AirLife!"

He said, "OK!"

I could see the helicopter making a pass to find the landing zone. I got on the radio, "841 to AirLife! Can you see the two cars on the road?"

The pilot responded, "Affirmative. Is that you waving between the cars?"

I responded, "Yes, that's me waving. I will assist you!"

I saw the fire truck arrive.

I told the Airlife crew, "I'm gonna let fire set you all down. I'm going back to the patient."

The fire crew got off the truck and started to guide the helicopter to the landing zone.

I yelled to the fire crew. "You guys got it?"

They said, "Yeah! We got it!"

As I was running back to the car, I could see the county deputies had pulled up and started directing traffic that was backing up from both directions. I had no choice but to block traffic so I could land the helicopter on the road.

I ran back to the patient in the car and saw my partner applying the C-collar. He, along with the bystander, who happened to be a nurse at a local trauma center, had trouble applying the C-collar as the patient was still combative. Her combativeness was indicative of a brain injury. She was still asking for her baby. I looked into the back seat and saw there was no baby or car seat.

Two of the firefighters came over to assist getting her out of the car. With the driver's door opened, we immediately placed the backboard under her buttocks and rotated her onto the backboard. When we placed her on the backboard, I yelled to my partner, "Let's start an IV now!"

He said, "Why right now?"

I yelled at him, "Just set up an IV so AirLife can give her some medication to intubate her! Just set me up!"

Instead of putting her in the ambulance and taking her out again, I opted to start the IV while outside the car. I started the IV without any problems, secured it, and got it ready for the flight crew.

One of the paramedics, Jim, ran up to us. "Need the Succs now?"

I yelled back at him, "She is calming down a little now!"

He said, "OK, we'll give it to her in the helicopter!"

"OK!" I responded. "Thanks, Jim!" I reported the details. "She got hit by a rock that fell off a truck. The rock bounced off the ground, went through her windshield and struck her head. She's got brain matter on her frontal area!"

Jim yelled, "OK, Conrad, thanks bud! We'll see you again!"

"OK!" I yelled.

We started walking to the helicopter. We had to take the backboard off the stretcher to make it easier to carry her over the grassy area. As we were approaching the chopper, I looked at the pilot to see if it was safe enough to approach the helicopter. He gave us the thumbs up. That was our safety signal from the pilot that ensured that we were safe to approach the helicopter. We carried the patient on the backboard to load her on the chopper. Jim, the flight paramedic, looked at me and yelled over the noise of the rotors.

"We're going to intubate her inside!"

I yelled back, "Perfect! Thanks again!"

He said, "Thank you for the LZ (landing zone)! Great thinking doing it by yourself!"

I replied, "I had no choice!"

We loaded her onto the helicopter and ran back toward the car and away from the chopper. They didn't take off for about another few minutes. I knew they were intubating her.

We approached the vehicle. The male trauma nurse that assisted asked, "It doesn't look too good, does it?"

I responded, "Well, we don't know. The good thing is that she was conscious and moving. It could have been worse. She could be dead."

He said, "Yeah, you're right."

I said, "Hey, thanks for your help. I really appreciate it. We sure needed the extra help."

"I was glad to be of assistance."

I heard the rotors to the helicopter revving up. They lifted off. I turned and looked and said to myself, "God, I hope she makes it."

She did.

In fact, a few months later, I received a phone call at the fire station. It was a writer from *Reader's Digest* that was calling me about the rock incident. He asked me if I would be willing to be interviewed about the call. I was surprised and quickly agreed, but I had to run it through my supervisor and the city.

Well, it was approved and I met with the writer at The Gunter Hotel in San Antonio a few weeks later. The writer actually told me that he was surprised that I remembered the call so vividly. I told him, "This call will be ingrained in my brain!"

The writer had interviewed just about everyone involved, including the patient and the Good Samaritans! The writer told me that the patient, a female that worked at Wilford Hall Medical Center at Lackland Air Force Base, survived the incident, and he was also able to interview her. I was elated that the outcome was positive.

Ma'am, if you are reading my book, I continue to think about you and your family today. I am glad the Lord placed us there in your time of need. God Bless.

The article was published in the *Reader's Digest* October 1995 issue.

Lesson Learned - Don't Get Burned

Everything with this call went smoothly, and it was God's intervention that assisted us in getting the patient to the hospital in a timely manner. This is what we had going in our favor:

1. It only took us a few minutes to arrive to the scene.
2. The nurse on scene gave us a good report, which allowed for the rapid request and response of Airlife.
3. Working with Airlife part-time, I knew we needed a proper landing zone and could help expedite treatment and transport.

The key here was everyone worked together as a team. From the Good Samaritans to AirLife, to our EMS presence, to the Sheriff's department, and the cohesiveness of all, we were successful at getting the patient immediate help.

How many times have you driven behind a gravel truck only to have your windshield cracked or shattered by a rock or debris? Big or small, it can be annoying, expensive and can also result in severe injury or death.

How many times have you come across debris on the road only to swerve in the last second, or worse, hit whatever debris was on the road?

Anytime you're behind a gravel truck, an eighteen-wheeler, someone pulling a boat, trailer, or trunk loaded with furniture, TAKE HEED! THEY MAY LOSE THEIR LOAD, AND YOU'RE GONNA HIT IT! You have to stay at least FOUR seconds behind them, if not further. This will give you ample time to move to another lane quickly and/or slow down to avoid hitting the object.

Whether you are a private citizen or driving a work truck with a load, SECURE YOUR STUFF! You can be liable if you do not secure what you are carrying, and it falls and hits someone. Be safe out there and leave plenty of room between you and those in front of you.

Chapter 26
The Wedding

Saturdays were typically busy shifts. In the mid-1980s, I was assigned to Station #6 which was located just north of the downtown area on West Russell Street. This area, Monte Vista, is known for its beautiful ornate homes with distinguished residential architecture. Built in the late 1890s and early 1900s, this neighborhood was high-style, with some homes having covered driveways that were used to park their horse-drawn buggies right next to the entrance of the house. Some were up to three stories and even had gargoyles protruding from the rooftops. Monte Vista housed many of the elite and prominent citizens of San Antonio back in the day. It was a rather interesting area to work in, and I thoroughly enjoyed working in a neighborhood that had so much history.

One particular Saturday at Station #6 my partner, Alfred (Fred) Casillas, and I were at the station kicking back and relaxing and mentally preparing ourselves for a long night. I called my parents just to check in on them. It was around noon. Mom answered the phone.

"Hi, Mom! How are you all doing?" I asked.

Mom replied, "Fine, Mijo! How are you?"

"Doing great! Just working today. I'm at the station and just kind of relaxing here. How's Dad?"

She replied, "He went to wash the car. We're going to a wedding this evening so he wanted to make sure the car was nice and clean. You know your Dad!"

"Yep, sure do." I said. Dad always made sure the car was clean. Whether he was going to a wedding or just going to the store, he always made sure the car was the shiniest car on the block, or in San Antonio for that matter. I asked Mom where the wedding was.

"The reception's gonna be at the North Ballroom," she replied.

"Wow!" I said. "That's not too far from the station."

"No... Maybe you all can come by and eat with us. They're having barbeque for dinner."

"Naw, that's okay, Mom. We don't want to crash the wedding. Besides, people would worry if they saw an ambulance there. I appreciate it, though."

Mom said, "OK, Mijo, I'll tell Dad you called. Have a safe shift and God be with you. Tell Fred hello for us!"

"I sure will, Mom!" I replied. "Take care, Mom. Love you both."

"Love you, too, Mijo."

Mom and Dad knew Fred very well. Fred and his wife were to baptize my son, Adrian, a few years later. Fred was my second partner in EMS and a great one, I might add!

After I hung up the phone, I thought, "Mmm, barbeque, rice and beans, tortillas, and wedding cake. And it's all FREE!" I knew Fred would have liked that. After I spoke with Mom, we responded to a couple of calls and returned to the station around 3 p.m. I figured I'd lay down and take a little nap to rest for the Saturday night knife-and-gun-club.

It was 6 p.m. when the call came in. I woke to the dispatcher's voice on the radio.

"806, 806, respond to a cardiac arrest at 3719 White Road at the North Ballroom for a cardiac arrest. That's 3719 White Road at the North Ballroom for a cardiac arrest. Fire is responding."

As soon as I heard the North Ballroom, I shot up from my bed and bolted out the door of our dorm room. I said to myself, "Shit! That's where Mom and Dad are!" My heart started pounding.

Fred was in the kitchen when he heard the call. I just about ran into him.

"Fred, that's where my parents are!" I yelled at him.

"What?!" he replied.

We climbed into the ambulance, and I quickly started the engine. I told Fred, "Yeah, I talked to Mom earlier and they said they were going to a wedding reception at the North Ballroom."

He said, "Okay, just take it easy. I'm sure they're OK."

I responded, "I hope so!"

I pulled out of the front of the station, turned on the lights and siren and quickly turned right onto San Pedro Street. The ballroom was maybe eight minutes away. Fortunately, I caught the first few green lights. Weaving in and out of traffic, I was literally traveling up to sixty miles an hour on a very busy street. I saw Fred out of the corner of my eye with his right hand holding onto the door and his left hand on the dashboard. His knuckles were turning white. He looked pretty frightened as I was barreling down the street!

My heart was pounding out of my chest. My hands were trembling. I was so nervous I wasn't even talking to Fred. I was hoping to hear the dispatcher call us to cancel us.

We were about two blocks away, when I heard the dispatcher call us on the radio.

"806, 806," the dispatcher said.

Nervously, I reached for the radio. Fred got to the radio first. He told me, "Just drive, Conrad." Fred replied, "Go ahead, Dispatch. This is 806."

The dispatcher replied, "806, you have a cardiac arrest. Bystanders are doing CPR."

Fred asked, "Is fire on the scene yet?"

"Negative," the dispatcher replied.

I quietly said, "Damn it."

Fred tried to reassure me. "I'm sure it's not your Mom or Dad."

"I hope you're right."

We arrived at the intersection and I quickly looked at the ballroom to hopefully see if Mom and Dad were standing outside of the ballroom. I couldn't see them because some cars and trucks obstructed my view. I didn't see the fire truck. The fire crew hadn't arrived yet. I pulled up to the front of the entrance. My heart was pounding out of my chest.

I kept praying, "Please, God, don't let it be Mom or Dad." I felt like my eyes were already starting to tear. There was a crowd of around ten people outside. They were waving at us. Then, in the crowd, there they were. Mom and Dad were standing amidst the crowd. My heart dropped. A big sigh of relief followed.

Fred said to me, "There they are. Thank God. Go greet them, Conrad, I'll get the equipment."

"Thank you, Fred."

I quickly got out of the ambulance and hurriedly walked between the crowd and right over toward Mom and Dad. One gentleman in the crowd yelled at me. "He's inside, sir! They're doing CPR!" he exclaimed.

I told him, "Thank you, sir." Then, briefly ignoring him, I walked up to Mom and Dad. They quickly and calmly told me, "We're fine, Mijo. We knew you'd be worried, so we came outside so you could see us."

Mom was crying. I can still see her tears today. I gave them a quick hug. I'm sure the patrons outside were wondering what was going on.

I told them, "I'm glad you all are okay."

Just then, I could hear the fire crew arriving. The other EMS unit, our backup, was pulling up to the parking lot. I walked past Mom and Dad and was escorted by the gentleman who informed us that someone was doing CPR. We walked inside into the ballroom. Fred was right behind me and literally carried the ECG monitor and the heart kit all by himself. He could have carried the stretcher on his back if he needed to!

As soon as we turned the corner, to the left I could see some people had moved tables from the area where our patient was. We found the victim on his back and a man doing CPR and another gentleman providing mouth to mouth ventilations. The music continued to blare as if nothing was going on. Family members stood around. Some were sobbing.

I looked at Fred and told him, "Fred, I'm gonna intubate him. Can you set me up?"

Fred replied, "Got it."

I told the helpers, "Thank you for doing CPR! Please continue while we set up our equipment."

The man doing CPR was doing excellent compressions. As I was getting the device to assist the patient's breathing, I started to check to see if the patient's chest was going up as the person was giving mouth to mouth breathing. I noticed the person doing the breathing did have the patient's head tilted back properly. Then, while the person was breathing into his mouth, I saw that the patient's chest was not rising.

I told the rescuer, "Sir, thank you for doing the breathing. I surely appreciate it. Can you tilt his head back again? His chest isn't going up and down when you breathe."

He said, "OK."

When he looked up at me, I could smell alcohol on his breath. The man doing CPR had been drinking, but at least he was trying to save this man's life. I took over for the gentleman doing the breathing. I tilted the patient's head back again and tried to breathe for him with the airway bag that we use to assist a patient's breathing. I could also smell alcohol on the patient.

As I placed the mask on the patient's face, I squeezed the inflatable airway bag. I could see that his chest wasn't going up and his cheeks were being "inflated." The air wasn't going in. I felt resistance. I tilted his head back again to make sure. Still, his chest wasn't rising.

Fred quickly said, "Here you go, Conrad."

Fred handed me the laryngoscope, a device that I would insert into the mouth to view the back of his throat and assist in getting the plastic airway tube into his lungs. He then placed the ECG electrodes on his chest and turned on the monitor.

Fred asked the bystander, "Can you stop CPR for a second?" The bystander stopped. We looked at the screen on the heart monitor. "He's in asystole," Fred said quietly.

"OK," I replied, "Continue CPR, sir." He continued doing compressions. I knew this wasn't good. In asystole, there is no electrical activity whatsoever. His heart was practically dead.

The fire crew arrived and so did the backup EMS unit.

"Can you all get the stretcher?" I asked the fire crew. I wanted to get the patient out of the ballroom as soon as possible. One of the firefighters stayed to relieve the bystander with CPR.

The backup EMS unit prepped to start an IV. Fred was getting the stethoscope so he could listen to the lungs to make sure I intubated the patient correctly. When intubating a patient, you had to make sure you were in the lungs and not in the stomach, in order to provide oxygen to the patient's brain and vital organs.

While CPR was continuing, I told Fred, "Fred, his chest wasn't going up when I was ventilating him."

"I noticed that," he replied.

I told the firefighter, "Hold CPR while I intubate him." The firefighter stopped.

I put the airway bag down. I picked up the laryngoscope and inserted the device into his mouth. With the light at the end of the device, I would be able to see the back of his throat, his vocal chords, his airway. Then, I saw why his chest wasn't going up when we were trying to assist his breathing. There, in the back of his throat, was a big chunk of meat.

He didn't have a heart attack.

He choked.

It was no wonder that his chest wasn't rising. He wasn't getting any air into his lungs because the piece of meat blocked any air from entering his lungs.

"Fred, his airway's blocked. He's got a piece of meat in there. I need the forceps."

He quickly got the forceps out of the bag and placed it in my hand. I reached into the back of the patient's mouth and quickly grabbed the chunk of meat. It was lodged in the back of his throat. It took me about thirty seconds before I was able to get it out. That's thirty seconds too long. And there was no telling how long he'd been unconscious.

As soon as I pulled it out, I grabbed the laryngoscope again and intubated the patient. Immediately after I inserted the tube, I told Fred, "I'm in the lungs, Fred, can you check breath sounds?" He quickly placed the stethoscope over the chest and listened while I breathed for the patient with the airway bag.

"You're in the lungs."

"Okay!" I yelled to the fire and EMS crew, "Let's go, guys! We're taking him downtown!"

They replied, "OK!"

The firefighters had the stretcher ready. We lifted the patient and placed him on the stretcher while we continued CPR. One of the family members, sobbed and asked, "Is he gonna make it?"

I told her, "Ma'am, we're doing what we can! Are you related?"

"That's my husband!" She cried harder.

"Ma'am! You can go with the other ambulance to the hospital or you can have someone drive you. We're taking him to the downtown hospital. That's the closest hospital. Okay?"

Still sobbing, she softly said, "Okay."

The other ambulance was our backup unit. Usually, it was the backup unit that would take a family member to the hospital, or, they would ride with another family member in a private car. We never placed a member in the back of the unit while doing CPR or if the patient was in critical condition. It would be too traumatizing for them.

One of the firefighters jumped onto the frame at the bottom of the stretcher and was doing CPR as we were rolling the patient out of the ballroom. I saw the bride and groom coming from behind us. The bride, sobbing with huge tears in her eyes, reached in between the firefighters and the paramedics. We slowed down to avoid hitting her with the stretcher. We were doing CPR and I was ventilating (breathing for the patient) with the airway breathing bag. She put her hand on the patient's hand and said, "I love you, Tio!" The patient was her uncle.

I exhaled a deep sigh. I told her as we rolled the stretcher through the doors and out of the ballroom, "Ma'am, we're doing the best we can." She turned around, placed her head on her groom's shoulder, and cried.

Fred jumped in the driver's seat as the firefighters and I were loading the patient into the back of the ambulance. We closed the doors to the ambulance and I stepped around to the side door of the ambulance to get in.

I heard my Mom and Dad, "Be careful, Mijo."

I turned around and saw them together. They gestured to me with the Sign of the Cross to bless me. It was a gesture that they always did before I would leave their house.

I whispered to them, "Thank you. I'm glad you're okay." I stepped in the ambulance. (Believe me, I felt like walking up to them and giving them both a huge hug again. I was thankful to God that they were okay. Just no time.) We continued CPR as we took off to the hospital. I had a firefighter with me to assist me on the way to the hospital. It was a long ride.

Unfortunately, the patient did not survive.

I still remember that day.

Thank you, Lord, for taking care of my parents. I pray for the wife, the bride and groom, and the family members anytime I drive past the ballroom which is still there today. This was at least forty years ago.

This was the wedding I "attended" while on duty, and I won't ever forget it.

God bless the family.

Lesson Learned - Don't Get Burned

Unfortunately, this patient did not survive. Fifty percent of adults that choke to death are under the influence of alcohol or drugs. The patient had been drinking during the reception and everyone thought he was "sleeping it off," with his head on the table, when in fact, he had the piece of meat lodged in his throat and was unconscious.

When one is drinking while eating, the alcohol tends to slow down your reflexes. Please, heed my advice: if you're going to drink alcohol, be extra cautious while you're eating.

Now, as a paramedic, one of my worst fears was responding to a call that involved a family member. I cannot fathom something happening to my family nor can any other firefighter, paramedic, police officer, or first responder. But, then again, those are the risks that we take in this profession.

Anytime you see an ambulance, fire truck, police officer or law enforcement, air medical rescue helicopter, say a prayer for them. They may be responding to a call to assist their own family, or a "family member" they work with. Or, maybe your own.

A quick message for my colleagues: SLOW DOWN! I look back and wonder what would have happened if I had run into someone or been in an accident on the way to the call. Many first responders have been killed responding to a call even with lights and sirens blaring. Please, colleagues, don't take unnecessary risks! Get to the scene safely.

My message to civilian drivers: If you see an ambulance or hear sirens, be aware of where they are! Pull over safely to the right. Look in your rear-view mirror and try to see which way they are going. If you must cross an intersection or turn left or right, do so slowly and carefully. Watch out for oncoming traffic as they may not realize there's an emergency vehicle behind you! Common sense will increase the chances of your survival and theirs.

Be safe out there!

Chapter 27
He Had My Whole Car in His Hand

This incident occurred after I retired. But this was one of the many post-retirement life lessons!

I remember some great friends of ours inviting my girlfriend, Alma, who is now my wife, and I to their parents' wedding anniversary. We were excited to be going to an event that reminded me of when my parents celebrated fifty years of marriage. The anniversary was going to be held in Uvalde, Texas, which is about ninety miles west of San Antonio.

A few weeks before the event, I told Alma, "We should probably stay in Uvalde so we don't have to make that long trek back to San Antonio after the reception." I knew we'd be having a great time because we love to dance and stay out late… and yes, we'd be drinking a little wine.

"We have to get back that night because I'm dog sitting and have to let the dog out when we get back," she replied.

I suggested, "Maybe you can call someone to come by your house and let the dog out in the evening. Then, they can come in the morning to let the dog out again. I just don't like driving ninety miles at night after we've been partying. There's a Holiday Inn a few blocks away."

She said, " I'd really like to get back after. Or maybe we shouldn't go."

"No, let's go but we won't stay too long but you have to talk to me all the way back to San Antonio so I can stay awake!"

"Ok!" she replied. We always have fun traveling together; we talk, laugh, sing, and joke around a lot! So, I thought it wouldn't be any problem and continued with my day.

The day of the anniversary came, and we hit the road to Uvalde. On the way to Uvalde, I was thinking that I should not be drinking and my plan was to be alert after the reception and buy coffee for the ninety-mile drive back to San Antonio.

We arrived in Uvalde about 2:45 p.m., just in time for the Mass at three o'clock. It was a great ceremony and we enjoyed our friends' parents renew their vows.

After the Mass, we knew that the reception wasn't starting till six o'clock. It was 4 p.m. I told Alma, "We have two hours to spare and I'm hungry now. What do you say we find a place to eat?"

She replied, "Yeah, I'm hungry too. There's gotta be a place around here."

"There was that steak house that we saw on the way in. Want to drive by there and check it out?"

"Sure," she said. "Let's do that! We don't have to eat that much so we can eat at the reception."

We drove to the steak house and walked in to get a table. I looked at the menu and saw they had a big picture of a sirloin steak.

"That's what I want!" I told Alma. The waitress walked up to take our order. "Where's everybody at?" I asked the waitress.

"It's still early. We usually get busy in the evening," she said.

I told her, "Cool. I'll have the sirloin steak." Alma ordered a salad. "And, can we have two glasses of wine?"

I figured it was early enough to have a glass of wine and I'd "dilute" it with water. Well, we ended up with two glasses of wine. Why not? The wine would "dissipate" throughout the night. We had two hours before the reception! We spent those two quiet hours at the restaurant enjoying the little break and our food and wine.

Around 6 p.m., we decided it was time to head over to the reception. We arrived in less than five minutes, since we were only blocks away. We worked our way over to the table where our friends' parents were sitting and offered our congratulations. They were a very cute couple and their eyes were still gleaming after renewing their vows and, of course, knowing they'd managed fifty years of marriage. Thoughts of Mom and Dad came back to me.

After wishing them congratulations, Alma and I turned around and sat at a table. With a full stomach, we decided to pass on eating. That steak was not going to digest anytime soon! We waited anxiously for the music to start, and when it did, we were on the dance floor!

Before we knew it, we'd only sat down for a couple of songs when we realized it was eleven o'clock! We had completely lost track of time. I told Alma, "I think it's probably best that we head back home. Don't you think?"

She replied, "Yeah, I think we should."

We walked over to our friends and thanked them for inviting us to a most memorable event. They were both excited that we had attended and sorry to see us go. We then walked over to the parents and congratulated them one more time. I told them, "We have to go back to San Antonio, but we wanted to congratulate you and wish you many more years of marriage before we left."

They responded, "Thank you very much and have a safe trip home!"

I said, "We will. Thanks again!"

We exited the building and got in my car. I told Alma, "We need to stop somewhere and get some coffee. I need caffeine! There's the McDonald's off the highway. We can stop there."

"Sounds good," she replied.

We pulled into the McDonald's drive thru and got my coffee. Alma, the sweetheart that she is, fixed my coffee with cream and sugar as we started to pull out of the McDonalds.

"Thank you, Darlin'! You gonna stay awake and keep me up on the way home?"

She said, "Of course!"

I pulled onto the highway and we began to chat. Well, that lasted for about fifteen miles. By the time I knew it, her head was resting back and out she went!

So, with coffee in hand, I was on my own.

I thought to myself, "OK, Conrad, you gotta stay alert and awake. We have a long ride home." I felt pretty good in that I didn't have any wine or beer at the reception. I drank water most of the night, and I was still in "adrenalin mode" after dancing all night. While driving, I would occasionally look at Alma and tell myself, "Gosh, she's so pretty! I've got me a catch!"

I was doing pretty good when we drove into Castroville which is about thirty minutes from San Antonio. The road was Highway 90 and we were headed east back to town. I was thinking, "Castroville! Yes! Thirty more miles and we're in San Antonio!" I was excited. Well, I was sleepily excited, I should say. I could see the lights of San Antonio in the distant horizon. It didn't take but five minutes, if that, to get through the town of Castroville.

After we drove past Castroville, suddenly, the sleepiness hit me. My eyes started to droop. I turned the radio on a little louder. I didn't want to wake Alma up as she was sound asleep. My head started to drop a little and my eyes were starting to close. I slapped myself a couple of times just to try to stay awake. (I didn't slap myself that hard!) I was thinking we should have stayed in Uvalde overnight. But I was thinking about the "dog that needed to go outside and pee."

I could see the lights of San Antonio get brighter. Then it happened.

Next thing I know, I woke up! As I opened my eyes, I was coming up to a stop sign!

I yelled, "OH SHIT!" I blew through the stop sign and not even looking to my left, I quickly turned the steering wheel to the right. I turned so abruptly that it knocked Alma toward me. I pulled over to the side of the road and came to an abrupt stop. I was AWAKE now and so was Alma! I must have looked as if I'd seen a ghost!

She looked back at me and asked, "Did you fall asleep?"

I replied quietly, "Yes."

Still grasping the steering wheel tightly, I was taking deep breaths. Finally, I looked ahead and saw a long dark road ahead of me. I looked in the rear-view mirror and saw nothing but darkness. I couldn't even see the highway I was on!

Alma looked up and asked me, "Are you okay?"

I said, "Shit... I fell asleep at the wheel. I can't believe I did that! That was stupid of me! What the hell was I thinking?" I was furious at myself. I could have killed us both.

Alma asked, "Are you okay? Do you want me to drive?"

I said, "I'm fine. No. Believe me. I'm awake now."

I got out of the vehicle. I told Alma, "I need some air." She stayed in the car. I walked around in disbelief. I thought, "God, thank you. You saved our lives." After a few minutes of getting some air, I got back in the car. I don't even remember if I turned the engine off or not. I put the car in drive, slowly turned around and worked my way over to the intersection of the highway. I stopped to evaluate what happened.

I looked to the left and saw what I had done. I fell asleep and somehow exited the highway. When I woke up, I opened my eyes to see that I came upon that stop sign. That's when I jerked the car to the right after I ran the stop sign.

Alma asked me one more time, "Are you okay?"

I replied, "Yeah, just can't believe it. I almost killed us. Let's just get home."

We headed back and got home without any incident. The dog was fine. I wasn't. At least we were back safely. We almost didn't make it home. Thank God for His protection.

Lesson Learned - Don't Get Burned

A few days later, I drove back to the area where we could've died. I drove west and went past the road where I had exited. I made the turnaround and headed east so I could retrace my route. As I approached the exit, I realized that if I hadn't exited, I would have possibly hit the concrete pillars of the bridge or run into the grassy median with the possibility of hitting someone head on coming from the opposite direction. I got off on the same exit to see the lonely road where the stop sign was at. We could've also been killed running the stop sign.

I should've insisted that we stay in Uvalde. I should have wakened Alma up and asked her to drive. I should have stopped somewhere just to get some fresh air and wake up! But you know, there are always those "should haves." Alma intended to stay awake but sleep overcame her. I also intended to stay awake but sleep overcame me and put us in danger. Don't let this happen to you!

Please, please, please - if you ever have to drive long distances, GET SOME REST OR STAY SOMEWHERE! It's not worth the risk to try and be somewhere in a hurry! It's not a driving marathon! Never did I imagine going through something like this. Next time, we will stay somewhere! This taught us both a lesson.

Today, I still thank God that "He placed His whole Hand on my car!" It's like the Lord placed His hand on my car and guided us safely off the road and onto the deserted exit. Because that's what the Lord does; He keeps us safe.

Chapter 28
Am I Dead Again?

This was another New Year's Eve call. This was in the mid-90s. I don't recall my partner's name here, so we'll call him "Pete."

It was around 6 p.m. on New Year's Eve. We had just eaten dinner at the station and I figured I would take a nap and prepare myself for the onslaught of calls. My partner, Pete, who was working overtime, looked at me and said, "You gonna take a nap?"

I told him, "Yep, just in case."

He responded, "You're gonna jinx us."

I replied, "It's coming sooner or later."

Seconds after I told him that, the sound of the tones of the radio blared. Pete commented, "See, I told you so! You jinxed us!"

The dispatcher called out on the radio. "841, 841, respond to the 4200 block of Robinridge for seizures. It is a sixty-five-year-old male. Patient is conscious at this time."

I picked up the radio and replied, "10-4, 841's 10-96, we're on the way." I told Pete, "It's right down the street."

He replied, "Maybe it's nothing."

I answered, "Maybe. We'll see."

I was hoping it was nothing. The fire crew at our station was out on another call and if we needed help or a backup, they would be coming from another station that was quite a ways off. It didn't take us more than three minutes to arrive. As I mentioned, it was right down the street.

Pete was driving and, as we pulled up, I noticed the front door to the house was opened. I thought, "Smart people inside. We have easy access to the house."

I told my partner, "I've got the kit. Would you grab the heart monitor?"

He said, "Sure thing."

With the age of the patient and the fact he had a seizure, I wanted to make sure we didn't have a heart patient that may need to be monitored. We both walked to the door. With the door opened, I felt uneasy so I quickly asked before going in, "Hello! EMS! Can we help you?"

I heard a female voice, "We're over here! In the bedroom! "

"Ma'am! Are there any dogs in the house?"

She replied, "No! Please hurry!"

We followed her voice to the bedroom. We peeked around the door and found a lady standing by the bed next to a male patient who was lying face up on the floor and next to the bed. He was conscious and wore not a stitch of clothes. I quickly grabbed the sheet and covered him. The female was in a robe. I knelt on the floor and placed my hand on his shoulder. I asked him, "Sir! What happened?"

He responded, "Hell if I know!" He seemed a little disoriented.

I turned around and asked the female, "Ma'am, can you tell me what happened?" I noticed she didn't really want to respond to my question. "Ma'am, I need to know what happened. We got the call for a seizure. Did he have a seizure, ma'am?"

"Well, kind of. That's what it looked like," she said.

"Ma'am, what was he doing?" I asked.

"Well..." she hesitated. Then she said softly, "We were making love. He was on top of me and he just had a seizure while he was on top. I couldn't get him off. I was finally able to push him off me, and he fell off the bed onto the floor. Is he alright?"

I told her, "Ma'am, we're gonna check him out and see what's going on."

She replied, "Okay."

I turned to the patient and told him, "Sir, we're gonna check you out, OK? What's your name?"

He replied, "Bill, I think. What happened?"

I told him, "You may have had a seizure. Do you know where you are?"

He replied, "No."

I said, "Okay, sir. I'm gonna take your blood pressure." I asked Pete, "Can you put the monitor on him? Let's see what his heart's doing."

He said, "Got it."

As I was placing the blood pressure cuff on him, I noticed he started jerking a little and his eyes rolled back and was beginning to have another seizure!

"Shit, partner, he's having a seizure!" I said.

I quickly turned him over so he wouldn't throw up. His seizure lasted about one minute. Then he stopped. I quickly looked at him and thought, "He's not coming around." I checked his pulse at his neck and his wrist. I couldn't feel anything.

I told my partner, "Get the paddles and do a quick check now! I can't feel a pulse!"

I started doing CPR while Pete was grabbing the heart paddles so we could quickly see what his heart was doing. I grabbed the radio that I'd laid on the floor.

"841, 841 to Dispatch, Give me a backup now! We have a cardiac arrest! We are doing CPR. I need the fire truck, too!"

The female nervously asked, "What's going on?"

I said, "Ma'am, can you step out? We are going to have to do a few things for him. You need to step out now!" She turned around and quickly ran out of the room. She started to cry.

Pete grabbed the heart paddles and placed them on his chest to do a quick check. I continued CPR. We looked at the heart screen. I told him, "He's in V-Fib! Charge it up!" V-Fib is a term that we use when the heart is out of rhythm, quivering and doing nothing. With this condition, the heart needs to be shocked right away so we can try to get the heart back in a normal rhythm. I continued doing CPR while the heart monitor was charging up.

Pete said, "OK, clear!"

I took my hands off the man's chest as Pete placed the paddles on his chest to shock him. I yelled "Clear!" My partner shocked him and the patient's chest rose off the floor. I check for a pulse and looked at the heart monitor.

"No pulse, he's still in V-Fib. Let's hit him again. Crank it up to 360," I told Pete as I continued CPR. The monitor charged up to 360. Pete said, "Ready! Clear!" I stopped CPR and took my hands off his chest. "Clear!"

We shocked him again.

"No pulse. Still in V-Fib." I hoped to see or hear the sirens of the fire truck or our backup EMS unit, but I heard nothing except the woman crying in the other room. I started CPR again. "Let's charge it up and shock him again at 360," I said.

"OK, getting ready to shock," Pete said.

"Ready! All Clear! Shock him!" I told him.

We shocked him again. Still nothing. He wasn't breathing. I told my partner to continue CPR as I was getting the intubation equipment ready. Since he wasn't breathing, I knew I had to get this tube into his lungs so we could breathe for him. Pete continued CPR. We hadn't started an IV yet so we couldn't give him any drugs. My first goal was to try to change his heart rhythm by shocking him and getting this tube down his throat and into his lungs. I got the equipment ready to intubate him.

I said, "OK, get ready to stop CPR for a second while I intubate him." I had the laryngoscope in my hand. The tool was used to insert into his mouth and slip this tube into his throat and lungs. When intubating, you have to literally have your face over the patient's face to insert the tube into his throat. With the patient lying flat on his back, this meant placing myself in a position where I am flat on the floor on my stomach. So, in other words, the patient's feet and my feet were at opposite ends. He is laying on his back and I'm on my stomach. (Hard to describe!)

I told Pete, "OK, hold CPR for a second!" I knew he was going to be easy to intubate and was only going to take maybe ten seconds to intubate him.

As Pete stopped doing CPR, I quickly opened the patient's mouth and began to insert the blade of the laryngoscope into his mouth. I was two inches from the patient's face when he opened his eyes and suddenly screamed!

"Aghhhhh!"

I screamed back in surprise, "Aghhhhh!" Right after I screamed, Pete screamed, "Aghhhhh!" Then the woman in the other room screamed, too!

The patient woke up! He opened his eyes and yelled, "What the hell did you do?!" as he clutched his chest. I was still trying to gain my composure after he scared the crap out of my partner and me! I looked at the heart monitor. He had a normal sinus rhythm, meaning his heart was back to normal. I felt for a pulse at his neck; he had a strong pulse!

I yelled at him, "Shit! Don't do that! We had to shock you to get your heart back!"

He yelled back, "Well, don't do that again! That f---ing hurt!"

I asked the patient, "Are you okay, now?"

He said, "Yeah! Just don't do that again, please!"

I responded, "Well, don't go unconscious 'cause we'll have to shock you again!"

"Okay!" he said. "I went out! I saw nothing but black. I just remember seeing black! Did I die?"

"No, but it was close!"

Finally, the fire crew and backup EMS unit arrived. I told them, "Hey, get the stretcher, quick! He just crashed on us and we brought him back! We're going Code 3." The firefighters quickly got the stretcher and came inside the house.

One of the other paramedics asked, "What happened?"

I summarized. "He crashed on us and we brought him back after three shocks. He scared the crap out of me. I was intubating him when he suddenly screamed!"

He said, "I bet that was funny!"

I replied, "Well, no, not quite!"

We quickly loaded him onto the stretcher and headed out the door. The woman asked, "What hospital are you taking him to?"

"We're taking him to University Hospital. You can either ride with the other ambulance or meet us there. We're taking him to the emergency room."

She said, "I'll meet you all there."

I replied, "Sounds good. We're gonna get him there as soon as possible, ma'am."

"Thank you," she quietly replied.

We loaded him onto the ambulance. We got an IV started on him and I asked the paramedic from the other ambulance, "Hey, can you ride with us just in case he goes out again?"

He said, "Sure, my partner will follow us out there."

I told him, "Yeah, that would be a good idea 'cause we don't know if he'll crash on us again!"

"I know what you mean."

We were quickly on our way to the hospital with the other unit behind us. My fear was, yes, he was going to crash on us, and we'd have to start CPR and do this all over again. I remember yelling to Pete as he got ready to drive off, "Just go back up Tezel Road, cross Tezel and go straight to Bandera Road. Once you get to Bandera..."

He interjected, "Don't worry, I got it from there. Thanks!"

"Okay, just don't get lost! Let's go Code 3!"

"Code 3. Don't worry, I won't get lost." Pete replied.

While we were in route to the hospital, I quickly got on the radio to turn in my report to the hospital. "841, 841 to University Hospital, I have a report for you," I said.

The ER nurse got on the radio and replied, "Go ahead, 841."

"University, we have a sixty-five-year-old male that apparently had a cardiac seizure. He crashed on us, and we shocked him three times. He converted to normal sinus rhythm after CPR and shocking him, and he is conscious at this time. We have an IV established, and we are headed your way Code 3. Our ETA should be about ten minutes. Do you have any questions for me?"

She responded, "No, sir, we'll see you in ten."

"Thank you," I replied.

I turned around and looked at my patient who was still conscious. The paramedic riding with me was taking another blood pressure. As I looked at the heart monitor, I could see he was still in normal sinus rhythm which indicates his heart was still beating normal. We had the shock paddles close by in the event he should go into V-Fib again. I kept praying to myself, "Please, Lord, don't let him crash on us again!"

Looking out the back windows of the ambulance, I could see we were on Bandera Road and just a few blocks from Wurzbach Road where we would make a left turn. I could also see the backup unit following a few cars behind us.

Bill, our patient, asked me, "How soon will we be there?"

"Once we turn left on Wurzbach, it should be around ten minutes. How are you feeling?"

He said, "I'm feeling fine but my chest is sore. Was it when you shocked me?"

"Probably. But we needed to. Your heart had stopped."

"You mean I died!" he exclaimed.

I told him, "Bill, let's say you almost did. The shock we gave you brought your heart back. And now your heart's beating normally. Which is a good thing."

"Geez," he said. "All I remember is everything going black. That was a strange feeling."

"Well, just stay with me and we'll have you at the hospital in no time."

With lights and sirens on, I noticed we were now approaching to make a left turn on Wurzbach. We got on the left turn lane but had to wait because there was some traffic. It's difficult for cars to move out of the way when the front car sitting at the light probably doesn't even see our lights or hear the sirens. The light turned green and now we were moving toward the light to make a left.

Since we had slowed, I alerted Bill, "Okay, Bill, we're moving now."

He replied, "Okay."

Then, suddenly, all the lights went out in the ambulance! The engine stopped. It was completely dark and pitch black! I thought, "What happened?"

Then I heard Bill, our patient.

"Oh my God! Am I dead again?! It's pitch black! I can't see! Oh no! I'm dead again!"

"No! No! No! Bill! You're not dead! Something happened to the ambulance!" I loudly reassured him. I yelled to my partner through the small open window between the box of the ambulance and the front cab. "Pete, what happened?"

He said, "I don't know! I lost all power. I can't even use the emergency flashers! I'm gonna have to put out some flares!"

"OK!" I shouted at him. "Call Dispatch and tell them we are 10-7! (out of service) We have the backup unit behind us. They can take our patient!"

He said, "OK!" I heard him get on the radio. "841, 841, to Dispatch. We are 10-7! We are 10-7! We need the mechanic ASAP!"

No response from the dispatcher.

Pete again keyed the radio, "841 to Dispatch, can you hear me?"

Again, no response.

In the back of the dark ambulance, Bill asked me again, "Sir, are you sure I'm not dead? 'Cause this is what I saw when I died! It was all black and dark!"

I told him, "Bill, you're with me and my partner. We're all alive, okay?"

He asked, "Are you sure?"

"Yes sir!" I shook his shoulder. "See! We're all alive!" I thought to myself, "Geez, Lord, don't let him crash on us again!" I asked my partner in the front, "Any response from Dispatch?"

He said, "No! I think the radio is out, too!"

"Okay, I'll use the handheld radio. "841 to dispatch! 841 to Dispatch! Can you hear me, sir?"

"10-4, 841, I can hear you!" the dispatcher replied.

"OK, our unit is 10-7! Don't know what happened but all power is out! The mobile radio is out, too! We need the mechanic. We have the backup unit behind us, and they'll take our patient."

Meanwhile, I could hear the cars behind us honking at us. Without any lights at all, the motorists couldn't tell what was going on. My partner stepped out of the unit to get flares out. He had to use his pen light from his pocket to let the car behind us know that we broke down. The cars started going around us not knowing what the hell was going on. Finally, the backup unit realized that something was wrong and turned their lights on and got behind us.

I opened the back doors to our unit. Fortunately, we could see with the backup unit's headlights beaming into the back of the ambulance.

I told the patient, "Bill, we broke down! The ambulance behind us is going to take you to the hospital. We're going to unload you and put you in their ambulance. It will only take a couple of minutes."

The paramedic driving the backup unit approached the back of our unit. "What happened?" he asked.

"I don't know! Everything just blacked out and we lost power!" I said.

Bill, seeming quite the guy with a sense of humor, added, "Yeah, I blacked out, too! But I seem to have *some* power 'cause I can see y'all!" I just smiled and shook my head.

I said, "Bill, these guys will get you to the hospital ASAP!"

He replied, "Are they gonna lose power too? I don't want to die again!"

I told him, "No, Bill! You'll be fine!" My backup partner and his driver proceeded to unload Bill from the ambulance. I said, "No sense in moving him to your stretcher. Just take ours and we'll get it from the hospital once we're back in service. He's got the electrodes but make sure you have your paddles ready just in case."

"Not a problem," one replied.

We loaded Bill into the backup unit. I told him as we were loading him up. "Bill, these guys are gonna take good care of you. I'm sorry about what happened but at least these guys were here. Hey, and they have lights in their unit!"

Bill laughed and replied. "Don't worry, it was nice meeting you! I bet it was your serpentine belt! I'm a mechanic!"

"Really?" I asked.

"Yep, it's a Ford and you only have one belt. If that goes out, everything goes out!"

"Okay, we'll check it out, Bill! Thanks! I'll see you again, Bill, God bless!"

I kept praying that he'd make it to the hospital. It was still going to be a ten-minute ride for him. I kept monitoring the radio to listen and hear if anything came up or if the unit taking him would have to stop and call for help. I knew that if they called for help in route, Bill probably crashed again. When I heard the unit arrive at the hospital without incident. I thought, "Great, he made it!"

Meanwhile, Pete placed flares out so motorists could see that we were stalled. We were literally at the traffic light and blocking traffic that was going to turn left. We were by ourselves for about five minutes when, luckily, a police officer drove by and rolled his window down.

"What's the problem?" he asked.

"We don't know! We lost all power!" I responded.

He said, "Okay, let me pull behind you about twenty yards. I'll have my lights on and direct traffic in front of you."

"I really appreciate it, brother! We have a mechanic on the way!"

"Sounds good!" the officer replied. I should've gotten his name. He was a lifesaver!

I thought, "Thank you, Lord, for placing this officer here for our safety."

After putting some flares out, I could see my partner was popping the hood to see what may have gone wrong. He opened it and we both pointed our little pen lights into the engine. Well, Bill was right! The serpentine belt was just hanging over a pulley! It had torn apart.

I told Pete, "That Bill is a genius!

"What do you mean?"

"He said it was the serpentine belt. He said he was a mechanic. What a guy!"

Pete replied, "He said it was the belt?"

"Yep, that's what he said in the back of the unit, and he was exactly right!"

We left the hood open so motorists could see we had an engine problem. It was funny. People were driving by us shouting, "Happy New Year, guys! Need some help or a beer?"

We answered, "No thank you! We surely appreciate it!" They continued honking as they went by. A car with some females shouted at us. "Need a ride? We're going to a party! Want to join us?"

"No thank you, ladies! We're working!"

They drove off honking and yelling, "Happy New Year!"

We heard Dispatch calling on our handheld radio. "841, 841, is the mechanic on scene yet?"

I said, "Negative. What's his ETA?"

The dispatcher answered, "Unknown at this time. He's working on another unit that's out of service, too."

It was around 8:30 p.m. We'd been sitting there for almost two hours. We'd been monitoring the radio and could hear that the city was getting pretty busy. We already had two other ambulances go past us with patients on their way to the hospital. A paramedic of one of the units that drove by us rolled his window down and yelled at us, "Hey you loafers! Get back in service! We're making all your calls!"

I just shrugged my shoulders at him.

There we were sitting in a dark ambulance with nowhere to go. Fortunately, we had plenty of flares to place on the road and the police officer stuck around as well. I spent most of my time writing my patient report after we got stalled. I gave the original patient report to the paramedics from the backup unit.

Finally, around 9:30 p.m., the mechanic showed up. Fortunately, we didn't have to get towed as he had a serpentine belt ready to install.

The mechanic asked us, "How long you been here?"

"For almost three hours."

He said, "Oops. Sorry."

"No problem. We've been entertained, offered a beer, and invited to a New Year's Eve party. So, it's been an interesting night. How long before we're back in service?"

"Eh, give me around twenty minutes," he answered.

I said, "OK." I looked at Pete and said, "We have to get our stretcher back some time. Once we get back in service, I'd like to go visit Bill at the hospital. It won't take but twenty minutes. Just wanna see how he's doing."

He said, "Fine with me."

Twenty minutes later the mechanic closed the hood and said, "Crank her up! You're ready!" I turned the key and, sure enough, it started! We were on our way! We had lights!

I said to the mechanic, "Thanks, and have a Happy New Year! Hope we don't see you till next year!"

The mechanic replied, "Yeah, I get off at midnight. I just might stay at the shops to avoid all these crazy people on the road!"

"Yep, I don't blame you! Take care!" My partner and I were off and running. Now that we were back in service, I got on the radio and told the dispatch office that we were headed to University hospital to swap our equipment. On our way to the hospital, I hoped we wouldn't get a call. I really wanted to see if Bill was okay and wondered what was going to happen to him.

We arrived at the hospital in the ten minutes we expected from hours before. We walked into the ER and went back to where they would have put Bill. I walked up to the ER nurse behind the desk.

"Hi, I'm Conrad from unit 841. Our backup unit transported Bill, the guy who we converted a few hours ago. What room is he in?"

She said, "He's in the room behind you."

I turned around and started walking slowly to the room. I walked in, but the curtain was closed. My heart was beating quickly, as I wondered what kind of shape he was in. I hoped he didn't crash. Was he dead? Again? I slowly opened the curtain.

He was awake!

He took one look at me and shouted, "Hey, Gonzales!" He remembered my name. "Hey, I made it! My lights didn't go out on me again!"

I took a deep sigh of relief. I asked him, "Bill, how in tarnation are you?"

"Better now that I'm here. I can't wait to get out. I'm ready for a beer!" he exclaimed.

"Well, Bill, you made our evening, bud. I'm glad your lights didn't go out like ours did! You don't know how ecstatic we are that you pulled through!"

He responded, "Hell, if it weren't for you all, I'd be meeting them pearly gates in Heaven! I'm glad you were there for me! Hey, I'm thinking I'm gonna live another fifty years!"

"I bet you have nine lives like a cat, huh, Bill?" I asked.

"Well, maybe not nine. I think this is my fifth. So, hell, I've got four more to go! Ha!" Then he said, "Hey, Gonzales, I owe you and your partner a beer! You all need to drive and visit me so I can buy y'all a beer or two! Let me know, and I'll show ya the town!"

I told him, "Thanks, Bill, I appreciate the invitation. Maybe one day!"

He replied, "Well, you just let me know. I have the mechanic shop right next to the bar by the highway. You can't miss it! If you miss me at the shop, you can find me at the bar! We can shoot some pool, too!"

"You are too kind, Bill. Maybe we'll see ya again sometime."

He said, "Yeah! That would be great! As long as your lights don't go out!" He laughed. "Hey, was it the serpentine belt that tore up?"

I responded, "You know what, Bill? You were absolutely right! It was the belt!"

"Dang it, I knew it!" he hooted, as he slapped his knee. He was getting me nervous. I kept looking at the ECG monitor on the wall next to his bed. I was hoping he wouldn't get too excited and crash here in the ER.

I said, "Bill, take it easy, bud. We're gonna take off. We just wanted to come by and see how you were doin'. We have to get out on the road. You have a Happy New Year, okay?" We shook hands.

He replied, "Y'all too! I'm gonna have one helluva year thanks to y'all!"

"Take care of yourself Bill and don't drink and drive tonight," I told him.

He said, "Naw, my wife or girlfriend will drive me. It don't matter!"

I laughed. No questions asked and no comments! I left it at that. "See ya, Bill!" I opened the curtain and walked out of the room. The nurse, who was taking care of Bill joked, "He must be your best friend. You saved his life and now you're lifelong buddies."

I responded, "Well, we did shock the hell out of him and saved his life. But, lifelong buddies? Maybe."

To Bill, yes, we were lifelong buddies. And come to think of it, yeah, Bill was my lifelong buddy, too. He made another New Year's Eve interesting.

Speaking of interesting. I said to Pete as we left, "You know, I've heard of patients sometimes having seizures when they go into a cardiac arrest. I believe this is a first! You know, thinking back, when his wife said they were making love and he was on top of her, she said he had the seizure and became unconscious. She said that she pushed him off and he fell on the floor. You know what? I bet his heart stopped when he was on top of her and when she pushed him off and hit the floor his heart was 'shocked' back into rhythm. Remember, when we got there he was conscious."

My partner said, "You know, you're right. I think she saved his life, too! She shocked him when he hit the floor! I bet that's what happened!"

Well, whether it did happen or not, he got one hell of a jolt.

Happy New Year, Bill! You made our night!

Lesson Learned - Don't Get Burned

Well, one thing we learned, as paramedics, you never know what kind of patient you're going to have. My suggestion to my colleagues, when you get a call for a seizure patient, remember that cardiac seizures do exist! They will have a seizure right in front of you and then... BAM! No pulse! Take the heart monitor with you at all times! This was a textbook case of being there at the right time! Bill actually didn't know what hit him until we told him!

One thing that Bill taught me was that no matter what happens in life, keep your sense of humor. Bill was a perfect example of someone who almost died, yet when he came back to life, he was just as normal as, I'm sure, he'd always been.

If someone has a cardiac seizure and you find no pulse, call 9-1-1, and start CPR.

By the way, readers, enjoy every day of your life. If you see the lights go out, let's hope it's the circuit breaker in your house and NOT the circuit breaker in your heart! It reminds me of a song by Willie Nelson called, "Turn Out the Lights...The Party's Over." Well, Bill's lights went out for a few minutes and after we turned his lights back on, his party was NOT over!

Here's to you, Bill, even if your lights are out now, I'm sure you turned them on in Heaven because, with your happy heart, positive attitude and great disposition, that's where you belong... in Heaven.

Chapter 29
Hotline to Heaven

This particular incident happened after I retired. It involved my father.

How many of you remember your parents being sick or ill and you had to remind them to make an appointment with their doctor and their response was, "It will pass," or "I'll take some aspirin and it'll go away," or "Nothing better than honey and lemon. That's a heal-all."? Do you remember your mother telling you "Don't tell your father I told you."?

Well, I remember Mom calling me one day. I answered the phone. "How's it going, Mom?"

She answered, "Just fine, Mijo."

"How's Dad?" I asked.

She said, "That's why I'm calling you."

Curious, I asked Mom, "What's going on?"

She said, "Let me go to the back room so I can talk." I knew something was up because she always made an excuse to use the phone in the back room or outside where Dad couldn't hear what she was saying. She told me, "Dad says he feels something in his throat. I don't know what it is, but he says it kinda bothers him."

"Can you see what it is?" I asked her.

"No, he won't let me look at it. He says it's probably his tonsils," she replied.

"But he doesn't have his tonsils!" I exclaimed.

"Yes, I know."

I told her, "Okay, I'll be by there later and I'll ask him."

She said, "Okay, but don't tell him I told you, or he'll get mad at me."

"Yeah, I know, Mom. I won't."

About an hour later I arrived at their house. Nonchalantly, I sat down and started to chat with them. I made some coffee and started a casual conversation.

"How ya doin', Mom?" I asked.

"Fine, son. How have you been?" she replied.

"Been pretty busy at work, Mom. Just the usual. Conducting classes at work. The grass looks great, Dad! You been watering?"

He answered, "Yes, son, you know me. I'll grab that water hose and sit out there and water." Dad has always been meticulous about his yard. Trimming, cutting, and ensuring that the grass was a lush green. I loved growing up and watching both Mom and Dad out there cutting grass. We'd all be out there together.

"How've you been feeling, Dad?" I asked.

"Been fine," he said quietly. "How about you, son?"

I replied, "I've been okay... I just have this nasty sore throat. I guess my tonsils have been acting up a little bit. I don't know. Maybe it's allergies. No cough or phlegm, though. I'll probably get some antibiotics or something to soothe my throat." I continued, "I've noticed your voice sounds a little different, Dad. Does your throat hurt, too? It sounds a little raspy."

He quickly turned and looked at Mom with the accusing glance. Mom just looked away and smiled. Dad, with his sense of humor answered, "I think my voice is finally changing. You know, like puberty?" He laughed. Mom did, too. I just shook my head and smiled at him.

He said, "No, it's probably my tonsils. They may be a little swollen."

"Dad, you don't have your tonsils."

"Well, you know son, they do grow back sometimes." He smiled.

"Dad, they don't grow back!" We all laughed. "OK, Dad, can I take a look right quick?" He quickly opened his mouth and said, "Aghhh," and closed his mouth again. "C'mon, Dad, let me take a look," I repeated.

"Well, you said right quick! That was a quick look!" he quipped. We all chuckled again.

"Nah Dad, let me get a flashlight so I can see what you have in there."

Jokingly he replied, "You'll find clean teeth, gums, my throat, and my tongue."

Boy, my dad was quick and clever. He had some great comebacks. He should have been a comedian! He was always kidding around. I'll never forget when we were kids we were having dinner one time. We were having green beans as a side. I remember he sneezed and we looked up at him and told him, "Bless you!" He took his hands away from covering his mouth and nose only to see two green beans sticking out of his nose! We all went, "Ooooh, gross, Dad!" We all laughed so hard our food got cold!

Anyway, Dad finally consented and let me look into his throat. I could see a small lump in the left side of his throat. It wasn't his tonsil. It looked like a mass. And it didn't look right. I asked him, "Does it hurt?"

He replied, "Just a little bit. Only when I swallow. I told you, son, it's my tonsil growing back!"

"Nope, Dad, it's not your tonsil growing back." I put my two fingers at the side of his neck and felt it. It felt hard and very unusual. I told him and Mom, "Dad, it's not your tonsil 'cause you don't have them. It's something else and you need to make an appointment with your doctor. I want you to make an appointment tomorrow. If you don't, I will make it for you."

Mom told him, "Honey, let's call tomorrow."

My dad said, "OK."

"How long have you had it, Dad?" I asked.

He said, "Hmm. Probably around two months. But I didn't tell your mother. Did she mention anything about this to you?"

"Well, kind of," I said, "but she was concerned about you. And I'm glad she did."

Mom just smiled and told him, "I needed to tell him because you don't listen to me sometimes."

Dad quipped, "Yes I do. I always listen when you say dinner's ready. I come and sit down to eat!" We all laughed.

"Okay, Dad, please call the doctor tomorrow and let me know what he says."

Dad replied, "I will. I'll call tomorrow."

Mom repeated, "We'll call tomorrow for sure, Mijo."

"Make sure, Dad! OK, gonna go now." I said as I walked out the door.

The following day, I called them around 10 a.m. Mom answered the phone. "Hello?"

"Mom, it's me. Did Dad call the doctor today?" I asked.

"Yes, Mijo. We're going in this afternoon. We were able to get in today."

I replied, "Great, Mom. Let me know what the doctor says. I'm glad he was able to take Dad in today. How's he doing?"

"Oh, he's fine. I guess he's a little worried."

"I know. I would be too. But let's pray it's nothing," I told her. "Call me tonight or I'll call you after I get off work."

Mom said, "Okay. Thank you, Mijo."

I told her, "No, Mom, thank you for telling me. We'll talk tonight."

I called them that evening to see what the doctor had said. Mom picked up the phone. "Hi, Mom. How did things go this afternoon?" I asked.

She said, "Well, the doctor wants Dad to see a specialist, Dr. Brown. He's an ear, nose, and throat specialist. He has an appointment next week with him."

"That's great. What day and what time?"

"It's during the day on Wednesday at ten in the morning," she said.

I replied, "Okay, let me see if I can go with you all to the appointment."

The morning of his appointment, the doctor saw dad and found the mass that I had seen. The doctor told us that it was unusual; since the mass was behind his tongue, he would have to remove a small piece to conduct a biopsy. The doctor made another appointment to have a small piece of the mass removed.

After the biopsy, we waited about four days to find out if it was cancer or not. It was the longest four days of our lives. The doctor finally called to set up an appointment to see us after the results came in. It didn't sound good. Mom had asked all of us if we could make the appointment with her. I didn't want her to go by herself. So, we all went! It was Mom, Dad, myself, my sister, my brother, and my Aunt Dorothy and Uncle Norris drove in from McAllen, Texas. It was going to be a consultation with all the family.

We were all waiting in the lobby when the doctor called us in for the results. We all sat nervously and hoped the results were negative. They weren't. The tumor was malignant. He had cancer in the back of his tongue. It was Stage 3 cancer. We were stunned. Mom started to cry, and so did my Aunt Dorothy.

I asked the doctor, "What's the prognosis, Doc?" Dr. Patrick Brown, a great ENT, was very positive and compassionate.

He told us, "We could knock this out with aggressive chemotherapy and radiation. Years ago, they'd have to literally break his jaw and go in to cut the tumor out. Disfiguration of that side of his face would have been common back then. But, with plans for aggressive radiation and chemo treatment, we can hopefully knock it out."

With his positive attitude and disposition, I felt very confident that he, along with a lot of prayers, would take care of Dad.

"Thank you, Dr. Brown. We trust your judgement and decision. We'll pray for you as well."

He said, "I am hopeful that this will work out. I have a great oncologist and she is awesome and will take care of your Dad. I will set up his appointments so she can start his treatments next week."

"Thanks, Doc," I replied. We left the office and the whole family met outside. I told Dad and Mom, "We'll knock this out, Dad. Everything will be alright. Let's just be glad that it's not worse than what it seems." Mom and my Aunt Dorothy agreed.

Dad was referred to a female oncologist, Dr. Rao. She was an Indian doctor who had the most positive attitude and demeanor and I knew that Dad would be comfortable working with her. I had the utmost respect for her and her staff. Her staff exhibited the same disposition to patients and their families.

Dad would be going for his chemo and radiation treatments three times a week. On Mondays, Wednesdays, and Fridays, Mom would drive Dad to his appointments. Sometimes, if I was off or available, I would go drop them off and pick them up. Sometimes when I had the opportunity, I would take Mom some tacos so she could eat breakfast as Dad had to be there for up to four hours in the morning.

The staff was phenomenal. They knew Mom and I loved our coffee and they made sure there was a fresh pot of coffee when we arrived on the days Dad had his appointments. It never failed; there was a fresh pot of coffee every time we arrived. Sometimes they'd even have donuts!

As we entered the door, the receptionist would look up and say, "Fresh coffee, Mrs. Gonzales!" What a welcoming! And, we felt welcomed each and every time. The other patients there were also grateful for the doctor and staff. Everyone talked very highly of Mom and Dad. The staff made sure there was an empty chair so Mom could sit right next to Dad during his chemotherapy. He had his IV pole next to him and, of course, Mom right there next to him, too.

Mom would take her Bible with her and read scriptures out loud to Dad while he was having his treatments. Mom and Dad are very religious and, I know for sure, have a hotline to Heaven, as they prayed every day next to each other. Mom would have her Bible, read to Dad, and Dad would close his eyes while she read. Also, in the room, were eight patients sitting next to each other getting their treatments.

Mom told me one day that another patient was so intrigued by Mom's scripture readings that she asked her if she could read louder because she was a little hard of hearing. So, Mom obliged. Next thing you know, they were all listening to Mom reading from the Bible. A few weeks later, almost every patient that was there had their Bibles, too! It looked like Bible study at the doctor's office! What an inspiration my parents were to these patients!

As a matter of fact, even some of the staff noticed a change in disposition of the patients. They felt more confident that they would survive. They continued to read the Bible with Mom and Dad for the following months during their shared treatment time.

I loved taking Mom and Dad to his appointments when I had the opportunity. It gave me inspiration watching them inspire everyone in that office.

The oncologist monitored the size of the tumor on a monthly basis. Thank God - each month that went by during his treatments, we could see the tumor dwindling and shrinking in size. We prayed every month thereafter that the tumor would shrink and eventually disappear. That day came. The tumor was gone and Dad had no signs of cancer at all. Truly a MIRACLE! Truly GOD IS GREAT! We cried with joy! We hugged Dad and hugged each other!

Dad started his radiation and chemotherapy in June of 2010. In December, six months later, he was taken off chemotherapy and radiation. He was cancer free. As of this writing in October 2018, Dad is still cancer free and has been in remission for eight years. He visits Dr. Brown on a quarterly basis and gets his blood work done. Still in remission and cancer free! Thank God... and thanks to Mom! She saved his life.

Lesson Learned - Don't Get Burned

The lesson I learned from this trying time with Dad and Mom was: communicate about health issues!

Don't be afraid to talk about your health issues especially when it comes to issues concerning your family. Males, being the macho guys that we are, don't want to tell our spouses about any health issues. From sore throats to headaches to "guy stuff," we tend to put off these very important and critical subjects until it's too late.

With Dad, it could have been too late if it weren't for Mom stepping in and telling me that there was something going on with him. There are many cases where people have died too soon as they suffered from some illness that, if seen by a doctor sooner, could have been treated or fixed. *If you're in doubt, get it checked out!*

Learn the early warning signs of cancer, heart disease or heart attacks, strokes, diabetes, high blood pressure, and, believe me, you'll be able to someday help save your life or the life of someone you love!

Also, we believed in prayer. Whether you do or not, always have a positive attitude. Always have hope. The more we know about health issues, the more likely we can save a life, possibly your own.

Chapter 30
The Day My Dad Saved Me

This particular incident happened when I was fifteen years old. Yes, it was way before my fire department career, but this was still a lesson learned.

It was summertime when my neighbor, Ricardo, had just bought a brand new 1967 Charger. Wow! I remember when he came home and pulled up in this avocado green Charger with a black vinyl top. Boy, was I impressed! I remember going outside to meet him.

"Dude, that is an awesome car! Did you just get it?"

"Yep," he replied. "Just got it today. Want to look inside?"

"Of course!" I looked around inside and asked him, "Can I sit in the driver's seat?"

He said, "Okay, but don't get it dirty!"

"I won't. Wow! Black leather seats, sound system with an 8-track stereo system! That is so cool! It has a standard shift! Wow! I wish I knew how to drive standard!"

He said, "Someday I'll teach you how to drive standard."

"Really?" I replied.

He said, "Yeah, it's easy. Well, I gotta go now. I'll let you know when we go cruisin'."

"I hope it's soon!" I exclaimed.

Ricardo was twenty-one years old. He was six years older than me, and he had just gotten a job with the federal government. He was making pretty good money at such a young age. Being fifteen years old, I thought I couldn't wait to turn twenty-one so I could buy me a Charger or a Mustang!

Well, it was the following Saturday, when Ricardo and another friend, Gilbert, came to my house. They rang the doorbell. It was around seven in the evening. I opened the door.

"Hey, Conrad, want to go for a ride? We're gonna go cruisin' downtown. It's gonna be fun. Come with us!"

Excited, I responded, "Yeah! OK, wait here so I can ask my dad. I'll be right back." Remember, I was fifteen years old. Ricardo was twenty-one and his friend, Gilbert, was twenty-two. I went to my parents' bedroom to ask my dad.

"Hey, Dad! Ricardo and Gilbert are here and they asked me to go riding with them. We're going in Ricardo's new Charger. Can I go?"

Dad stood up and walked to the door. I followed behind him. Ricardo asked my dad, "Mr. Gonzales, can Conrad go riding with us? We'll be back around ten o'clock. We're only going downtown and back. We won't be long."

I jumped in, "Dad, can I go please?! We'll be back soon! Please, can I go?" I felt like a small kid pleading with him. Dad looked past Ricardo and Gilbert and saw the car. He thought for a minute and turned to me and said, "No, you can't go."

I answered, "What?! Why not? We're only gonna be gone a couple of hours! C'mon, Dad. Just for a little bit!"

Ricardo pleaded, too. "C'mon, Mr. Gonzales, it'll be fun! I don't drive fast at all."

Dad replied, "No. He's not going with you all tonight." Dad turned toward me and said, "No, you're not going."

"Dad, please!" I pleaded.

Once again, Dad repeated, "No, you're not going and that's it."

Dad closed the door on Ricardo and Gilbert. I stormed back into my room, infuriated. I locked the door and never came out. Dad went back into his room. I laid in bed still upset that I couldn't go with them. I heard them take off. I thought, "Nice engine." I fell asleep still in a pissed off mood wondering why I couldn't go with my buddies.

The next morning, Sunday, it was around seven when I heard a knock on the front door. I woke up and thought, "Who could be knocking at the door so early on a Sunday morning?" I stepped out of my room to see that my dad had answered the door. It was my friend Ricardo's mom.

Still sleepy-eyed, I heard her say, "Is your son, Conrad, home?"

Dad replied, "Yes, he's right here. What's going on?"

"I'm glad he's home," she said.

My dad asked her again, "What's going on?"

She replied, "Just be glad your son didn't go riding with my son and Gilbert last night." My dad and I were both looking at her, puzzled. She continued, "They're both in jail."

All of a sudden, I was very awake. Dad asked, "What happened?"

"They killed someone."

"What?!" Dad and I exclaimed together.

"Yes, the police told me they were at an intersection on the east side of town. They were sitting at a traffic light and Gilbert, who was the passenger on the right, rolled his window down and started cursing at a man that was waiting for a bus. The man started cursing back at them. My son yelled at Gilbert to stop cursing at the man. Suddenly, Gilbert pulled out a gun from his waistband and shot the guy several times and killed him right there. He was maybe five feet away when he fell from the gunshot wounds."

Still in shock, Dad and I kept listening.

She continued, "They drove off and sped away. There was a drunk man sitting by a fire station. Startled by the gunshots, the drunk man saw the car speed away and, surprisingly, looked at the license plate, memorized it, and gave it to the police. They were caught not too far away in the downtown area and arrested. They found the gun. Gilbert had thrown it in the back seat where the police found it after searching the Charger. So, they're both in jail. Be glad that your son didn't go with them. Your son would be in jail, too."

She turned to leave. "Have a good morning and pray for my son and Gilbert. They will be in jail for a long time, I think." She walked away.

Dad closed the door, turned around and looked at me and said, "That's why I told you no. I had this bad feeling about them and the car."

I was still reeling but replied, "Thank you for telling me no, Dad. I will always listen to you." I went back to bed still in shock. I couldn't go back to sleep. I kept remembering Dad telling me "No, you can't go." The word "no" is still etched in my mind and in my heart.

Ricardo got twenty years in prison. He was the accomplice and driver of the getaway vehicle. Although he had no idea Gilbert was carrying a weapon, he paid the price. Gilbert, the shooter, received a forty-year sentence. He died in prison of unknown causes.

And me? I got a "no" from Dad and a life with a great future ahead. Thanks, Dad, you saved my life and my future.

Lesson Learned - Don't Get Burned

Listening to Dad was a life-changing and a life-saving experience. At fifteen years old, I would have been a juvenile accomplice. I would have gone to a juvenile detention center until I turned eighteen then gone to prison as an adult. I wouldn't be writing this book or sharing my experiences as a firefighter, paramedic, consultant, son, brother, uncle, friend, husband, or father.

I won't forget the look on Ricardo's mother's face when she came to the door that Sunday morning. She mourned the loss of her son for twenty years.

Now, you tell me. How many times did you get mad at your parents for telling you "no"? How many times did you storm into your bedroom and started throwing things around because you were upset that you couldn't go to a party? At that point, we can't see that they helped us by saying "no".

My message to parents: "Say no when you need to say no. And don't change your mind later."

What's happening today, and this I've noticed for the past thirty to forty years, parents want to be "friends" with their children. Parents want to be the coolest parents on the block or the best parents at the school. Parents are giving in to the whims of their children.

Parents: you've got to stand your ground, and don't let your kids shove you around. Your children will learn to respect you for teaching them about respect and discipline. Teach them about love and consideration for others. They, in the long run, will appreciate it when you told them, "no."

And, tell them "I love you" every day, too.

Chapter 31
Get Out Of The Way

Ah, the life of the paramedic in EMS was always interesting and exciting. Never knowing what the next call would be about was always a mystery and sometimes unnerving. However, that's what this profession was all about. You never knew what your shift was going to be like. Very unpredictable!

One early morning, I'd say around 2 a.m., we were called for a shooting in the 1100 block of East Elvira. The call came over the radio, and I was awakened to the blaring of the tones.

"806, 806, respond to a shooting. Eleven hundred block of East Elvira. That's 1-1-0-0 East Elvira for a shooting. Be advised that there might be active shooting at the scene. Proceed with caution."

I got up from my bed, put on my shoes, picked up the radio and walked out the door.

"806 is 10-96. Did you say there was active shooting?" I asked.

"10-4, active shooting at this time. Proceed with caution." Dispatch replied.

"10-4. 806 received." I replied.

I don't remember who my partner was (so we'll call him Jim) but we both got in the unit and responded with lights only. We didn't want to startle anyone, especially the shooter, with our presence!

It didn't take but a few minutes to get to the street. I remember turning left onto Elvira Street and turned the lights off. We were at the 200 block.

I said to Jim, "Why don't we just stage close by and wait till we get cleared by PD?"

He agreed. So, I slowly drove to the 700-block and decided to stage there. For safety reasons, I figured it would be best to stay as far away as we could so we wouldn't get in the crossfire in the event they were actually still shooting. Four blocks from the scene was a good safe distance for us. All we had to do now was wait for PD to call us in if there were any patients.

"I'm gonna turn the engine off so we can at least maybe hear what's going on ahead of us," I told Jim.

He said, "Good idea."

I turned the engine off. It was summertime, and it was hot. I rolled the window down. It got eerily quiet. I couldn't hear anything at all up ahead. Then, suddenly, from our right and in the darkness, someone whispered, "Get the f--- out of the way."

We both turned to the right.

We heard the voice again, only a little louder, "Get the f--- out of the way!"

In the dark were two police officers hiding behind a tree. They had their guns drawn at us! One of the police officers said, "The shooter is in the house to your left and you're between us! He's gonna shoot your ass! So, get the f--- out of the way!"

You don't know how fast I turned the engine on; I actually think I burned rubber as I screeched out of there! My heart was pounding as I sped down the block! I think I did a quarter mile in 2.3 seconds!

Once we were blocks away, I got on the radio and called Dispatch, "Hey, guys! What the hell are you doing? We were in the line of fire! You sent us to the wrong address!"

The dispatcher replied, "806, that's the address the caller gave us. He gave us the 1100 block of East Elvira. Standby, 806, we're calling the caller back."

After a few minutes, the dispatcher came on the radio. "806, 806."

I responded, still pissed off, "This is 806, go ahead."

"The caller was mistaken. He meant to say the 'seven hundred block' of East Elvira. But he said, 'eleven hundred block.' The caller apologized. We're sorry, too." The dispatcher told me.

I thought, "Well, it wasn't the dispatcher's fault if that's the information they were given." But, yes, it could have been worse. We could have been caught in the crossfire and possibly injured or killed. I actually believe the shooter was probably taken by surprise. The shooter may have been thinking, "What the hell are those stupid paramedics doing? Am I on TV or what!?" Well, I thank the shooter that he didn't decide to shoot us because he certainly could have!

As it turned out, the shooter finally gave up after a three-hour stand-off. This time, we were parked *far* away... like the ELEVEN HUNDRED block of East Elvira! That's 1-1-0-0!

Lesson Learned - Don't Get Burned

The biggest thing I learned was... if it's too quiet at the scene, something is up! Also, I should have asked Dispatch to call the caller back to ensure that the right address was given. Yes, the caller was mistaken. As it turned out, the caller was visiting his neighbor and the neighbor told him that there was a shooting. So, it was the visitor who was unfamiliar with the address of his friend's house that called 9-1-1 and gave the wrong number. So be it. We didn't get shot and all turned out well.

In this case, communication was the key, or lack thereof. When it comes to any call, it is imperative that all communicate in order to avoid any catastrophe or missteps.

Now, have you ever had to call 9-1-1? Do you know your home and work address? Nowadays, with great technology, when you call 9-1-1, the dispatcher will be able to tell where you are calling from and even have your number at hand.

Here are some helpful hints if you ever have to call EMS: (know where you are!)

- If you are in an apartment, give the apartment and building number, gate code and any directions to get through the complex, including how many flights of stairs. Circling the complex wastes time.
- If you work in an office building, can you describe the location of the office, parking situation, security on the bottom floor, suite number, etc.? Give as much info as possible.

- If you are at home, does your neighborhood have a gate? Where are your children and pets? Will the ambulance be able to park in front of your house?

We all hope and pray that we never have to call EMS for an emergency but knowing what to expect and teaching your children what to do is imperative. In the meantime, think about taking a CPR or First Aid class. You must do something pending the arrival of the paramedics and firefighters. You can save someone's life!

Chapter 32
The Overhang

Working just north of the downtown area at Station #5 brought many challenges. From small streets and alleys, to downtown traffic, the night life at the Riverwalk, and tall buildings, I knew that if we made a call in those areas, it was going to be interesting. I recall many times trying to maneuver our ambulance around cars with inches to spare on each side of our unit. We had to ensure that we didn't "get stuck" in between parked vehicles, dumpsters, or even getting blocked at scenes by drivers trying to get into their own homes or driveways. We were also located in an area where we had easy access to the highway to go north, south, east, or west.

I remember once having to park on the driveway of a home because there were cars parked up and down the street. We had to get as close as we could to get to the patient. It was at a party and someone was having a heart attack. When we came back to the ambulance with the patient on the stretcher, a car had literally parked right behind us and blocked us from getting out! The host of the party had to go inside and look for the "fool" that had parked and blocked us! Well, needless to say, no one claimed the car! It turned out that a neighbor was so upset that someone had blocked his driveway at his home down the street so he decided to park and block the ambulance!

Knowing that we had to take this patient to the hospital and couldn't get out, we had to call another ambulance to pick up our patient! Well, after an hour of being blocked, the owner of the car was ticketed by a police officer for obstructing an emergency vehicle. He was not a happy camper, or I should say, a happy home owner.

Back to the overhang story. It was a late evening at Station #5 when we were called to a sick party in the downtown area.

The dispatcher stated, "805, 805, respond to St. Mary's and East Market for a sick party. We don't have any details as the caller hung up. All they said was that they felt sick."

"10-4. 805 is 10-96. You say you have no details at all?" I asked the dispatcher.

The dispatcher replied, "Negative. No details."

I replied, "10-4. Thank you. I'm sure they'll call back soon." I hoped they would.

Unfortunately, technology hadn't caught up with us and the dispatch office didn't have "caller ID" and the only way we could get back with the caller is to wait for them to call back. OK, I know what you're thinking. "That is so prehistoric!" Yep, it sure was! There were no cell phones either! We had to stamp a card when the call came in, when the call went out, when the EMS unit was on the way, when they were at the scene, when they were in route to the hospital, when they were done at the hospital, and when they were back in service! Can you imagine, time stamping a card every time a call came in? Compared to today, yes, it was very prehistoric! This was in 1983.

Well, it didn't take us but maybe five minutes to get to the intersection.

"805 is 10-97 at the corner of St. Mary's and East Market. Did the caller call back?" I asked the dispatcher.

"Negative..." the dispatcher replied.

"10-4. We'll look around." I answered.

Well, at the corner of St. Mary's and East Market stood a parking garage, the San Antonio Library, and two buildings. One was a bank and the other a building with offices. Everything was closed and we saw no one in sight. I thought maybe it was a homeless person or someone that may have gotten off the bus. We looked and saw a couple of pay phones with no signs of anyone around.

I told my partner, "Hey, Bob, we should go down the street. Maybe we'll find someone down there."

He said, "Sure."

Bob was driving. We drove down one block and saw two buildings. One was a building on the right that housed some elderly and on the other corner, there was a small motel. There were some lights on at the office of the motel. I suggested. "Hey, Bob, pull into the parking lot at the motel. I'll get down and ask someone at the office if they called or if someone called from the motel."

He pulled into the parking lot. I got out of the unit and walked into the office where an attendant was looking at me rather surprised as we had the red lights of the ambulance on. I said, "Good evening, sir. We received a call for someone that was sick. Do you have any idea if it may have been someone staying here?"

The attendant, a male, answered passively, "No one here called," and turned around. Then he asked me over his shoulder, "Can you turn the lights off on your ambulance? You're going to scare my patrons that are staying here."

I looked at him and felt like asking him, "Are you kidding me?" but I replied, "No, sir, I cannot turn the lights off. We are on an emergency call and until we find this patient, we'll need to have our lights on."

He just looked at me and turned back around. I thought, "What a jerk." Then again, he was probably thinking the same thing about me. I walked out and headed toward the ambulance. Bob rolled the window down (yes, "rolled" the window down - we didn't have electric windows!).

He asked, "Did they call?"

I answered, "No. He said no one called from here. I'm thinking they may have called from the elderly home. Why don't we turn around and check it out?"

Bob replied, "Okay. No need to back out. I'll just go straight and go around the block."

I said, "Okay. Just beware there's that overhang that we need to watch out for."

He said, "No problem. Just make sure I can clear the top."

This overhang was a walkway that led from the second story of the motel office across to the second story of the motel. It stretched about thirty feet. The walkway was used by patrons to walk across to their rooms on the second floor. Surely, it was a convenience for them.

I stood ten feet from the front of the ambulance, "OK, Bob. Just inch forward and I'll check the top so we can clear it."

He said, "OK." Bob put it in drive and started moving forward inching toward the overhang which was at least a good fifteen feet clearance. Or, that's what I thought. I was walking in front of the ambulance and off to the side. I just wanted to be safe and ensure that Bob didn't run over me. I started walking backward carefully watching the top of the ambulance work its way toward the wooden overhang.

I called out, "OK, Bob! Looks good so far! I think you're gonna clear the top."

He kept coming closer. Finally, the overhang was just around two inches above the roof of the ambulance. I thought, "Looks good so far." The top of the ambulance was under the overhang and past the front part. All we had to do now was clear the middle and the rear of the top of the unit. "OK, Bob! Looking good! I think you're gonna make it!" I said.

Bob kept moving slowly forward.

"CRRRUNNNNNCCCHHHHHH!"

I yelled at Bob, "Stop, Bob! Stop!" He stopped. Then I yelled at him again, "Go back, go back!" He put it in reverse and then again, I was shocked when I heard another, "CRRRUNNNNNCCCHHHHHH!"

After the second crunch, I ran to the back of the unit and looked up at the top. There it was! The vent cover of the air conditioner on top of the ambulance was crushed and wrapped around an eight-foot 2x8 board that came off the overhang! The vent cover was around eight inches tall and caught the overhang and literally tore the board off the walkway and was just laying on top of the ambulance. The vent cover was also falling off! We had cleared the top of the ambulance but I failed to see the vent that was protruding from the top!

Bob got off the ambulance and looked up to see the board. "Geez. Is that what I heard? Didn't you see that, Conrad?"

I responded, "Of course I didn't see it, Bob! Maybe you should have been out here 'cause you're taller than me!"

Bob was six feet and three inches tall and, well, he may have seen it, maybe not. So, Bob, being as tall as he is, stepped up onto the running board on the back. He reached up and grabbed the 2x8 board. He also grabbed the vent that was crushed.

I asked him, "Whatcha gonna do with the board?"

He said, "No problem."

He opened the back doors of the ambulance and placed the board, and the crushed vent, into the back of the unit on the floor next to the stretcher! We peeled out of the parking lot! Of course, we didn't tell the attendant what happened since it appeared he had no idea what went on!

I said, "Damn, I didn't see the vent! I should have climbed onto the hood to check the top!"

Bob replied, "That's okay. I'd rather explain the board than explain you falling off the hood of the engine!" Bob was right. I could have fallen off the hood and how would we explain that?

Just as we peeled out of the parking lot, we received a call from Dispatch.

"805, 805, the caller called back and said that she is across the street from where you are. The patient states that she can see the lights of your ambulance across the street. She's on the seventh floor."

"10-4," I replied. I turned to Bob. "Do you think she saw us?"

He said, "Nah, she probably saw the lights but she didn't see what happened."

"I hope not. Damn, we'll be in deep doo-doo."

We turned around the block and came up to the location across the street from the motel. Little did the attendant know what was going on. Actually, when we arrived at the building across the street, we could see the attendant standing in his office. Now, how close was that! He had no idea that we had dismembered his overhang and left with his 2x8 board!

Parked in front of the building where we were supposed to be, Bob and I stepped out of the ambulance. We opened the back doors of the unit to unload the stretcher. We figured we might as well take the stretcher and some equipment knowing that we'd probably transport the patient.

I asked Bob jokingly, "Want to take the board down, too?"

He just chuckled.

As we were walking toward the building, I kept looking back to see if the attendant was outside checking anything out. I was hoping he wouldn't be curious and look up at the walkway!

Once inside, Bob and I made our way to the elevator. I looked at Bob and asked, "What are we gonna do?"

Bob replied, "Not to worry, it's just a board and a vent. Who's gonna look on top of the ambulance anyway?"

"I can only wonder." I replied.

We reached the seventh floor and walked over to the apartment number and knocked on the door. "Ma'am! EMS! Can you open the door?" Bob yelled. She came to the door and opened it. "Ma'am, what seems to be the problem?" Bob asked.

The lady was an approximately eighty-five-year-old female who said, "I just haven't been feeling well. What took you all so long?" she asked. "I could see you all from my window. I thought you knew where to come?"

"Ma'am," I replied, "We didn't know where you were because you hung up and didn't leave an address or apartment number or building. That's why we were across the street." I paused, "But we're here now. So why don't we just take you to the hospital?"

She answered, "OK. Let me get some makeup on."

"Ma'am, you don't have to. You look just fine and pretty, too!" I told her.

"I'm not worried about you. I'm worried about those good-looking doctors there. You never know. They might be single and want to date an older woman!"

I chuckled a little and said, "You know, ma'am, you're right. Where is your makeup bag? I'll get it for you."

She replied, "Right there with my suitcase." Yes, she was ready with suitcase and all.

We went down the elevator and loaded her into the ambulance. We slightly turned our heads toward the motel to see the attendant still at the counter and oblivious to what happened! As we loaded her in to the back of the ambulance, she saw the broken vent hood and the big piece of the 2x8 board.

She asked, "What's that big board for?"

Bob quickly answered, "That's for people who don't behave and we have to hit them!"

She said, "What?!" I looked at Bob in horror.

"I'm just kidding, ma'am. We don't hit people over seventy-five years old!" Bob said jokingly.

She enjoyed that one! She laughed, and we laughed.

We took off and made the short drive to the hospital. As we unloaded her from the ambulance, she asked, "You all gonna keep that board?"

"Of course!" Bob quipped. "I'm glad you behaved, ma'am!"

"Me too!" She replied.

After we left the hospital, we returned to the station, and we still had the crumpled vent cover and the 2x8 board in the back of the unit. In the darkness, we put the vent in the garbage can and the board behind the station. End of story.

So, to make this long story short, and to my surprise, we never heard anything from the maintenance shops or heard from the motel. Today, I'm sure, the missing board and the missing vent cover is still a mystery. Only Bob and I know what happened that evening with the overhang.

Well, now you know too.

Lesson Learned - Don't Get Burned

Well, there are a few lessons here that we can learn and one lesson that I can pass forward to my brother and sister firefighters and paramedics.

Let's start with the little lady that Bob threatened to hit if she didn't behave. I still can't believe he said that! That was not becoming of a professional paramedic!

The lady, obviously, hung up the phone before the dispatcher could get any information from her. The dispatcher had no details and that played a critical role in not responding in a timely manner. As mentioned previously, whenever you call EMS, don't hang up! Let the dispatcher ask all the questions first!

When you call EMS and there is a dire emergency, it will feel like it takes an eternity for EMS or the firefighters to arrive. And, speaking of firefighters, the firefighters will also respond to the call. So, if the firefighters get there before EMS does, don't wave them off and tell them, "Hey, we called EMS not the firefighters! There's no fire!"

They are called and trained to be the first responders if EMS is a long way out. They have practically everything except the ability to transport a patient to the hospital. They can start IVs, shock a patient, take vital signs, and they can also give Dextrose (sugared water) to a diabetic patient. They are there to help!

Now, my message to my colleagues: Make sure you clear the overhang! How many times have you come across an incident where the top of the vehicle does not clear? Now, you damaged the ambulance or fire truck!

This incident with Bob and I could have been prevented. All we had to do was put the unit in reverse and back out. If we would have done that, we would have backed up right to the door of the elderly home!

In summary, remind yourself and your children how to call 9-1-1 in the event of an emergency, including the not-hanging-up part. And, watch the top of the ambulance or fire truck!

Chapter 33
Nice Doggie

"I've fallen and I can't get up!"

Have you all ever seen that commercial? Of course, you have! It happens all the time! The little lady falls and activates her alarm that she's wearing on her chest. With the invention of these devices, many patients have been saved throughout the years. I can attest to that as we were called to respond to a "lady that had fallen and couldn't get up."

I was working at a station on the east side of town when the call came in.

"818, 818. Respond to 4500 Dice Road for a lady that has fallen. She activated her medic alarm hanging on her chest and is laying on the living room floor."

I picked up the radio and answered, "818, we're 10-96."

"10-4" the dispatcher replied. "All we have is that she's on the floor and she couldn't get up."

I answered, "10-4. Thank you."

We got in the unit, turned on the lights and siren and took off. When we arrived, we noticed there were no vehicles out front. The house was well kept as was the front yard. A wooden privacy fence surrounded the home. We got off the ambulance and walked toward the front door. The door was locked.

We knocked on the door and yelled, "Ma'am! We're EMS. Are you still on the floor?"

We heard a faint response. "Yes, I'm on the living room floor. I can hear you!"

Nice Doggie

I walked over to the front window and peeked inside. I could see her laying on her right side. I yelled through the window, "Ma'am, I see you. Can you move any at all?

She cried, "No! I really need some help! Can you help me?"

I told her, "Ma'am, we have to get in but your doors are locked. Is there a back door?"

She said, "Yes! And the door is unlocked, too!"

"Great! I'll come in the back door!" I told my partner, "I'm gonna go around to the gate and into the back yard. I'll open the front door for you."

He said, "Okay. Be careful."

"I will."

I took the medical kit with me in the event I needed it once I got in the back door. The kit was a large "Plano" box that actually looked like a large fishing tackle box. It was pretty sturdy. As I walked to the gate to the right of the house, I tried opening the gate. It was locked.

I yelled to my partner. "I'm gonna jump the fence! The gate's locked!"

He said, "Okay."

I placed the medical kit on the ground right up against the privacy fence. I stood on the kit and reached up and placed my hands on the top of the fence. I figured I was just going to jump up and place my foot on the top and jump over. As my right foot was on the fence, I looked down to see what I was going to be landing on. I was hoping there weren't any holes or anything that would injure me when I landed. Just as I was getting ready to clear the other side, two Dobermans came running around the corner of the house toward me.

I yelled, "Shit!" The two Dobermans ran up to the fence, barking and snarling with their razor-sharp teeth. It seemed like they were just waiting for me to jump onto their feeding ground! They looked hungry! I immediately jumped back and almost fell over the medical kit under me. They continued to bark through the fence and attempted to try to jump over the fence. I could see them trying to tear the wooden fence through the small gaps between each piece of wood. Yikes!

I picked up the medical kit and ran to the front of the house. I told my partner, "There's no way I'm going into the back door! There's two Dobermans that want to tear me apart!"

My partner laughed and told me, "Just look at them and tell them, 'Nice doggie!'"

I responded, "Then YOU jump over the fence!"

He shook his head. "Nah, that's ok."

I could still hear them barking and saw their heads as they were jumping up and down to get a glimpse of "dinner" ... me!

We had to wait for the fire department to show up and cut the burglar bars so we could get to the woman via the window. Once inside, I asked the woman, "Ma'am, why didn't you tell me you had dogs in the backyard?"

Her reply was, "Well, Sonny, you didn't ask!" I shook my head. She was right. I didn't ask and I should have! While we tended to her, I could see the two Dobermans barking at the back glass sliding door. Yeah, they were still mad, barking, and looking hungry.

I asked one of the firefighters, "Hey, can you lock that sliding door? You never know, they just might find a way to open it!"

The firefighter slowly walked up to the sliding door. As he was getting closer to lock the door, the dogs were getting even more aggressive and showed every tooth in their mouth! He locked the door.

Nice Doggie

The patient had a fractured hip. She tripped over a throw rug that she had on the living room floor. We immediately packaged her and placed her on the stretcher. When we were leaving out the front door, she asked, "Can you all put some dog food out for me? My dogs haven't had their breakfast."

I told her, "Ma'am, they almost had breakfast when I almost jumped over the fence!"

She responded, "Oh, they always do that but they really don't bite. They just try to scare people off. They're really nice dogs."

I told her, "Let's just get you to the hospital, OK? We'll tell the neighbor to feed them for you."

She said, "Okay."

We took her to the hospital. On the way to the hospital she told me once again, "They are really nice doggies."

I replied, "Well, I know they are, but they didn't seem to like me."

She said to me, "Not to worry, once they know you, they'll like you."

I thought, "You mean, once they eat me, they'll like me!"

Once we arrived at the hospital, I told the patient, "Ma'am, it was a pleasure meeting you. Please be careful at home and put those rugs away, OK? We don't want you to trip and fall again and then have to take you back to the hospital again. And, I don't want to excite your dogs either!"

She replied, "Okay."

We unloaded her into the ER and went back to restock our ambulance. We got into the unit and left the hospital.

10-96 (We're on the way)

I told my partner as we were headed back to the station, "No, they were not nice doggies. They were *hungry* doggies."

He laughed.

Lesson Learned - Don't Get Burned

Now, don't get me wrong. I love animals, including dogs. But this time, I could have done without the Dobermans. I can still see their teeth poking through the small spaces in between each wooden slat of the fence.

To my colleagues: Always look to see if there are any signs of animals in or around the house! How many of you have been approached by menacing dogs when entering a home to care for a patient? How many of you have been bitten by a dog or any other animal?

To families that have pets that can be territorial or aggressive: in the event you ever have to call EMS or the fire department, lock the dogs up in a room or place them somewhere safe and away from the firefighters or paramedics.

A sign that reads "BEWARE OF DOG" helps in preventing injuries and death, too. In the case with this lady, there were no signs on her property. I had no idea that she had dogs in the yard. With the privacy fence, I couldn't see anything like dog bowls, dog toys, a doghouse, or any remains of other paramedics that jumped over the fence and didn't make it back out! (Just kidding.)

I should have been more careful, too. Common sense, ladies and gentlemen, will definitely prevent any tragedy.

Now, this, I have to mention, too. I understand many families have dogs. There are, and have been, many children that have been injured or killed by the family dog. Also, there have been many incidents where a neighbor's dog has gotten loose and attacked someone who just happens to be walking by. Please ensure that your children not do anything to agitate or annoy the dog.

Please educate yourself and your children about dog safety. This could have been worse.

"Nice doggies" can still hurt you.

Chapter 34
He Looked Like My Son

One early morning, it must have been around 2 a.m., we were called to respond to a house for seizures. I was sound asleep at the station when the call came in.

"841, 841, respond to the 3200 block of Timberhill for seizures. It's supposed to be an infant. Respond to the 3200 block of Timberhill for an infant having seizures."

I sprung up out of my bunk, grabbed the radio and told the dispatcher, "10-4, 841 is 10-96."

My partner and I ran to the unit, climbed in and were on the way in less than two minutes. Knowing it was an infant, it seemed that we just went a little faster. Thinking about my son, Christopher, ten years old, my daughter Andrea, who was three years old and my son, Adrian, just around eighteen months, we sped to the scene. I was hoping by the time we'd arrive; the infant would stop seizing.

We arrived in less than seven minutes.

"841 is 10-97," I told Dispatch. We arrived.

Dispatch responded, "10-4. 841 is 10-97."

The front door was already opened as my partner and I rushed into the house. "EMS! Where are you?" I yelled.

"I'm in here. In the bathroom!" I heard a woman call out.

"Ma'am, keep talking so I can hear you!" I shouted back. I wanted to work my way to the bathroom by listening to her voice. We turned down a hallway and found the bathroom. I walked in to find a young mother holding her infant son, around a year old, who was wrapped in a wet towel. The baby was shivering.

"Ma'am! What happened?" I asked.

"My son had a seizure. He's had a fever since yesterday evening. He's never had a seizure like this!" She began to cry.

"Don't worry, ma'am. He'll be ok." I said. Then I looked at her son's face. My heart stopped for a few seconds. He could have been my son; they looked so alike.

She yelled at us, "I've been trying to cool him off. He had a temperature of 102 last night. I had him in bed with me and felt him shaking. Suddenly, I saw that he was having a seizure! Please do something!"

I grabbed him from the mother's arms and quickly opened the faucet to cool him down with tepid water. I took the towel off. My heart sank as I held him. I almost told the baby, "Mijo, (son) you're gonna be OK!" I felt like I was holding Adrian. I wanted to cry.

As I waited for the water to get a little warmer, he suddenly arched back, and with his eyes rolling back, he started to have another seizure.

The mother screamed in my ear, "Oh my God! He's having another seizure!"

I turned the water on even more. With the baby in my arms, I had to make sure that he didn't fall out of my grip. He was having a grand mal seizure which is one of the worst seizures anyone can have.

I placed him under the faucet carefully. The water was tepid and I had to monitor his breathing as I was bathing him mid-seizure. I was still in shock. I looked at his face and was thinking, "Mijo, you'll be OK!" I still couldn't get over that he looked exactly like my son.

After about a minute, his seizure began to subside. I continued monitoring his breathing. He was breathing well, and he was getting cooler. After around two minutes, he opened his eyes. He looked at me, locking his eyes with mine. He reached for my face with his little hands. I started to tear up. I gave him to his mother who, with outstretched arms, looked at me and asked, "Is he OK?" She was still crying.

With my eyes watering, I said, "He needs to go to the hospital. Get some clothes for him. Grab his diaper bag and make sure he's got some diapers and a bottle. I'll carry him to the stretcher."

As I picked him up, he continued to stare at me. I'm sure he was wondering who I was. He was still in a postictal state, which means he was still incoherent and confused. We walked out to the ambulance with the mother behind me with diaper bag in hand. I instructed her, "Ma'am, sit on the stretcher and I'll have you hold on to your son. I will strap you in and we'll take off."

"Okay," she replied.

I told my partner, "Let's go. Code 3 (lights and sirens). I don't want him to have another seizure on the way to the hospital."

As we were in route to the hospital, I had the mother hold a small oxygen mask inches from his face. I could see that, while he was in his mother's arms, he was staring at me and looking at me as if he knew me. I can still see his little eyes that had confusion and fear, but yet, he looked at ease knowing that he was in the care of his mother as she held him in her arms. I almost felt like asking her, "Can I hold him, too?"

I wanted to hold him to comfort him as much as I would have if my own son had seized. Thank God, Adrian never had a seizure.

I had to take the baby's temperature to see if it had gone down. He didn't like that I had to take a rectal temperature to get an accurate reading. His temperature was now 100 degrees. Fortunately, his temperature had stabilized with the tepid bath I gave him before we left the house.

We arrived at the hospital and the mother asked me, "Do I need to get off the stretcher?"

"No ma'am, just sit on the stretcher and we'll take you in with your son."

She obliged, "Okay. Thank you."

We went into the ER and were directed into a room by an ER nurse. I gave her my report. The nurse was talking to the mother with her son still in her arms.

I waved at the mother as we walked out of the room, "Take care, and I hope your son gets better soon!"

The mother replied, "Thank you very much." She said to her baby, "Say bye to the man. Can you say bye to the man?" He looked at me as he peeked around the nurse. He slowly picked up his little hand and waved with his fingers. I wanted to cry.

I waved back, "Bye, little guy! I hope you get better! Bye, Mijo!" We walked out and hopped back into the ambulance.

On the way back to the station, I was rather quiet. My partner asked me, "You okay?"

I responded, "Yeah, this kid looked like my son."

"I figured that," he said. "You looked nervous."

"Was it that obvious?" I asked him.

"Yep, pretty much," he replied.

I told him, "I don't let my emotions get to me, but this was different. It's much different when you see someone that looks like your kid. It gets to you."

My partner replied, "Yeah, it would get to me too."

We arrived at the station and I went to bed. It was four o'clock in the morning.

That morning, when I got home, I woke my kids up. Still sleepy-eyed, I snuggled them in my arms and gave them big hugs and told them, "I love you very much."

They replied, "I love you, too, Daddy. Can we go back to sleep?"

After I hugged them and told them "I love you," I felt better. Thank God.

Lesson Learned - Don't Get Burned

Every child is different. Every *body* is different. In the case of this child, his temperature spiked and suddenly caused a febrile seizure. A febrile seizure is a convulsion caused by an elevated temperature that affects the body and the brain. A seizure, depending on the body temperature, can last from seconds to minutes. The seizure will deprive the brain of oxygen which is dangerous. After a seizure, they will relax and possibly go unconscious. They may urinate or defecate on themselves.

What can a parent or caregiver do to prevent a febrile seizure? Here are some tips:

- If the infant or child starts to feel ill, always monitor their temperature. It is best to have a rectal thermometer for infants and small children, in order to have the most accurate reading.
- Call your **pediatrician**. They will know what medication to prescribe for the fever. Keep up with the dosages and times that you administer the medication.
- Don't wrap an infant or child with a blanket! It only makes them hotter. The goal is to cool them down.

Once an infant or child has a febrile seizure, they are susceptible to having more. **Call EMS in the event of a seizure!**

Treat a seizure as something that is urgent. Give as much information as you can to the first responders. Include temperature readings, times of medication, and whether or not the child has any allergies.

Hug and love your child every day. I don't care how old they are! Enjoy them.

Chapter 35
"Who Was That Masked Man?"

Do you all remember that phrase? If you're a baby boomer, you probably do. The "Masked Man" was the Lone Ranger who would come in and save the day. The victims, who were rescued by the cowboy in white would ask as he rode off in the sunset, "Who was that masked man?" Everyone would say, "That's the Lone Ranger!"

Here is my updated version to the masked man story.

It was a Sunday afternoon and I was working at a station just south of the downtown area. Fire Station #13 was a cool station that was built in 1929. This station was small and housed a fire truck and an EMS unit. I was working overtime.

The call came in from the dispatcher right around 2 p.m.

"813, 813, respond to The Little Red Barbeque Place for a choking victim. That is for a choking victim. A bystander is trying to do the Heimlich Maneuver. The patient, a 40-year-old female, is still conscious."

"813 is 10-96," I replied on the radio.

The Little Red Barbeque Place is a well-known restaurant that has been around for years. It was popular for its steaks and waitresses who wore cowgirl outfits, including holsters with toy guns. They looked like they just came out of a Western movie!

With a patient choking, I knew we had only three minutes to get there before the patient would go unconscious. Being a CPR instructor too, I knew that if an adult is choking they only have three minutes before they pass out due to lack of oxygen, and once they pass out, they have another three minutes before their heart stops and they go into a cardiac arrest. Unfortunately, it would take us five minutes.

When we arrived at the restaurant, we pulled up right to the door. The manager was outside waiting for us.

"How's the patient?" I asked.

"She's better now. She's just a little scared," The manager replied.

"Is she breathing now?" I asked.

He replied, "Yes, someone did the Heimlich Maneuver."

"Great!" I answered.

As he escorted us inside, we arrived to find a female sitting at a table not far from the cashier. She looked pretty terrified. I asked her, "Ma'am, how are you?"

She replied, "I feel better now. I was choking on a piece of steak when this man came behind me and did the Heimlich Maneuver on me. He saved my life."

As I looked behind me, there was a gentleman standing there who I thought was the lifesaver. I turned around and said, "Sir, thank you for saving her life. Is this your wife?"

"No, sir," he replied. "I was sitting at this table," pointing to the table close by, "when I heard her get up and started banging on the table. Then this man came from the counter, where I guess he was paying, noticed that she was choking, walked over, and did the Heimlich on her."

"Where did he go?" I asked the man.

He responded, "He went back to the counter to get his change and just left."

"Just left?" I asked him.

He said, "Yep, just did the Heimlich on her, went to get his change, and walked out the front door. He was like the Lone Ranger. He just disappeared."

Well, this is what happened. There was a gentleman that was at the cashier paying his bill. When he heard the woman banging on the table, apparently, he turned around, walked up behind her and administered the Heimlich Maneuver. After the piece of meat came out, he walked back up to the cashier, got his change, and walked out the door.

It was just like the Lone Ranger. I would have asked, "Who was that masked man?" The case of the "masked man" still is unclear today. No one knew what happened to this "Lone Ranger."

"Hi-Yo Silver! Away!" That's what the Lone Ranger would say as he pulled on the reins of his horse, and the Lone Ranger would wave and ride off into the sunset. I wish there were more "Lone Rangers" out there. He saved this lady's life. My thanks to this heroic "Lone Ranger."

Lesson Learned - Don't Get Burned

Once again, here is someone that could have died from choking. Fortunately for this lady, there was someone there that knew what to do: the Heimlich Maneuver. Actually, I did tell her about doing the universal sign of a choking victim by grabbing her throat with both hands. She said she knew it but she panicked.

You never know when you have to do this lifesaving technique. This is why it is so important to take a CPR class so you can be prepared in the event someone should start to choke. With the average response time of seven minutes for a fire truck or paramedics, this is just too long to wait to do something. As new parents or grandparents, it is imperative to know what to do in the event your child or grandchild is choking. Learn it as soon as you can. Enroll in a CPR class. Believe me, you'll never regret it.

CPR is like a smoke alarm. You have it there just in case and you hope you never have to use it. But, if you do, you'll be prepared.

I have been a CPR and First Aid instructor for almost forty years and I am proud to say that since then, I know of sixteen people who been saved after their rescuers took my class. Most have been saved by doing the Heimlich Maneuver.

I know of many infants, children, and adults that would be alive today if someone close by might have known how to do CPR or the Heimlich Maneuver. Please, don't let this be you. Enroll in a class today. I'd rather you live

317

and regret that you took a class than see someone die and regret that you didn't. At least try. You may be a "Lone Ranger" someday.

Chapter 36
What? Not Again?

Well, after we left The Little Red Barbeque Place for the choking patient, we headed back to the fire station. I thought I'd lay down for a while and take a little nap. While we were pulling back into the bay, we got another call.

"813, 813, return to the Little Red Barbeque Place for another choking victim. A bystander is attempting the Heimlich Maneuver and the patient is still conscious. Do you receive?" the dispatcher asked.

"10-4," I replied, "We're 10-96."

The dispatcher repeated, "Be advised, the patient is still conscious."

"10-4," I answered.

I looked at my partner and exclaimed, "Not again! What's going on over there?"

My partner jokingly responded, "They're all choking!"

"I guess so," I replied.

We got in the ambulance and took off again. We knew that it would take us no less than six minutes to arrive. As mentioned before, that is still too long for a patient to go without any oxygen.

We were about one block away when the dispatcher called us back.

"813, 813, you've been cancelled. 813, you can cancel."

My partner picked up the radio and replied, "10-4. 813 cancelled." We turned off the lights and sirens. We were only half a block away, and we could actually see the parking lot of the restaurant.

I asked my partner, "Hey, since we're actually here, why don't we go check if the patient is OK?"

"What for?" he answered.

"Well, now that we're turning in the parking lot, we should just go in and see if the patient is alright. Hey, you never know. Let's go in real quick. I might order a steak or something."

He reluctantly replied, "Okay. It's up to you." It was apparent that he didn't want to continue on this call.

"813 to Dispatch. 813 to Dispatch. We're in the parking lot and we're gonna check the patient out," I radioed.

"10-4." Dispatch replied.

We pulled up to the entrance of the restaurant to find the same manager waiting for us. I asked him as I opened the door, "Sir, what's going on?"

He replied, "I have no idea. This isn't good for us! Anyway, did you get the notice that we cancelled you?"

"We did, but I wanted to see if the patient was okay. Can you take us to the patient?"

"Sure," he replied. "But he seems to be fine now. He can breathe."

"That's great. Let me just take a look at him if you and he don't mind..."

The manager led us to the back of the restaurant, and we found a patient sitting on a bench at the table. He was an approximately seventy-year-old male. I introduced myself.

"Sir, my name is Conrad, and this is my partner. I understand you almost choked on something."

"Yes, but my nephew got behind me and just about crushed my ribs." He then looked over his shoulder and pointed at him. "That's him!"

I went over to congratulate him. "Thank you very much, sir. You saved your uncle's life!"

"I took a CPR class a few weeks ago. I kind of remembered what to do," he said.

I told him, "Well, you did great! Your uncle owes you dinner!"

The uncle replied with a laugh, "I'm having fish this time. It's easier to chew and swallow."

Just then, I noticed his uncle grabbing his chest.

I asked him, "Sir, are you okay?"

As he clutched his chest, he responded, "I'm feeling a little chest pain." I wondered what might be ailing him and asked if he had a history of heart disease. "Sir, have you ever had a heart attack before?" I asked.

"Yes, I had open heart surgery six months ago. I guess I got a little excited. My ribs hurt, too."

I nodded. "Sir, why don't you sit down. Let me take your blood pressure and pulse. I want to make sure you're okay."

I asked my partner, "Can you get the stretcher and the heart monitor?"

My partner rudely responded by asking the patient, "Sir, do you want to go to the hospital with us or don't you?"

I asked my partner again, "Can you just go get the stretcher and the monitor?" I was a little annoyed as it seemed he didn't want to transport the patient. He just kind of rolled his eyes and slowly turned to the door to go outside.

I got on the radio and told Dispatch. "813 to Dispatch. We have a patient that needs to be transported. Our patient is now having chest pain."

"10-4," Dispatch responded.

I told the patient, "Sir, let us take you to the hospital just to see if everything is alright."

He said, "Well, I think I'll be okay."

I checked his pulse. It was not normal. His pulse was irregular; there was something going on. My partner came in with a "I don't give a crap" look on his face. I took the heart monitor and placed the ECG electrodes on his chest.

"Sir," I said, "Let's take a look at your heart. I want to check to see what your heart is doing." He obliged. As I was placing the ECG electrodes on his chest, I told my partner to get oxygen on the patient. Again, he kind of rolled his eyes. Looking frustrated, he motioned and handed the oxygen mask to me. I thought, "Okay, that's it."

"We're transporting him right now and we're taking him Code 3 with lights and sirens. Do you have any questions, partner? Put the O2 mask on him." I demanded.

Silently, he obliged. I couldn't believe I had to demand we transport this man. My partner was annoying me but I had to concentrate on my patient.

As I was looking at the heart monitor to see what his heart was doing, I noticed that he was "throwing PVCs." He had an irregular and abnormal heart rhythm which explained the chest pain. He was having another heart attack. Now, it seemed that my partner was a little more interested.

I told the patient, "Sir, you are having an issue with your heart. We're taking you to the hospital so they can check you in."

"Okay," said the patient, still clutching his chest.

We gave him a nitroglycerin tablet to see if the pain would subside. Fortunately, it did. We put him on the stretcher and wheeled him to the ambulance. As I was setting up to start an IV, he asked if he really needed the IV. I told him it was necessary in the event he needed some medication. We loaded him up and transported him in Code 3 mode.

Fortunately, the patient survived his heart attack again.

I am glad I decided to continue to the restaurant after we were canceled. And, fortunately, I didn't work with that partner again. I am also glad my "sixth sense" kicked in. If we ever got cancelled and were close by, I would check on the patient anyway... just in case.

Lesson Learned - Don't Get Burned

With the excitement of almost choking to death, the patient's heart had a "near death" experience. His heart was suddenly deprived of oxygen while he was choking, and with his recent open-heart surgery, I made the decision to transport. Although his airway was cleared by the abdominal thrusts, it put a strain on his heart, which induced another heart attack.

Also, this patient didn't really want to go with us. His statement of "I'll be OK" did not suffice for me. He was in denial and much too excited. This is dangerous because it will only cause a delay in treatment or transport which can prove to be fatal.

If someone complains of signs and symptoms of a heart attack, call 9-1-1. Always remember, these signs and symptoms may go away, but there can be some underlying issues going on! If in doubt, check it out!

Another lesson I learned was one that I lived by: go with your gut instinct. My gut instinct or "sixth sense" told me to continue with the call.

I learned that partners have different personalities and there can be times when you have to make a "command decision." I made the decision to transport this patient, and I made the decision to never work with that paramedic again. If one of your partners makes the decision to transport, "Let's go" should be the response. You and the patient have a lot to lose. You can lose your job and the patient could lose his life.

Chapter 37
The Riverwalk

Have you ever been to the Riverwalk here in San Antonio? What a sight to see! The river meanders through the downtown area, surrounded by restaurants, historical buildings, the River Center Mall, hotels, and much more. The sights can certainly be joyful, peaceful, and eventful. It was also the Riverwalk that could have been my uncle's last sight to see…

In the summer of 1985, my Uncle Leonard and my Aunt Connie, my mom's sister, were visiting from Riverside, California. Back in the 60s, they had moved from San Antonio to Riverside to look for a brighter future and job opportunities.

Every time they came down to San Antonio, one of their favorite spots to visit was the Riverwalk. That and eating Bar-B-Q! Yep, every time my Uncle Leonard visited, he'd say "Let's go eat Bar-B-Q! I want some barbeque ribs!" So, we'd make sure that we made plans for barbeque as soon as we pulled out of the airport. We were "10-96" to eat ribs!

One afternoon during their summer visit, they wanted to go take a stroll down the Riverwalk. I picked up Mom and Dad, my Aunt Connie and my Uncle Leonard. We drove into the downtown area, and I knew I wanted to park as close as I could to the Riverwalk so they wouldn't have to walk too far. What I did was drop them off on Market Street which is adjacent to the stairs leading to the river.

As they closed the door to the car, I told them, "I'll be right back. I'm going to park the car and then I'll meet you at the bottom of the stairs. OK?"

Dad replied, "Okay, son."

My uncle quipped, "Don't get lost!"

I told him, "Don't worry, Uncle Leonard! I know the area pretty good!" And I did. Working in the downtown area with EMS, we responded to many calls in and around the Riverwalk. It seemed that every shift I worked, we were called to either a fall, heart attack, seizures, construction sites, or just about anything around this attraction.

I pulled away from dropping them off and drove to the nearest parking garage, which was a block away. I wanted to be sure I was close enough that, after we were done, I wouldn't have far to go to retrieve the car. I parked the car and walked the one block back to the stairs. I went down the stairs to the Riverwalk and found them sitting on a bench waiting for me.

Uncle Leonard asked, "You ready, Conrad Jr.?" He'd always called me "Jr." or "Conrad Jr." That was my Dad's name and he never wanted to get confused, not that he would. He said that my dad and I looked and talked the same. He couldn't tell the difference when Dad or I would call him on the phone. He even told me one time that Dad and I had the same walk! Do you look like your dad or mom or walk and talk the same?

Anyway, I replied, "Yes sir, Uncle Leonard! Ready when you are!"

He got up from the bench and told my Aunt Connie, who was also sitting on the bench, "Let's go, Connie!" He always called her by her first name.

There were quite a few people walking along the Riverwalk. It was a Saturday and a bright and sunny day, which accounted for the crowds enjoying the beautiful weather and scenery. I was walking behind Mom, Dad, and my aunt and uncle. Then, after walking around fifty feet, I noticed my uncle holding on to my aunt as he stopped at a bench to sit down. It seemed he was struggling to breathe.

I looked at him and asked, "Uncle Leonard, are you okay?"

He had his hands on his knees, looked up at me and replied, "Just a little hard to breathe, but I'm OK. Just give me a few minutes to catch my breath."

I told him, "Let me check you out. I'll take your pulse real quick."

He replied and waved me away, "I'll be OK. I just need a few minutes. I'll just sit here for a little bit."

Aunt Connie told him, "Let Conrad Jr. check you out. Maybe there's something wrong with you."

My uncle replied, "No, it's okay. I'm ready to go now."

I replied, "Uncle Leonard, just take it easy. We're in no hurry."

He slowly got up from the bench and started to walk. He said, "Let's go. I'm ready." But he still huffed a little. I grabbed his arm and assisted him as he tried to continue.

Mom said, "Maybe we should just go home. We can come back tomorrow."

My uncle replied, "No, what if I'm not here tomorrow? I want to see the Riverwalk."

As we walked a few more feet, he held on to my aunt's arm which was kind of unusual. I never really saw them hold hands, much less walk arm in arm. I walked behind them again. Mom turned around and said, "He doesn't look too good."

I asked her, "How did he do when he was coming down the stairs?"

"He said he was a little short of breath. Then he sat down to rest."

I walked up to my uncle and looked at him more closely; he was a little pale now. "Uncle Leonard, sit here while I check your pulse. You don't look well." This time he sat down. "I'm gonna check your pulse. Are you having any chest pain or discomfort?" I asked.

He replied, "No, just a little short of breath. I'll be OK."

I checked his pulse. It was irregular. It seemed to skip a beat which indicated something was wrong. He started to look even more pale and somewhat ashen. At that point, I knew he was in trouble.

"Uncle Leonard, you need to get to a hospital. I'm gonna call EMS so they can get you to a hospital really quick."

He refused. "No, I just need to rest. I'll be okay. I don't need to go to a hospital."

I replied, "Please, Uncle Leonard, you really need to go. I'm afraid you may be having a heart attack. Your heart is beating irregularly, and that is not good. Let me call EMS so they can take you to the nearest hospital."

Even Mom and Dad, along with my Aunt Connie, tried to persuade him to let me call EMS.

Adamantly, he said, "I'll go only if you take me. I am not going in no ambulance!" He was getting a little excited. Not the thing to do right now. It would only make him worse.

"Okay, Uncle Leonard, I will take you, but you must stay right here so I can go get the car. I don't want you to over exert yourself. Please stay right here." I ordered. I turned around and told Mom, "Don't let him move. I'm gonna go get the car. If he passes out, check for a pulse at his neck. Fortunately, I had showed Mom and Dad how to check for a carotid pulse when Mom was taking care of my grandmother. "If he goes unconscious and you don't feel a pulse, call EMS and start CPR."

She said, "Okay, son."

I turned around and told my uncle, "Uncle Leonard, I'll be back in five minutes. Don't move!"

He said, "I won't go anywhere."

I immediately turned around and ran like a bat out of hell up the stairs and turned the corner racing to the parking lot where I parked the car. I ran so fast my heart was beating a hundred miles per hour! I finally got to the car which I had parked on the third floor of the parking garage. I started the car, pulled out of my parking space and raced through the parking garage. Once I got down to the first level, I arrived at the gate to find the parking attendant standing by the gate. He looked at me with wide eyes, as if I was going to fly past him and tear the gate down.

I opened my window and yelled at him, "Please, open the gate! My uncle is having a heart attack, and I have to drive him to the hospital now! I am a paramedic with San Antonio. Please open the gate!" He gave me a puzzled look, but he could see the fear and anxiety on my face. He opened the gate. "Thank you, very much! I'll come back and pay you later," I yelled.

He replied, "Don't worry about it! I hope he's OK!"

I pulled out of the parking garage, turned the corner, and raced down the one-way street and headed toward the area where I had dropped them off. I took a quick left and literally made a U-turn on a one-way street. I knew if a police officer would have seen me, he would have stopped me and given me a ticket. But then again, that would not have been bad since I could have used him as a police escort!

As I approached the area where I had dropped them off, I figured I'd stop, put on my emergency flashers and run down the stairs to meet them on the Riverwalk. As I was stopping, I suddenly saw Dad and Mom coming up the stairs. Behind them, I saw my aunt and Uncle Leonard coming up the stairs, too. I thought to myself, "Oh no! I told them to stay down by the Riverwalk!"

My uncle looked like crap. He was pale and sweaty. His shortness of breath had worsened. He didn't look good at all. As a paramedic, I'd seen these patients and, unfortunately, some of them would die on me. I didn't want that to happen. Right then, I thought I'd call EMS but it would have taken them longer with all the traffic in the downtown area.

My dad explained, "He wanted to come upstairs to meet you. He was feeling worse."

I responded, "OK. Thanks." To my uncle, I said softly, "Uncle Leonard, let's get in the car." I didn't want to get him too excited. I tried to stay as calm as possible. His heart didn't need any more excitement.

I put him in the front passenger seat so I could keep an eye on him. I put on his seat belt. Mom, Dad, and Aunt Connie got in the back seat. I ran around the front of the car and quickly got in, put on my seat belt and drove off. I raced down East Commerce with my emergency flashers on and headed west toward Santa Rosa Hospital which was ten (long) blocks away. At every stop light, I started to honk my horn to let people know I had an emergency. I was weaving in and out of traffic. The worst that could happen right now was my uncle passing out and going into a cardiac arrest. Or, another nightmare would be getting into a car crash.

My uncle had worsened. The excitement of going through traffic probably got him excited too. However, if EMS had picked him up, they too would have their lights and sirens on. Not to mention they would have delayed transporting him so they could start an IV, put him on oxygen and a heart monitor. And, that would have excited him also. I took a big chance by driving him.

Finally, I could see the hospital to my right. "Great! Two more blocks!" I thought. I took a quick right and almost didn't see a car coming from my left. I slammed my brakes. He honked at me as he went past me and made a hand gesture. If he only knew why I was in a hurry.

I proceeded slowly and took a right. Two more blocks... that's all I needed. Up ahead, I needed only one more traffic light. It was green. I thought to myself, "Please stay green! Please stay green!" It didn't change. I went through the traffic light and took a quick left into the emergency room entrance. I quickly stopped right where the ambulances park. Fortunately, there were no ambulances there.

I stopped the car. I looked at my uncle and told him, "Uncle Leonard, don't get out. I'm going in to get a wheelchair and tell them I have you in the car. Please, don't get out!" I turned to my mom to make sure, "Mom, don't let him get out."

I ran around the front of the car and up to the emergency room doors. Fortunately, being a paramedic and working with EMS, I knew the code to open the doors. As the doors opened, I ran in and yelled at one of the ER nurses. "I have my uncle in the car. He's having an MI! (myocardial infarction, medical term for heart attack). He's gonna crash. I'm getting a wheelchair!"

She ran around the counter and ran behind me. The nurse knew who I was and what I was talking about. She ran out behind me and yelled to another nurse behind her, "Get the doc! We've got an MI!"

I ran down the ramp with the wheelchair and could see my uncle with his head back and eyes closed. I thought, "Oh no! He's crashed!" Mom and Dad were outside the car with my Aunt Connie. My dad quickly opened the door.

"He closed his eyes. He felt tired," Dad said.

I said, "OK." Then I looked at my uncle and said, "Uncle Leonard!" He slowly opened his eyes. "We're gonna put you on this wheelchair. Just take it easy." Thinking back, I should have rolled out a stretcher to him so he could just get on a stretcher, however, it would have taken two people to roll it out. I helped him get out of the front seat. The nurse inched the wheelchair close to the door. I slowly helped him stand up.

"OK, Uncle Leonard, turn around and just sit down." Another technician came out of the ER to assist. I asked him, "Is the doctor right inside?"

He replied, "Yes, he's getting everything ready. The nurses are setting up an IV and they're also calling for chest X-rays. He's going into the first room to the left."

The "first room to the left" is usually the room where critical patients go in when transported by an ambulance. There, they have everything in the event a critical patient should crash, or EMS comes in doing CPR. I told my Aunt Connie, "Tia, we're going right inside to the room. One of the staff members will take you to registration to get some information from you. Mom and Dad will follow you."

She said, "Okay. Is he gonna be alright?"

I said, "They're gonna check him right away, Tia. He's having a heart attack, but they'll take good care of him."

I pushed the wheelchair up the ramp and into the "room to the left." As we got him into the room, all the staff was ready. I knew most of them, but the doctor was a visiting doctor that I didn't know. The doctor asked me as we were getting him off the wheel chair, "What happened?"

I told him, "We were at the Riverwalk and he suddenly complained of shortness of breath. He has no previous history of heart attacks and only has high blood pressure. He has no allergies and takes medication for his hypertension. My aunt is right outside getting him registered."

"Let's do a 12-lead ECG on him and notify the cath lab just in case," the doctor ordered. He continued. "Also, get some cardiac enzymes and chest X-rays now."

Everyone was working in unison. The techs were undressing him. I was looking for a vein on his right arm. A nurse was getting oxygen on him while another nurse was documenting the information I was providing.

The administrative secretary asked me, "Does he have family here?"

I replied, "Yes, she went to see you. Did you see her up front?"

"No."

I said, "This is my uncle. My aunt will have all the information for you. He's retired military if you were going to ask about insurance. She should be outside with my parents. They're probably in the waiting room."

She replied, "Well, I didn't see them."

"Ma'am! Can you step out, please? I'm working on my uncle." I turned away from her; she had a poor disposition and seemed to have a poor attitude. "I found a good vein over here. Can you hand me a tourniquet?" I asked the tech.

With the doctors and nurses knowing that I was in EMS, they had no qualms about my working on my uncle with them. I started the IV. I reported: "IV's in! Eighteen gauge. Left AC (antecubital area of the arm)."

"Everybody clear. I'm taking X-rays!" the technician exclaimed.

We stepped out of the ER room to allow them to take X-rays. Everyone looked concerned as my uncle was still very cool and clammy. The doctor was looking at the ECG.

"ST elevation," he said. "Let's get ready to take him to the cath lab."

Damn, I thought. He was in bad shape. ST elevation indicated he was having a massive heart attack. "Doc," I said, "I'll talk to my aunt and let her know what's going on."

The ER staff was preparing to take him to the cath lab. He still wasn't looking well. He was in no pain and his shortness of breath had subsided. He still looked pale and clammy. I said a quick prayer. "Dear Lord, take care of Uncle Leonard, please. I pray to you that he makes it." He had no history of any previous heart attacks which was good, however, due to the abnormality of his heart and the severity of this episode, it was going to be touch-and-go.

The ER staff wheeled him on the stretcher to the cath lab. I stepped out into the waiting room where Mom, Dad, and my aunt sat and held hands praying. I had a lot of faith in Mom and Dad as they ministered to the injured, sick, and dying. I always told them they had the hotline to Heaven!

The doctor mentioned that it would take a couple of hours to do the procedure which included prepping him and go into recovery. But that was if everything went right. We waited anxiously in the waiting room... praying. We also reminisced about good times with my Uncle Leonard.

Here's one great time we talked about:

There was a time when I was eighteen years old and had just graduated from high school. My dad made a down payment on a 1970 Ford Mustang as my high school graduation gift. It was burnt orange and it was the coolest thing on the block! Boy, I didn't know I had that many friends until I bought it! Dad made the down payment and I made the payments of $62 a month! Unreal, right?

I wanted to take a trip to go see my aunt and uncle in Riverside, California. I told Mom and Dad that it was going to be my graduation present to myself, to take a trip to California in my Mustang! They didn't mind at all. I was taking my brother, Abel, with me. Yep, I was eighteen years old and my brother was thirteen! Two young Hispanics driving thirteen hundred miles! Hiiiijole (pronounced: E-hō-lě, English translation: Wow!) I had $500 in cash for the trip. That should be enough! Wrong.

While visiting my Aunt Connie and Uncle Leonard for a few days, my brother and I seemed to have run out of money. So, God Bless them, my aunt and uncle decided to "help us" by following us back to San Antonio. They also wanted to make the trip to ensure we returned home safely and not have to sell my car to get back! And, it was another great opportunity for them to go to San Antonio and visit Mom and Dad.

So, we loaded up our cars and headed back to San Antonio with my aunt and uncle following behind us! My uncle had two walkie talkies that my cousin lent us. It was funny as we gave ourselves code names. My aunt's car was yellow and, of course, my car was orange. Their code name was "Yellow Bird" and mine was "Orange Goose." While we were on the road and we needed to go to the bathroom, we'd say, "Orange Goose to Yellow Bird, Orange Goose to Yellow Bird! Come in!"

My uncle or aunt would answer, "Come in, Orange Goose, this is Yellow Bird!" That was so cool!

"Yellow Bird, we're making a pit stop to make a drop. Do you copy?" I would say.

They would respond, "10-4, Orange Goose. Copy that. We're right behind you!"

So much fun. We made it back safely back to San Antonio. One thousand three hundred miles of "Yellow Bird to Orange Goose!" It was a blast!

With all the reminiscing, time had passed quickly. Suddenly, we saw the doctor come out into the waiting area. He had a big smile on his face. We felt a great relief. Mom and my aunt hugged each other as the heart surgeon walked up to us.

My aunt asked him, "How is he, doctor?"

The doctor replied, "He did well. He had a severely clogged artery and we had to unclog two more. He's not out of the woods yet."

"What do you mean?" my aunt asked.

The doctor replied, "He will need open heart surgery because his arteries are too clogged. We were able to unclog them; however, they are damaged as well. We have no choice. I understand you are from California."

"Yes, we are. Do we need to do the surgery here or can we go back to Riverside? His doctor's there."

The doctor answered, "We can stabilize him here and give him medications. I talked to his doctor and gave him my report. He will need to go to the hospital as soon as you get to California. He needs surgery ASAP. I'd say within the next three or four days. His doctor told me he would schedule his surgery as soon as you get to Riverside."

My aunt confirmed, "We can make plans to leave tomorrow."

"Let him stay overnight so we can watch him and make sure all is going well. As I mentioned, I've talked to his doctor and he recommends that as soon as you fly into Riverside, he goes straight to the hospital and he'll do the surgery the day he arrives or soon after."

My aunt started to cry. My mom hugged her. Dad hugged both of them.

The heart surgeon said, "You got here in the nick of time. Another thirty minutes, he would have gone into a cardiac arrest and he could have died. You got him here alive."

"The Lord got him here alive," Dad told him. "And so did my son."

I said, "We got him here together, Dad. We all did."

My Aunt Connie and Uncle Leonard flew back to California two days later. He did so well he didn't even have to fly back by an air medical plane. He had a quadruple bypass the following day and did very well. Yes, the physicians there told my aunt that he could have died while visiting San Antonio. "He was very fortunate" was a common quote from his physician and surgeon.

I was able to see Uncle Leonard a few times when he came down to visit with Aunt Connie. Still, every time he came to San Antonio, it was barbeque time! He just didn't have that much brisket. My uncle would say, "I'm having a salad, too." Then he laughed.

10-96 (We're on the way)

All this happened in the summer of 1985. Uncle Leonard died on March 21, 2001. My Aunt Connie passed away four years later.

Today, every time I drive past the Riverwalk or eat barbeque, I think about both of them. I am indebted to them for accompanying us and our little "convoy" back to San Antonio. It is a memory I cherish.

This story is dedicated to you, Uncle Leonard, I'm glad I was with you visiting The Riverwalk. Rest in Peace to you and Aunt Connie. Love you both.

Lesson Learned - Don't Get Burned

As I finished writing this story, I was trying to think of the lesson I learned, or, what we could learn from this. One mistake that could have been fatal was my uncle walking back up the stairs to the street level above the Riverwalk. But, thank God, he made it. Another one was not calling EMS when I should have even if my uncle would have gotten upset. But, then again, all turned out well.

My recommendation: Whenever you have a family member that complains of signs and symptoms of a heart attack, don't hesitate to call EMS. Or, for that matter, call EMS for any condition that would warrant being taken to the hospital.

Once again, familiarize yourself with signs and symptoms of a heart attack. Time is of the essence. I took a chance when I drove Uncle Leonard to the hospital. Ask any emergency room doctor or nurse about people that have driven their loved one to the hospital only to have them arrive in worse condition, or much worse, die along the way.

I took a chance with my own life once. I won't do that again. I'll put that story in my next book!

Chapter 38
As Strong As Kong

Working in the downtown area brought many interesting calls. The downtown area was full of visitors from out of town, office personnel, students at the local community college, and locals who worked there. Station #6 was located just north of the downtown area on West Russell Street among very nice homes that are worth over a million dollars. The station was built in 1929; as a two-story firehouse with three sliding poles, it was a unique building that was nestled between a two-story home (that is now a four-plex apartment) and a home that was built in the late 1800s that supposedly had a wine cellar that was over three thousand square feet.

One late morning, while we were waiting for one of the firefighters to cook lunch, our EMS radio went off and we heard the dispatcher say, "806, 806, respond to the corner of Evergreen and San Pedro, Evergreen and San Pedro for a psychiatric patient. PD is on the way."

"10-4, 806 is 10-96," I responded. It was 11:30 a.m. I told my partner, Fred, "Well, so much for lunch!"

I could smell the bacon cooking as the firefighter was preparing BLT sandwiches for us. Bacon, lettuce, and tomatoes on toasted bread with mayonnaise was one of my favorite sandwiches! I hollered at the cook, "Hey, save a sandwich for us!"

"We'll try!" he joked.

We hurried to the ambulance. I still had the smell of bacon in my nostrils... I hoped this would be a quick call! Thankfully, the location wasn't far at all. As a matter of fact, it was around seven blocks away and would only take us three minutes to get there. Even with lunch time traffic, we'd have no problem.

I recognized the location when we arrived. It was a local restaurant and bar. I'd never been there but had driven past it many times. "806 is 10-97. We're at the scene," I told Dispatch.

As we pulled up, we could see two police cars, cars parked on the street and a truck. It was a utility vehicle belonging to the city. It appeared to be a popular place to eat for many who worked downtown.

"Great. PD is here. I'm sure they have everything under control," I said. We got our equipment from the back of the unit and entered through the front entrance. As we walked in, the manager approached us.

"He's on the back patio with the police. He's going crazy!" he yelled.

I asked him, "What's going on?"

"I have no idea! I think he's on drugs or something!" he replied.

I opened the back door to the patio. Suddenly, I saw two police officers struggling and trying to restrain this guy who looked like he was on drugs. The officers were trying to subdue and handcuff him, but with his size, that wasn't working!

One of the officers shouted, "We have a backup coming! We don't know what's going on!"

Fred and I jumped in to assist the officers. Another manager joined in, as did a patron. Even with the six of us, it was a struggle to restrain this guy who was around six feet four inches tall and weighed around 250 pounds, if not more.

He was so strong, he literally tossed me over; I tumbled into a chair. It was like "King Kong" throwing little men across the patio! I got back up and joined in the struggle again only to be tossed aside! My partner, who was as strong as an ox, was also thrown back. Then one of the officers finally grabbed his feet to bring him down. The other officers arrived.

Between all *eight* of us, we finally had this man wrestled to the cement floor of the patio. In the struggle, I noticed he was wearing a uniform with his name on it. He worked for the utility company. I noticed that the other patron who was helping us was wearing the same uniform.

"Do you guys work together?" I asked him as we held the patient on the ground. Even then, it was still tough to keep him down.

He replied, "Yes, that's my friend! I don't know what happened. We were waiting for our food and suddenly he just got up and started getting violent!"

Fred asked, "Does he do drugs or take any medication?"

"I don't know!" the co-worker answered.

"What's his name?"

"Robert."

We still had him on the ground. He was still fighting to get up. With his uniform on and his utility truck outside, I thought if this guy is working, he can't be on drugs. Then, I noticed that one of the officers was standing on his arm. He had his foot on his wrist and one above his elbow. I was actually sitting on his left leg while my partner and the coworker had his other leg restrained. In between the officer's two feet, I could see a couple of huge veins sticking right out on his arm. Then it dawned on me.

I asked the patient's friend, "Sir, is he a diabetic?!"

"Not that I know of, sir!"

I had an idea. "Fred! Set up an IV real quick for me! I want to give him some Dextrose!" Dextrose is sugared water that comes in a prefilled syringe used for diabetic patients.

Fred answered, "Got it!" If he was a diabetic, this would help him. I hoped.

Still struggling to keep him down, I wished we had some kind of sedative to give him to calm him down, unfortunately, we didn't even have Valium at the time. Valium would come a few years later. Also, with his violent behavior, the officers would have used a Taser on him. However, they didn't have Tasers back then either!

Finally, Fred yelled, "IV's set up, Conrad!"

"OK! Give me an 18 gauge. He's got a great vein here!" I said. I turned to the officer, "Keep your foot on his arm! I'm gonna start an IV! Please don't let him move!"

I sat close enough to the patient's arm and could see that the officer was positioning his feet to where he couldn't move his arm at all. I didn't even need a tourniquet with the officer putting his weight on his arm. I inserted the needle - pop! I got the IV as I saw the blood return in the chamber of the IV catheter. I advanced the catheter. I was in!

I hollered, "Fred! Give me the tubing and get the Dextrose ready for me!"

"It's ready!" he yelled back.

I connected the tubing to the needle in his arm. I quickly taped it down to ensure that it was secure. My worst fear was losing the IV.

"Don't let him move!" I yelled at the officers. To Fred, I instructed, "Fred, push the Dextrose, now!" Fred popped the caps on the huge vial that contain fifty milliliters. He inserted the needle into the tubing and began to push the Dextrose medication into the IV. The patient continued to struggle as the Dextrose was going in.

Then, I noticed something. As the first half of the Dextrose was going into his vein, his struggling began to subside slightly. He was reacting to the Dextrose!

I told Fred, "It's working, partner. Push the rest of it. Let's give it all to him!" I figured his insulin was too high and, therefore, he was in insulin shock. He was now starting to relax. I heard one of the officers say, "Shit! It's working!"

We all breathed a sigh of relief. The patient stopped struggling. He was relaxed now. Fred had pushed all the Dextrose into his vein. We loosened our grip on him. I had forgotten his name. I asked his friend, "What's his name again?"

"Robert," he replied. Just as his friend said his name, the patient heard his name called and said, "What?" The patient, Robert, looked up and saw us all sitting and standing over him. He looked dazed and confused.

"What's going on? What are you all doing here? Am I being arrested?" he asked.

I took a deep breath and said, "Robert, we had to give you some medication to take you out of your insulin shock." He still looked dazed and confused. "Robert, do you know where you are?"

"Yeah, I'm at work." He started to sit up. An officer and I were behind him holding him up and supporting him. He looked at all of us and said, "Damn, you all look like shit. It looks like someone beat the crap out of you all."

I looked at him and replied, "Yeah, Robert, you did. You beat us all to crap."

Still a little dazed, Robert looked at his friend. "Gilbert, did we get our food yet? We have to go back to work."

Gilbert just said, "Dude, you scared the crap out of me. I had to call EMS. Then you beat up on the officers and these paramedics. Man, you went ballistic on me! You could've been shot, dude! You want me to call your wife?"

Robert, now a little more aware of his surroundings, answered, "Naw, she'll get mad. She gets mad when I don't eat enough after I take my insulin. If there's anyone that can kick my ass, it's her."

An officer asked him, "Dude, is your wife bigger than you? If she is, don't make her mad, brother!" Everyone kind of chuckled.

Robert responded, "She's six feet tall. Just a few inches shorter than me."

Another officer quipped, "Yeah man, don't make her mad!"

I jumped in, "Go ahead and sit on this chair, Robert. You need to just sit down and relax. Let's take your sugar level."

He said, "Sure," and we helped him onto the chair. I grabbed the Glucometer to check his sugar level. It was 119. I thought that was perfect. When we arrived, I can assure you that it was well below 40 or 50. It's normal to have a reading of 100 or above. But, every person is different. With him standing over six feet, even a level of 50 or 60 could not have been enough for him.

I told Robert, "Your sugar level is normal now, Robert. I recommend that you go to the hospital with us and they can check you out. The hospital is close by, maybe five minutes away. Would you like us to take you?"

Robert responded, "No, this has happened before at home and usually I'll just fix me something to eat. Or my wife will put some sugar in my mouth or give me a Coke or orange juice. I'll be okay, thanks."

"Are you sure?" I asked.

"Yes, I'm sure."

The police officers, who were still recovering from the scuffle, said "You're lucky that we didn't shoot you. We thought you were spacing out on some drugs or something!"

Robert answered, "I appreciate you not shooting me. I'm sorry this happened."

"No need to apologize, Robert," I said. "Diabetics go through this all the time. You were lucky to have your friend here who called us. If he hadn't called, you could have gotten worse. People have died from insulin shock, you know."

"Yeah, my doctor told me that, too." he said.

I asked one more time. "Robert, are you sure you don't want to go with us?"

"I'm sure."

"Okay Robert, just remember. You've got to make sure you eat when you take your insulin. This could also happen when you're driving or even up in the bucket or ladder working with electricity. You can't afford to get hurt or killed while driving or working. You could also kill someone else while driving."

His friend Gilbert jumped in, "Hey, Robert, they're right. Dude, I'm driving now."

I asked Gilbert, "Was Robert driving?"

He responded, "Yep."

I silently thanked God nothing happened.

I looked at Robert. "Robert, if this had happened before you got here to the restaurant, you could have injured or killed someone. There's a lot of traffic out there and there are a lot of college students walking around. You could've run over someone. This is why it's so important for you to listen to me and listen to your wife, otherwise she'll kick your ass, right?"

He smiled and said, "Right."

Well, the result was Robert was back to normal. He refused to go to the hospital, and he stayed and waited for his lunch with his friend, Gilbert. More results: one officer suffered a busted lip; another officer had a scratch over his right eye; his friend, Gilbert, had a swollen finger; my partner, Fred, had his badge torn from his shirt; I had a bruised back since I tumbled over a table. I felt like a stuntman flying over the table and chairs. I also lost a couple of buttons from my shirt. Fortunately, no one suffered any serious injuries - just a few bumps and bruises. Could it have been worse? Yes, it could have been tragic.

I thank God that nothing worse happened. I thank God that my hunch was right. We went back to the station and had our BLT sandwiches.

Another day, another call, another life saved. Oh, I should have nicknamed Robert "Kong." He sure fought like him!

Lesson Learned - Don't Get Burned

Robert's diabetes was nothing new. However, what was new to me was the fact that I had never seen a diabetic in insulin shock exhibit bizarre behavior. I knew that diabetics could respond differently, but Robert was a first for me; that was the first time I'd seen a diabetic act so violently. In the downtown area, we were used to seeing this type of behavior with patients that were high or coming down from drugs.

Now, if you're a diabetic or have a family member that is a diabetic, be aware of what can happen. In Robert's case, this could have been prevented. He didn't eat well after taking his insulin in the morning. Diabetic patients need to take their sugar levels in the morning. They must eat well especially if they are taking units of insulin.

Also, if your parents are diabetics, it is likely you may become a diabetic as well. Your parents having diabetes is a red flag. Make sure you get checked on a regular basis. Rapid weight loss, excessive thirst, and excessive urination are precursors or signs of diabetes. Watch what you eat. Take care of yourselves and exercise regularly. Don't wait to be diagnosed with diabetes as this is a very debilitating disease.

Young children are also at risk. Remember, be a role model for your children. What you eat, they will eat. What you drink, they will drink. What you feel, they will feel. When you don't exercise, they won't exercise. Think about the health of your children. Would you like them to become diabetics and live on medication or injections every morning and evening?

Research the side effects of diabetes. You will be shocked. Take care and educate yourselves. Again, prevention is key.

Chapter 39
The Lady in Red

Back in 1999, one year after I retired, I started working as a marketing director for a private ambulance company. It was a rather unique job as my role was to visit hospitals and nursing homes. It was one evening in December around six o'clock when I stopped at a nursing home for an appointment with the director. I remember walking toward the building. From outside the building, I could see through the glass entrance doors.

Through the doors I saw beautiful Christmas lights, a Christmas tree, and many decorations. Walking in through the doors and into the lobby, I saw to my right a resident of the senior citizen home. She was probably around eighty years young. She was the prettiest little woman in a red dress and matching red shoes. She wore white gloves with snowflake earrings and a red hat. She sat in a lounge chair as if waiting for a date.

I couldn't help but speak to her when I entered.

"My! Young lady, you sure are looking pretty! Where are we going tonight?"

She quipped, "I ain't goin' anywhere with you, that's for sure!"

I laughed. "Of course, we're not! It seems like you're waiting to go out tonight, though."

"Yes," she said. "I'm waiting for my son who's going to pick me up shortly. We're gonna go have dinner and afterwards go to a movie. He should be here anytime."

"Well, you have a great time! He sure is lucky to have a mom like you!"

She smiled from ear to ear and turned toward the glass doors to see if her son would be walking in. I walked toward the receptionist and told her I was there for a meeting with the director. "Mrs. Brown will be right with you," she said.

I sat down and looked over toward the lady in red waiting for her son. She was staring out the doors with anticipation. I was happy for her.

"Mr. Gonzales?" The director stepped out of her office, and I stood up to greet her. "How are you? Why don't you step into my office?"

"I'm fine. Thank you, Mrs. Brown. How are you?" I asked.

"I'm great, thank you. Looking forward to the holidays?"

I replied, "Yes, the holidays seem to come and go so quickly." I followed her into her office. Before I sat down, I said "Mrs. Brown, you know I saw the most beautiful lady out in your lobby. She was all dressed up waiting for her son to pick her up. Isn't that sweet? She looked so excited waiting for her son."

She looked at me and took a deep breath. I thought I'd said something wrong. She said in a soft voice, "You know, Mr. Gonzales, she dresses up every night. She puts on her makeup, wears a different dress, comes out and sits in the lobby every evening to wait for her son." She exhaled another deep sigh and sat down on her chair, looked at me and said, "The sad thing is her son never comes. She comes from her room and sits in the lobby up to three hours. Sometimes till ten o'clock at night. There are times when she'll come to me and ask me to watch out for him as she goes to the bathroom. She'll even ask me if he's called. It hurts to tell her no. She always has an excuse for him."

"'Maybe he's running late,' she'll say. 'He is a doctor and sometimes he's on call and he has to go see patients at the hospital. You know doctors get very busy. They work all hours of the night and sometimes he's so tired that he falls asleep at the hospital...'" Mrs. Brown continued. "But you know what really bothers me, Mr. Gonzales?"

I looked at her in silence, waiting for her response.

"Her son works about a half mile away. The only time he comes to visit is to write a check at the beginning of the year and pays for the whole year. He'll sit with her at lunch and barely even talk with her. He's on the phone all the time he's here for that whole hour during lunchtime."

I was stunned. Speechless. I could feel my heart falling apart for her, and at the same time I felt rage. What kind of son would just visit once a year?! If I saw him, I'd probably tear right into him and ask him "What kind of son are you?"

I turned toward the lady in red. She was still in the lobby. I felt so empty. I felt like asking her if I could take her to the movies myself. I said, "It irks me that many people out there don't visit or call their moms and dads. Yeah, there may be some issues, but we must forgive. Our parents took care of us. The least we can do is continue to care for them somehow. Even a phone call will brighten up the elderly."

Mrs. Brown nodded, "I wish everyone had that same attitude toward their parents. We have residents here that see their families maybe two or three times a year. It's disheartening. Some of my staff members come by on their off time just to visit with the residents they care for."

We changed the subject for some time, and our meeting lasted about an hour. We walked out of her office to give me a tour of the facility. The lady in red was still in the lobby waiting.

"Mrs. Wilson?" the director called to her.

The lady in red turned around. "Yes?"

"I'm going to show Mr. Gonzales our facility. Are you okay?"

"I'm fine. I'm sure he's on the way. He's probably running late," she said.

Mrs. Brown and I looked at each other. We continued our tour.

After touring the facility for about forty-five minutes, we returned to Mrs. Brown's office. Mrs. Wilson was still in the lobby waiting.

"I think he's running late again. I'll go to my room in a while." Mrs. Wilson said.

"Okay. Just don't stay up late. Our night nurse will escort you back to your room."

"Oh, I know how to get back to my room."

I told Mrs. Brown thank you for allowing me to visit the facility. As I walked out toward the lobby, I looked at Mrs. Wilson, the lovely lady in red.

"Mrs. Wilson, you have a great evening and have a Merry Christmas, too, okay?"

She responded. "Oh, I will! My son will be picking me up and we can go Christmas shopping."

My heart fell to the floor.

I replied, "Good night, Mrs. Wilson."

She said, "Good night."

I walked out to my car. I opened the door and sat in my car for a few minutes. I felt like walking back in again just to chat with her. I stepped out of the car and started to walk into the building. I approached the front doors and looked in to where she had been sitting. She was gone. I didn't see her at all. I looked down the hallways. Not there.

"Where did Mrs. Wilson go?" I asked the receptionist.

"She went back to her room. She said she was tired."

"Okay. Thanks."

As I walked back to my car I was thinking that I should have stayed there to chat with her. But I didn't. I felt bad for her, excusing her son all year long. I fastened my seat belt, started the car and drove off.

The following week, I called the director.

"Hi, Mrs. Brown. How are you?" I asked.

"Mr. Gonzales, great to hear from you."

"I'm calling to see how Mrs. Wilson is today."

There was a pause.

"I'm sorry, Mr. Gonzales, but she passed away the day after you visited."

"Oh, no."

"Yes. She passed during the night in her sleep. We found her on her chair. She was wearing her Christmas dress, the red one you saw her in. Sad. It took us a few days to get a hold of her son. He was on vacation."

I held the phone and took a deep sigh.

"I'm glad you called about her, Mr. Gonzales. She was a nice lady."

I replied, "I bet she was a nice mom, too. Thank you, Mrs. Brown. I surely appreciate it. Have a nice day, and I hope you have a great Christmas."

I hung up the phone.

I will never forget the lady in red.

Lesson Learned - Don't Get Burned

This story was hard to write. I can still see her sitting there anxiously waiting for her son... the son who never came.

Sometimes we take our parents for granted. We make excuses for not calling or visiting. When our parents call us, we sometimes say, "Oh, it's Mom again. She must call me a thousand times a day! That's so annoying!" Yes, but they're anxious to talk to us. They love us.

I'll never forget when we were called to respond to a nursing home. A gentleman was having a heart problem and we decided to take him to the hospital. As we were rolling him down the hallway of the nursing home, a lady in a wheelchair grabbed my arm and yelled at me, "Please take me with you! Please take me with you!"

While holding onto my arm, I was literally pulling her down the hall in her wheelchair. I didn't know what to do or say. A staff member from the nursing home grabbed her arm and pulled it away from me. She then grabbed the lady's wheelchair and whisked her away. The lady was still yelling to take her away from there. I felt helpless. She did, too.

What can we learn from this? Plenty. Call or visit your mom and dad whenever you have the opportunity. When was the last time you told them "I love you, Mom or I love you, Dad.?" When was the last time you gave them a big hug and told them "I appreciate you and all you did for me when I was a kid?" Yes, things happen like divorce or separation or disagreements. Is it hard to forgive? Of course, it is. But how long will you go on living with unforgiveness?

If your parent is in a nursing home, take the time to visit them. They're anxious to see you. Don't forget about them. There's a mom, dad, aunt, sister, brother, uncle, husband, wife, or friend waiting for you to visit them. Or, why not volunteer to sit and chat with a senior at a nursing home? Company can brighten peoples' days.

Chapter 40
Please Call Me

Being an advocate for children and seniors, I have always tried to do whatever I could to promote their health and safety. And this following story is a testament about my compassion for the elderly.

It was an early morning of October 2003. It was around five o'clock when I was awakened by a voice. I don't know if I was dreaming or actually heard God's voice.

I heard, "Son, please write a song about the senior citizen. No one ever visits them."

I sprang up and sat at the side of my bed. I was having a hard time speaking. My heart was racing. I remember looking up toward the window to see if maybe someone was peeking through the window and whispered something. I looked around the room. My door was closed. I looked to see the time on my digital clock. It showed 5:00. The voice in my head kept repeating, "Son, please write a song about the senior citizen. No one ever visits them."

It was a message from God.

I got up and walked to my desk. I turned on my computer and started writing. I titled it *Please Call Me*.

It took me two hours to write the lyrics and put guitar chords to the song. After I wrote it, I looked at it and said a prayer: "Lord, this song is for you. This song is for the senior citizen who is waiting for that one short visit or a phone call."

10-96 (We're on the way)

I sang quietly. I didn't want to wake my parents who were asleep down the hall. I'd been staying with them while I was going through a separation. When I heard them in the kitchen, I thought, "Great. They're awake now." So, I picked up my guitar and the song I'd written and stepped out of the bedroom. I wanted to sing it to them to see what they thought about the song.

I walked into the kitchen and greeted them. "Good morning!" They were fixing coffee. "I was wondering if I could sing this song to you... I was awakened by a voice and I know it had to have been God. He told me to write a song about the senior citizen."

Mom replied, "Sure, son. Just to let you know, it was God that woke you up."

Just by the look on Dad's face, I could tell that he totally agreed with Mom.

I sat and placed the paper on the table. I picked up my guitar and started singing. Here are the lyrics:

Please Call Me by Conrad Gonzales | October 19, 2003

I've watched you grow up for many a year.
We shared laughter and sadness and many a tear.
As I look out the window of this nursing home.
I ask you please call me, I'm feeling alone.

The days and nights go by very slow.
This feeling I hope you'll never know.
So please call me soon and brighten my day.
Please call me soon. Your phone call I await.

The months are long as I go through each season.
When I don't get a call, I know there's a reason.
But all it takes is to pick up the phone.

Please Call Me

I'd love to visit the children at home.

(Chorus)
I've watched you grow up for many a year,
We shared laughter and sadness and many a tear.
As I look out the window of this nursing home.
I ask you please call me, I'm feeling alone.

I know you have friends and a big family.
But always remember don't forget about me.
Please call and forgive me if I talk way too long.
I'm here just waiting and I'll try to be strong.

It's dark now and I've waited as long as I could,
I was by the phone like I told you I would.
Please call me tomorrow as I lay down to sleep.
Please call me before God does, for my soul to keep.

If you're now crying or have a lump in your throat,
I don't blame you. It took me six attempts to sing the song
to my parents. I started crying before I even got to the
second verse. My parents cried along with me. After
gaining my composure, I finally had the strength to finish
the whole song. Mom and Dad just stood there when I
finished the song. I stared at them.

Mom, still drying her tears, said, "That's a beautiful
song, Mijo." I knew she was thinking about her mom, my
grandmother, who Mom cared for the last thirteen years of
my grandmother's life.

I said, "It's dedicated to God and all the elderly
around the world who are being neglected by their own
children."

Mom replied, "And there are many, son."

"I know."

Three months later, I asked a friend of mine who had a small studio in his home if he could produce and mix the song. I wanted only guitar, bass, and drums. Very simple. Very solemn. And, simple it was. The melody was a waltz. He agreed the melody was appropriate for the song.

A week later he called me to let me know the music was ready. All he needed was for me to go to his house and record my voice.

When I arrived at his home, he led me to his sound room. It was a closet that he had converted to a sound booth. He had a microphone and all the sound equipment he needed to record. The walls had gray foam and extended from the floor to the ceiling.

"Conrad, listen to what I put together and let me know what you think," he said.

I told him, "I'm sure it will be fine." I put on the headset as he turned on the music. I was speechless. I knew it would turn out great. "Beautiful music," I said.

"Let's do it."

As he started the music, I knew exactly when to come in. He didn't have to cue me at all. I sang the song. As I was singing, I could hear myself. It was sounding great!

After I sang the last few words, I waited for him to let me know when we were done. I stood there quietly not wanting to breathe so my breathing wouldn't be recorded.

Through the window, I could see him. He just stared down at the sound board and looked up at me. He looked like he was in shock. I thought, "Oh, no. He didn't turn on the recorder!"

He softly said, "Conrad, I think that's it."

I agreed. It couldn't have gone any better. We did it on the first take, and I was pleased.

Unfortunately, no one wants to play *Please Call Me* on the radio. "It's too sad," they tell me. "But my song has a message," I tell them. Still no response.

One day, you'll hear it on the radio. One day, the message will get across. When they do listen to the song, folks will stop whatever they're doing and call their mom or dad. One day, my song will make a difference. One day, the mom or dad at the nursing home will get that phone call or visit from their kids.

One day. I have hope.

Epilogue:
Using Songs to Save Lives

As a firefighter and paramedic, unfortunately, I witnessed many injuries and deaths. From my first three years as a firefighter, to my eighteen years in EMS, and even in my last year as a fire inspector and public educator, I concluded very early in my career that the common denominator with these events was *lack of education*. Even as a flight paramedic with AirLife, there was always this last quote "if they only knew."

If they only knew….
- o how to do CPR
- o how to do the Heimlich Maneuver
- o about wearing their seatbelts
- o about the dangers of not having a smoke alarm
- o that there was someone out there to talk to them about suicide
- o about the dangers of leaving medication within the reach of children

If they only knew…

Therefore, I decided to do something different and unique.

When my three children were small, I loved to entertain them. Making them laugh with silly faces and "accidentally stumbling" and acting like a clown inspired me to make them laugh even more. I recall when my

daughter, Andrea, and my son, Adrian, would tell me, "Daddy, you're silly!" I remember when my older son Christopher was eight years old. I put a football helmet on him to protect his head when he was learning to ride his bicycle. I also made sure that they knew about fire safety and buckling up when they got in the car. Early safety education was instilled in them and they knew what to do if their clothes caught on fire... Stop, Drop and Roll!

I would go to their schools to conduct safety demonstrations and put on my firefighting gear. I still have a picture of my daughter, Andrea, dancing with Sparky the Firedog when he, along with the firefighters, went to talk to the children about fire safety.

I always felt the need to educate children about safety because they were the most vulnerable to injuries and deaths from fires, car crashes, falls, drownings, and more. We can talk to the parents about fire safety until we're blue in the face, but I felt that it would also help to educate the children.

So, with that and my guitar skills, I decided to put my talents together. I wrote two songs that I could sing at their schools. The first song is called *Stop, Drop, and Roll* and the second song was called *Buckle Up*. Very simple and catchy, I wrote the songs with the intent to be repetitive and have an upbeat tempo.

As a matter of fact, I was approached by a teacher after a presentation.

"Mr. Gonzales, where did you get those songs?"

"I wrote them."

"You wrote them?" she asked.

I said, "Yes ma'am. I wanted a creative method of educating children. And, with music, you can't go wrong."

"Those are great songs!" she exclaimed. "You should write some more!"

I told her, "Thank you, ma'am. I just might!"

Well, it took me a few years to finally put some songs together. In 2003, I finally had some safety songs written. Actually, I had twenty-four songs written!

My goal was to eventually record them. And I did. Well, not all of them. The process was rather tedious. I had to pick my favorite songs that I was going to record. So, I picked fourteen. The songs covered fire and bicycle safety, car seat and seat belt safety, and I even wrote a song about train safety called *Don't Beat That Train!* This particular song I am proud of because it has a Johnny Cash flare to it. Really cool!

Included in my CD is a song about fire safety for grandparents. The title of the song is *Be Careful Grandma and Grandpa.* It is a message from the grandchildren to the grandparents to remind them to check their smoke alarm, don't cook with their robes on, and don't get close to space heaters.

Another song that I felt was needed is titled *Yes, Ma'am, No, Sir.* It's a song about manners and respect. Yes, something that is greatly needed in today's world! It featured my then twelve-year old niece, Ally Brooke. What an angelic voice!

Once I had my fourteen favorites, I knew that my goal was to have children sing with me in the background. So, I recruited my nieces, a friend's children, and children that spoke Spanish. Altogether, we had nineteen children as back-up singers! They were called "The Lifesavers!"

Included in the group of children was my own niece, Ally. She was special as, of course, she was my niece. I'll talk a little more about Ally later in my story. She's a big surprise and was a huge addition to "The Lifesavers!"

364

Then came the task of looking for a producer and mixer.

I recall meeting a good friend of mine, Joe Trevino and his wife. Joe and I attended the same high school here in San Antonio and Joe had a production studio called Blue Cat Studios. He produced many songs for some of the great Tejano artists in Texas. Some of them even won Grammys for their songs. It was a very good friend of mine, George Arispe, with whom I attended eighth grade and high school, that told me about Joe. George, my best friend, passed away a few years ago. He was part of my dream for this project. Rest in peace, my friend.

I met with Joe at his studio one day and told him, "Joe, I have a special project that I'd like for you to consider. I'm looking for someone to do the producing and search for musicians for my songs."

I remember him asking me, "What kind of songs do you want to record?" I told him, "Safety songs for children." He looked at me and asked, "Safety songs for children?" I said, "Yep. These are songs I wrote and I want to record them. I have fourteen songs that I've recorded on a cassette tape." (Yes, cassette tape! Remember those?)

He didn't even have to listen to my songs to say "Yes, let's do it!" He told me, "I'd love to be involved in your project! I've never produced or helped anyone record anything for children, much less safety songs. I'd be glad to do it!"

Although he hadn't heard my songs, I still remember taking my guitar out and singing just a few notes from one of my songs. He was even more enthusiastic!

"Conrad," Joe said, "I've got the perfect musicians for your project!"

I replied, "Joe, I knew you would."

Finally, the day came. It was in the Spring of 2005. All were able to come to Joe's recording studio on a Saturday morning. I remember arriving at his studio around 8:30 in the morning. The children started trickling in at 9:00 a.m. I provided tacos for them, and I had planned to get pizza for lunch. Yes, nineteen children, with some of the parents there to see their kids sing, was very exciting for me. "The Lifesavers" were also excited that they were going to become a part of my CD!

All the microphones were set up in the recording booth. Fortunately, Joe's studio was so big we were able to accommodate all the kids in the recording room. I could see the anxiety in their faces. They had never stepped into a recording studio before much less be a part of a singing group!

We practiced some cues and some of the songs, and I couldn't believe it.

I told them, "You all are... AWESOME! This is going to be a great CD! You all sound great!" They smiled from ear to ear. I knew then, we would have a great product that was going to make a huge difference!

We recorded songs for the rest of the morning. Right around noon, it was apparent that the kids and me, were getting hungry! They looked famished. They had worked hard; we recorded half the songs in the morning which was pretty good considering the kids ranged from 6 to 12 years old!

At noon and after recording the last song before lunch, I shouted, "Pizza time, everyone!" The kids and adults all gobbled down their lunch with happy smiles. A little boy around 7 years old tugged at my pants, looked up and told me, "Mr. Gonzales, it's really hard being a singing star!" I smiled at him and told him, "Yep, it sure is!"

After lunch, we all went back into the studio and continued recording. I could tell Joe was having a great time. I saw him through the window in the engineering room tapping his feet and the parents that were there were also having a great time watching their kids recording their first CD! We didn't get done until around 4 p.m. A long day, but it was well worth it.

After fourteen songs, nineteen children helping, and I believe around ten pizzas, we were finally done! I gave them all a high five as they walked out of the recording room.

It was a long day but my dream had come true. I finally recorded safety songs that I'd written on my own. It was an accomplishment, dream, and goal that I'd achieved. It took me almost ten years to finally write the songs and put them on a CD. I have to thank all the kids for being a part of this dream. Unfortunately, I have not recorded the last ten, however, I still have it on my bucket list and my bucket list continues to grow.

Now, for the surprise. As mentioned before, Ally, my niece and my cousin's daughter, had a special voice and a special background. Ally was born premature and weighed not even two pounds when she was born. She literally was so small, my cousin Jerry and his wife, Pat, could hold her in the palm of their hands. However, my cousin tells me that Ally was special. The doctors said that, for being so premature, she had lungs that no one could believe! She cried so hard and so loud for a preemie!

Ally was twelve years old when she recorded with me. She had such a beautiful voice; she sang harmony with me and sang along with several of my songs. What a voice!

I told her one day, "Mija, you are going to be a great singing star someday! I know it!"

"Thank you, Uncle Conrad! I sure hope so!" she replied.

I told her, "No, you will be!"

Fast forward eight years. As you might recognize, Ally Brooke Hernandez became a member of the all-girl singing group, Fifth Harmony. My niece is now a star!

She accomplished a goal that she had for years. I'm proud to say that Ally Brooke Hernandez, from Fifth Harmony, recorded with me at twelve years old and made a huge difference then and is making a huge difference now!

Additionally, I must thank all those that participated and made my CD come true. From the musicians and children who sang with me, to George who told me about Joe and his studio, to Joe, to Ally, who provided her beautiful voice, and to the Lord, who gave me the strength, patience, and perseverance to push forward with this project. And to the teacher who told me I should write more songs. As my passion is to save lives, with these songs, I hope to continue saving lives with music, songs and by making learning fun.

I also have to thank my partner and compadre, Fred Casillas, who "partnered" with me in this project!

I recall Fred, my partner, telling me that he has a friend whose grandson loves the CD and his favorite song is *Don't Beat That Train!* His grandson keeps telling his father as they approach the railroad tracks, "Hey, Daddy, don't beat that train!" I love hearing that the songs work!

Thanks for getting this far, dear reader. I hope you've enjoyed this book. God bless you and stay safe.

And don't forget to buckle up!

Acknowledgements and Thanks

{*Editor's note: Conrad wanted to thank every person (I mean every person!) along the way... so if you aren't mentioned by name, know that he probably had you here and I had to trim it! He's an amazing man and so grateful for all those who helped him along the way.*}

When it comes to acknowledging and thanking folks for this project, it's difficult to begin as there are so many people that I'd like to recognize and thank for their support in the past forty-five years since I joined the San Antonio Fire Department in 1976.

To my partners: Alfred Casillas, Lee Carrola, Mike Rodriguez, Bob Ebner, and others, thank you for teaching me "the ropes" of being a paramedic and for sharing a positive attitude on the job. We were a great team as we knew what to expect from each other and never questioned any decisions made.
Thank you.

Thank you, Richard Olivarri, you inspired me to be a paramedic. My gratitude to you, brother.

Thank you to all of my former colleagues and leaders within the agencies and organizations I served or worked with, including: The San Antonio Fire Department, the EMS Division of the San Antonio Fire Department, the Fire Prevention and Public Education Division of the San Antonio Fire Department, San Antonio AirLife, San Antonio College, the National Latino Children's Institute,

10-96 (We're on the way)

News 9, KTSA AM Radio Station, Any Baby Can, The Children's Shelter, University of Texas Health Center, and my very good friend, Gabriel Cano at the National Highway Traffic Safety Administration.

Thank you to the news media who aired a safety interview, published an article of mine, or assisted in any way with the safety education of others. Many lives have been saved because of your willingness to spread the message.

Thank you from the bottom of my heart to all of my instructors, teachers, and spiritual leaders, including folks at: St. Matthew Catholic School, Holy Family Catholic Church, Our Lady of Guadalupe Church, Holy Cross High School, the Archdiocese of San Antonio; priests: Father David Garcia, Father Emmet Carolan, and those who have passed on, Father Albert Storme, Father Charles Pugh, Father John Flanagan, Brother Rene, Bishop Patrick Flores; instructors: Dr. Lance Villers, Leslie Hernandez, Joe Lindstrom, Marte Eager, Mark Dieterle, John Phelps, and Mr. Butterfras, thank you. I am grateful to my fellow instructors and adjunct faculty who helped me along the way.

Thank you also to the fellow students who were part of my experience. From classes in the 80s until now, those who sat next to me or across from me, I thank you. It's been a privilege to teach you and learn with you. Additionally, I'd like to recognize the current and past Army flight paramedics; thank you for your service.

Thank you to Stephanie Rodriguez for your unwavering dedication and efforts in editing the book. Thanks to your family for letting me borrow you!

Now, for the finale of thanks!

To my parents, Conrad and Frances Gonzales

I call them Servants sent from Heaven. Mom and Dad, I love you both and thank you all for providing what we children need... Love. The Lord blessed me with great parents!

To my children, Christopher, Andrea, and Adrian

You are the purpose of my being a father. My safety songs, and this book, are dedicated to you. I love you and always remember... I was always there in heart, mind, and soul and always will be. Love you all!

To my step-son, Greg

Thank you for your patience. I knew I woke you up in the wee hours of the morning when I woke up to write my book. Your computer skills came in handy!

To my grandchildren Amber, Jeremiah, and Jonathon, and to my new grandson, Alonzo!

Thank you for being my grandchildren. You continue to inspire me to always move forward and be happy. Always be safe. I love you.

To my sister and brother-in-law, Marina and Jeff Marquez

Marina, if you wouldn't have choked, I would have one less story to write about you! I love you... Jeff, thank you for bringing happiness and joy to my sister. She's lucky!

To my brother, Abel, the bike rider

You always inspired me. I pray for you every time you ride and race your bike! (not a motorcycle!) I'll write a story about you in my next book!

To all my nieces and nephews

Jeremy, Briana, Diandra, Liana, and their kids; And to Drew, Cassie, Erin, Scott, and Jenny. I'm sure you may remember your Uncle Conrad telling you all to buckle up!

A very, very special thank you to my wife, Alma

Mi Corazon, you were the one that told me, "With all the stories you have, you should write a book!" If it weren't for you, this book would not have been possible. You listened to me as I retold my stories. You were my best critic when it came to writing my stories and even writing my songs. You were my guiding light and continue to inspire me today. I am grateful to you for your kindness, love, compassion, patience, and continued "nudge" to keep moving forward with my projects and education. If it weren't for you, I would not be here doing what I am doing today. You saw the best in me!

You have been at my side 24/7 laughing, joking, cooking, working, crying, listening, and being my rock and confidant. I love you and thank you.

My final thanks is to God.

Dear Lord, thank you for keeping me safe throughout my life, my career, and now that I'm retired. You held your hand over me and protected me the times when I thought I was going to meet you and St. Peter in Heaven. You put your hand over me when I thought I would get injured or killed on and off duty. You watched over me as you wanted me to go home and protect my children. You watched over me as you guided me when I was taking care of critically injured or ill patients. You placed your hands on my shoulders as I placed my hands on the shoulders of those that lost family members and comforted them in their time of loss. You put words of comfort in my heart and mouth when I spoke to patients who were dying in my care. You placed your hands over me as I cried for some of these patients as I thought about my own children. You placed your hands over me as I wrote my book to share my experiences with your children, and with Your will, save more lives.

I know You will continue to place Your hand on me when I start writing my next book. For, it is for You, and Your children Lord, that I am doing this. You, Lord, are the reason I am here and the reason for this book. Thank you.

A last note to my readers:
Thank you, be safe, pray and thank God each and every day that you're alive. I hope you enjoyed my book, and I pray it made a difference. Please, take a moment each day and hug your kids and tell them "I love you" no matter their age. And for those of you with troubled children, don't give up on them. They need you. Don't forget to call your Mom and Dad, and pray for their health, safety, and well-being. They would appreciate a phone call. And, remember, tell your spouse "I love you" every day.

Stay safe and don't forget to BUCKLE UP!

Love you all,
Conrad

Appendix A
A Poem

In November of 2014, I decided to write a poem about finding positivity when grief and turmoil abound. I hope this poem keeps you safe and sound:

The Lighter Side of Darkness

There are times in life when we suffer pain and sorrow
And it seems like there will be no tomorrow.
Pain is inflicted into our hearts and mind
And solutions to despair may be impossible to seek or find.

There are times in life when tears will flow
And when it will stop no one really knows.
Life will seem to be shadowed and obscured
And in vain we search for reasons and a cure.

There are times in life when darkness seems to take over
And no one seems to be there to lean on or cry on their shoulder.
We never know when our time shall arrive
So, we must take charge of our feelings and our lives.

Darkness is a shadow cast upon our light;

Appendix A

What can we do to make things right?
Darkness is temporary only if we want it to be,
So, we must make a change to live forever happily.

We must move from the shadow of darkness and seek the
light
We seek in ourselves peace and the God of Might.
The Lord allows us to see darkness to learn about Love
And pain is an ingredient of strength from above.

So, love to be free and be free to love
As we feel the breeze cast from a flying white dove.
The key to life from suffering and pain,
Is to heal through love and be happy again.

Let darkness be gone and be shed aside.
Let light shine upon us and be rid of our strife.
We move forward and ahead with love and happiness
And always look at the lighter side of darkness.

Appendix B
Personal Baby Stories

A note from the author:

I remember calling my mother because my young son, Christopher, was crying so much that I didn't know what to do. Christopher was six months old. I frantically called Mom, and Dad answered.

"Hello?"

"Dad! Dad! Where's Mom?" I was yelling at Dad while Christopher was in my arms crying and crying.

Dad replied, "She's not here."

I yelled, "DAD! I NEED TO SPEAK TO MOM RIGHT NOW!"

"I SAID, SHE'S NOT HERE!" Dad yelled back.

"WHERE IS SHE! I NEED TO SPEAK TO HER RIGHT NOW! WHERE IS SHE!"

Dad, again, yelled back, "SHE'S NOT HERE! SHE'S AT THE STORE!"

There were no cell phones back then. I know what you're thinking. No cell phones! What year was this?

I yelled to Dad again, "BUT I NEED TO SPEAK TO HER, DAD! CHRISTOPHER'S CRYING AND HE WON'T STOP!"

Want to know what Dad told me?

He said, "WELL, YOU WANTED TO HAVE BABIES, RIGHT?" Click. Dad hung up.

I just stood there with the phone in my hand and said, "Dad? Uh, Dad? Hello? OK. I love you, too."

I was stunned at Dad's response. I just turned to Chris and held him while he cried. I held him for almost thirty minutes until he stopped crying.

Dad called me back an hour later. "Mijo, how's Christopher?"

I replied, "He stopped crying, Dad. He's asleep now."

Dad told me, "Great job, Mijo. You're a great father. It's tough having babies, right?"

"Yeah. Thanks, Dad."

"You're welcome, son. You have to be patient. Now, go sit down and relax. You'll have to feed Christopher when he wakes up. He'll be hungry from crying so much. Want your Mom to call you back?"

I answered, "That's OK, Dad. I got it. Love you."

"Love you, too, Mijo." We hung up. I learned my lesson... be patient.

A note from the editor:

I recall vividly my six-week appointment. My OB/GYN looked me in the eyes and asked, "So how are you, really?" and I burst into tears. I was having a rough go of it after delivering our son. The labor was traumatic. He was our first little guy, and I had no idea what to do. I was terrified. I never slept. Everything hurt. I shook with fear when I drove him the first time. I thought we would die.

Ladies, there is no shame, I repeat zero shame, in struggling with your new baby. Your body pains, your hormone levels, your lack of sleep, your fears, your anxieties, your Googling - they can sometimes be classified as postpartum depression (PPD) or postpartum anxiety (PPA).

I didn't understand why they called it the "baby blues" until I had them, too. I didn't understand why I wasn't "good enough" to just be happy and in love with my precious child. I didn't understand until my visit with my doctor that this is a medical condition and can sometimes require treatment.

Thankfully, I never got to where I needed medication or wanted to hurt my baby. But there were times early on when I didn't think I would survive. Really. Like this mothering thing would kill me.

But we made it. I am here. I spoke up. I had help in understanding why and how my body would respond this way. I shared my feelings with good friends, and ultimately, they admitted to feeling the same way! No one talks about it, but it's real, and it happens to a LOT of women. And like Chapter 22 highlights, it's okay to call 9-1-1. It's okay to ask for help. It's okay to see your doctor again… and again. Becoming a mother is hard; a lot of it is truly out of your control.

I've heard all the stereotypes (seriously, who thinks this way?!). But it doesn't make you less than, or not a good Christian, or ungrateful, or unhealthy when you admit you may be struggling with a mental health problem, especially after having a baby. It makes you brave, strong, secure, and smart.

Please, if you're reading this and you or someone you know may be struggling to adapt to a new baby - even if it's your fourth! - seek help and counsel. Call your doctor.

I'm happy to report that now, five and one-half years later, we have three beautiful kids. Each pregnancy was different. Each delivery was different. Each baby was different. Each postpartum journey was different. But one thing that remained the same: I sought help when I felt like I needed it. Without shame. I hope you will, too!

Best wishes on your parenting journey! God bless.

Stephanie Rodriguez

(Conrad's editor; Mommy to James, Joseph, and Saida)

Appendix C
Photos Through the Years

Partners Lee Carrola and Conrad Gonzales, mid-90s

Conrad giving a report in the back of the ambulance.

In the middle, second row: Conrad with the EMS class of 1980. Photo taken at the University of Texas Health Science Center (now The University of Texas Health Center)

From Left to Right: Lee Carrola, Fred Casillas, Conrad Gonzales, Michael Rodriguez

About the Author

Conrad M. Gonzales, Jr. was born and raised in San Antonio, TX, where he has served its citizens for over forty years. He began his career as a San Antonio firefighter, then became a paramedic. He also worked as a flight paramedic with AirLife. After twenty-two years, he retired and worked with various nonprofit agencies and provided safety education locally and at the national level. He has been a CPR and First Aid Instructor since 1980. Conrad is an adjunct faculty staff member teaching the paramedic program at the University of Texas Health Center and is now launching another career as a writer.

In his free time, Conrad enjoys songwriting and singing at local venues. He and his wife, Alma, spend time together traveling, cooking, and dancing (as you can see above!). He enjoys being with his children and family. His book is available on Amazon and selected bookstores.

To purchase any CDs or books, visit
www.LifeSavingMethods.com

Made in the USA
Columbia, SC
01 December 2018